SUPERSTITION

SUPERSTITION

**The True Story of the Nanny
They Called a Witch**

Carole Compton
with Gerald Cole

*with an Afterword
by Guy Lyon Playfair*

EBURY PRESS
London

First published by Ebury Press
an imprint of the Random Century Group
Random Century House
20 Vauxhall Bridge Road
London SW1V 2SA

British Library Cataloguing in Publication Data
Compton, Carole
  Superstition: the true story of the nanny they called
  a witch.
  1. Persons accused of attempted murder – Biographies
  I. Title   II. Cole, Gerald
  364.1523092

  ISBN 0–85223–802–9

Typeset in Sabon by Tek Art Ltd, Addiscombe, Croydon, Surrey
Printed and bound in Great Britain by
Mackays of Chatham Plc, Chatham, Kent

To Sergio Minervini
with thanks

Acknowledgement

This book could not have been written without
the prompting and research of Stephen Volk
who first decided my story deserved telling,
persuaded me to go ahead with it and wrote a
screenplay based on it.

Contents

Preface

I am an ordinary Scottish housewife and mother. Today, at the age of twenty-seven, I have what I've always dreamed of – a loving husband, children, a home of my own.

I have never wanted, never expected anything else.

And yet, barely seven years ago, this ordinary, everyday ambition led me into a nightmare; a nightmare that is still as bizarre and inexplicable to me now as it was then.

People said I was a witch, that objects fell, that cold water boiled when I was nearby, that I made fires happen – including one that had threatened the life of a young child. A child no older than my own son is now.

I was pilloried by the foreign press, abused by the people around me, and, on evidence that was never more than circumstantial, imprisoned and held without trial for seventeen months in a country whose language I didn't know, and whose system of justice seemed obscure and unfair.

Finally, on 15 December 1983, I was put on trial in an Italian court, accused of arson and attempted murder. I was found guilty of one charge of arson and two charges of attempted arson. The charge of attempted murder was dismissed due to 'insufficient proof'.

Obviously the court must have believed enough of what the prosecution witnesses were saying to convict me, but I insisted at the time of my arrest, through my long imprisonment and right up to the end of my trial, that I was innocent.

I still insist on my innocence now.

But, when I left Italy, all I wanted to do was put the terrible experience behind me, despite the fact that I had made good friends inside prison and out, including the hundreds of strangers who wrote to me from all over the world offering sympathy and support. I even destroyed most of the letters I had received, as well as diaries I had kept from my earliest days in gaol.

In September 1988, when I was first approached to tell my story, my reaction was a blank refusal. The memories were too painful and, in any case, previous attempts to tell the truth had always been distorted.

Even more important, I didn't want to risk putting my family through any more of the hardship they had already suffered.

But the more I thought about it the more it occurred to me that this was a unique opportunity. Even though I never expect to return to Italy, my convictions remain on Italian records. Even in Britain my story is half-remembered by a surprising number of people.

I have never had a chance to reply fully – and in a language I understand – to the charges I was accused of.

Until now.

Through long conversations with Stephen Volk, who wrote a screenplay based on my experiences, and with Gerald Cole, who helped me write this book, I pieced together my story.

Perhaps it will be a warning to others that, even in one of the most modern countries in the world, superstition can still be a force for evil.

Perhaps it will simply be a way of explaining to my children, Imran and Nasreen, when they are old enough to understand, how something extraordinary once happened to their mummy.

I don't know. All I do know is that this is the truth as it happened to me.

Just before my trial I remember telling a journalist: 'The only thing I am guilty of is falling in love.' I still believe that is true.

But eight years ago, as a teenager in my home town of Ayr, I never dreamed that love could bring you anything but happiness. Love was simply my goal and my fulfilment.

1

Ayr

DECEMBER 1981 – MAY 1982

Rattling and banging, the elderly coach crawled past the bus station and swung carefully left by the Gaiety bingo hall. On the front passenger seats my friend Valerie and I looked at each other and winced.

'Looks like we're going to break another world speed record today, Mr Quinn,' Val called out.

'*Don't*—' I hissed at her.

'You worry about your job, and I'll worry about mine,' grumpy old Mr Quinn growled from the driver's seat. 'This is a safe service and always will be while I'm running it.'

Val made a face. 'Go any slower and this lot will have popped their clogs before we get there,' she murmured.

'*Sssh*—' I said, glancing back and grinning.

The coach was full of old folks, wrapped up tight against the winter cold. We'd spent half the morning collecting them from all around Ayr to bring them into the Carrick Street Day Centre in the middle of the town.

As the centre's two youngest assistants, it was what Val and I did every weekday, along with teasing Mr Quinn about his ancient coach, his grubby collars and the missing buttons on his shirts.

But today the coach was fuller than usual. It was Friday, and the afternoon on which the day centre had its weekly dance.

The centre was an old church hall, L-shaped with dingy, grey walls and tall, pointed windows. We rolled through the iron gates and juddered to a halt in the little car park by the main doors.

'All change!' Val called, getting up. 'Don't forget your dancing shoes!'

There were giggles behind us as we jumped out and started to help the old folks down.

'Are you coming down the Kyle disco tonight, Carole?' Val asked.

'No,' I said. 'I think I'll have a quiet night for a change.'

'Oh.' Val looked surprised.

When everyone was safely in the hall, we went into the kitchen and helped Essie, Rita and Margaret get the lunches ready. They were older than us but a good crowd. Lunch was always a bit of a panic.

Afterwards, while Essie and the others washed up, Val and I pushed back the formica tables from one end of the hall and cleared a space for the dance floor. It was nearly three o'clock by the time we finished. Our boss, Mrs Paterson, led in the band. There was a young, blind drummer who was excellent, and an elderly, blind accordionist. The singer was elderly, too, but at least he could still see.

As the band struck up and the others had a break, Val and I took over the kitchen serving-hatch and started to pour tea. A queue quickly formed.

'And I'll have one of those wee rolls with the cheese and tomato,' said a little old man in a striped bobble hat.

'Ah, well, I don't know about that,' I said, passing him a cup. 'The Centre has strict rules, you know, Mr Robertson.'

He blinked at me through his glasses. Val leaned past my shoulder.

'What are you doing, Carole?' she said. 'Give the fellow his roll.'

I pointed at a notice pinned next to the counter. 'It says, "Filled rolls are for *pensioners* only". Mr Robertson looks a bit young and sprightly to me.'

Mr Robertson's blank face crumpled into a grin. 'You cheeky wee lass.' I chuckled and gave him his roll.

Val nudged my elbow. 'What's this *flirting*, Carole Compton? You've been quiet all day, refuse to go bopping with my sisters and me for the first time in donkey's years, and now you're grinning all over your face! What little secret have you got tucked up your sleeve?'

I shrugged, and poured another cup as the queue moved up one. 'I don't know what you're talking about.'

'Oh no? Oh no?' My grin gave me away as Val's elbow nudged me again. 'It's *Marco*, isn't it? A romantic evening *alone* together, eh? You sly boots! I didn't think you were like that, Carole.'

'I'm not! What do you think I am?' I felt myself redden. Val might be my best friend, but sometimes she could really annoy me.

A grey-haired lady reached across her walking frame for her tea. 'Oh, sit yourself down, Mrs McEvoy,' I said. 'I'll bring it to you.'

'You're very kind, dear.'

'Sorry.' Val handed me some fresh cups. 'I'm just jealous, that's all. I think Marco's gorgeous.'

I went on pouring. 'He's got the evening off from the Turnberry. Mum's down with baby Sean. She's going out with Gran. Marco and I'll babysit. It'll give us a chance to talk.'

'Talk?' Val's eyed widened. 'He's not popping any questions, by any chance?'

I felt my face burn again. 'Don't be daft. I'm just cooking us a meal. A real Italian meal.'

'Oh Carole.' Val's face dropped. 'Do you think that's wise?'

'You cheeky—' I laughed and elbowed her instead.

Marco and I had been going out for almost two years then. We'd met at a disco not long after I'd come back from Aberdeen. Mum had moved there when I was eleven, two years after she had divorced my dad. Things had been so bad for her then that she'd had a breakdown, and needed to get away.

My younger brother Billy and I had stayed on in Ayr where we'd been born, moving in with my gran in Galloway Avenue just a few doors away from our old house.

When I'd finished my schooling, though, I hadn't been able to find a job. I wanted to be a hairdresser, but all I'd managed was some YTS work, helping out with the old folks at the Carrick Street Centre. I liked it well enough but, even there, no vacancies were coming up.

Meanwhile things were a lot better for Mum in Aberdeen. She even had a boyfriend, a tall, big-boned Irishman called John

Dillon who was obviously very good for her. She'd been asking me to move up there and live with them for some time. So now I did, hoping I'd be luckier, too, with work.

But none of the hairdressers there seemed to be taking on apprentices, either. Instead I joined Mum 'in the fish', which is what they call the fishing industry in Aberdeen. I had to pack wet fish in boxes on a conveyor belt. The money was OK but the work was cold and wet, and I had to wash my hair every night to get rid of the smell. I found Torry, the area where Mum lived, a bit windswept and bleak as well. And, of course, I was a long way away from my friends and the rest of my family.

One day a conveyor belt snapped and put me in hospital for a couple of days. They said I was lucky not to lose my leg. About the same time I heard from Ayr that the Carrick Street Centre was now looking for staff. That decided it for me. Mum wasn't too happy, but I made up my mind to move back to my gran.

I got the job in the day centre with Valerie, who lived just across the road from Gran with her three sisters and her two brothers. She was a bright, cheeky girl I'd known for years. We always had a laugh together.

I really enjoyed the work, too. I liked helping people and, because of my gran, I was used to talking to old folk; they had so many stories to tell. The money wasn't bad either.

One Saturday night I went out dancing with Val and her sisters. At one disco three boys from Oman asked to sit next to us. They were trainee waiters at the Turnberry Hotel, which is an enormous place with a famous golf course, about fifteen miles down the coast from Ayr.

Some of the local boys started making remarks about them because they were black. I've always hated that kind of thing. Perhaps it's because Dad was an Orangeman and Mum was Catholic and they had terrible rows about religion, but I can't stand prejudice of any kind. People are people to me.

So Val and I went out of our way to be friendly, to show them not all Scottish people are like that. They said they'd look out for us the next Saturday if we went dancing again. So we did. This time they brought along three other trainee waiters, Italian boys. One of them was Marco Vitulano.

He asked me to dance. He had dark, curly hair and lovely

eyes. I thought he was very good-looking. But he wasn't arrogant, like some good-looking boys are. His face was actually quite soft. He seemed kind, and his English wasn't at all bad. The second time I saw him at the disco he asked me out.

'Talk of the devil,' Val murmured when I got back from delivering Mrs McEvoy's tea. She glanced towards the kitchen window behind the counter.

I glimpsed Marco crossing the car park towards the main doors. My heart gave a little jump. Marco's head bobbed over the tea queue.

'Hello, Carole.'

'Hello, Marco.'

His smile lit up his whole face. Even Mum admitted it was his best feature. It made you melt inside and want to scoop him up, all at the same time. But it was embarrassing with Val and half the queue gawping at us and grinning.

'Ah,' Val sighed, 'true Romance.'

'Is this your beau?' A tiny little old woman at the head of the queue smiled at me.

'Sure is,' Val beamed. 'He's come to take Carole to the ball.'

'Don't listen to her, Mrs Montgomery,' I said. 'She's teasing. She's jealous!'

'Of course she's jealous,' Marco said. 'I've come to dance with the most beautiful woman in the room.'

He suddenly grabbed the little old lady's arms and began to dance round her in time to the band. She burst into laughter and so did the rest of the queue.

'That chappie's never over sixty,' said another woman at the back.

'If he is, I want to be introduced,' said her friend. They both roared.

'Thanks for being so nice to the old folks,' I told Marco on the bus home. 'They really appreciated it.'

'*Non é niente*,' Marco said. 'Don't mention it. It's my warm Italian nature.' He shivered suddenly, wriggled down into the collar of his leather jacket and widened his eyes.

'What's up with you?'

'I'm freezing! How can you bear this cold?'

'This is quite mild.'

'Aaagh!'

I burst out laughing. The Scottish climate was a running joke with us. Marco never had got used to it, partly because he insisted on wearing what he wore at home. 'But I'm an *Italian*, Carole,' he'd say. 'Not an Eskimo.'

'When we get in I'll make you a nice hot cup of tea,' I promised. 'It'll give you a chance to chat with Mum.'

'Your mother's at home?' He looked at me warily.

'Marco, I *told* you she was coming. I'm really looking forward to seeing little Sean again. He looks so like John.'

'I don't think your mother like me too much.'

'Don't be silly.' It was a sore point. We looked out of the bus window. The High Street was strung with decorations, and the shop windows were ablaze with Christmas lights.

'This year,' Marco smiled, 'I buy you a very special present. I think you like it very much.'

'I'll keep you to that,' I grinned.

At Gran's there was the usual chaos of a family visit: Mum and Gran scurrying about, my little half-brother Sean — all of two now — chattering away nineteen to the dozen, making no sense at all, Sean's father, John, snatching his chance to catch up with the racing on telly, Billy disappearing upstairs to his records, and Marco slumped at the end of the sofa, eyes on the box.

I looked up from the carpet where I was showing Sean a soft toy I'd made for him. 'Anybody want more tea?'

John shook his head. Gran stirred from her armchair. 'No, Gran,' I said. 'I'll do it.'

'Coffee,' said Marco. I gathered up the empty cups. Mum followed me into the kitchen.

'I notice his English hasn't stretched to "please" and "thank you" yet,' she said, tight-lipped. 'Not too good at picking up his own cups, either.'

I sighed. 'Marco works long hours at the Turnberry, Mum. He deserves a rest.'

'You don't, I suppose?' She took the cups off me and piled them in the sink. 'You're too soft on that one, child. I don't like to see you taken advantage of.'

I turned away for the kettle. Mum had very clear ideas about the boys who deserved to take me out. Trainee Italian waiters weren't very high on her list. When I didn't say anything else, she began rinsing the cups.

'Do you ever see your dad?'

I could see we were going through the whole gamut today.

When the marriage had broken down, Mum had got Dad to sign over the house to her when he came home drunk one night. Then she'd called the police and had him thrown out. He'd only moved to the next street and he was still there now. He saw Billy more than me, but we got on well enough.

'I can't help seeing him, Mum. He's working for Lochside Dairies. He's been delivering the milk.'

'Ever talk to him?'

I leaned past her to fill the kettle, and shook my head. I didn't want to get involved. There were memories I didn't want to bring back – shouts and screams in the night, Dad bawling *The Sash My Father Wore* and other Orange songs at the top of his voice, drunk as a lord, Mum complaining about the housekeeping she never had, then wrapping Billy and me in a big tartan blanket and rushing us up the street to Gran's because she knew another row was brewing.

'Don't have anything to do with him, Carole. He'd have put me in an early grave that pig, I swear—'

'Yes, Mum,' I interrupted. 'Do we all have sugar? I forget.'

Mum looked at me. 'We miss you, love. Little Sean asks after you all the time. Why don't you come back to Aberdeen? Your gran's got enough to do with her cleaning job as well as you lot.'

'Mum,' I said, 'I'm not going back to Aberdeen. I'm happy here. I've got everything I want.'

'You mean you've got your Italian waiter? That's all he is.'

I knew I'd made her angry, but where Marco was concerned I didn't care. 'I love him, and he loves me. That's all that matters.'

'You're sounding like a Mills and ruddy Boon, girl,' she snapped. 'Grow up!'

Now *I* was angry. 'I *am* grown up, Mum. Believe it or not.'

The kettle whistled. I turned my back and splashed hot water into the pot. In the living-room I heard Gran and Sean chuckling together.

Mum sighed. 'Aye, you are, love,' she said quietly. 'I just can't help worrying about you, that's all.'

'Tarantara!' I cried, pushing open the living-room door. Marco looked up from the dinner table. He'd lit the two candles I'd put on it. The rest of the room was dark, but Marco's eyes brightened as he saw the pizza I was carrying.

'Well, sit down, then.'

I put the plate in front of him, and settled opposite.

Grinning, Marco raised his knife and fork. He lifted the edge of the pizza and smacked his lips.

'Thin like they make them in Italy,' I said. 'With a bit of a charcoal underneath. That's right, isn't it?'

'Sure.' He nodded, and pushed his fork into the pizza. There was a crack and a wedge shot off across the tablecloth. Marco snatched it up and popped it into his mouth.

'Is it OK?'

'Mmm. Mmm.' Marco nodded again, chomping quickly. It crackled in his mouth like a giant crisp.

'Just like Mama used to make?'

'Mmm. Mmm.' Our eyes met. I couldn't hold back my laughter. The thing was obviously *awful*. Suddenly we were both roaring uncontrollably.

'Mama never made one like this,' Marco managed at last.

'Never mind,' I said. 'I'll give it to little Sean. He can use it for a frisbee.'

Marco's face softened. 'I will miss you when I go back home this time, Carole. I will miss your laugh. You have good laugh.'

And then I didn't want to laugh any more.

This is what had been lurking in the background all day, all autumn. Marco's military service. Every Italian young man had to spend a couple of years in the forces. Marco's service would start in the new year and his time at the Turnberry, and in Scotland, would be over.

'Well,' I said as brightly as I could, 'you can hear me laugh when you phone me from Italy. And we can write to each other. It's not as if you haven't made trips home before.'

But, even though those trips had been months at a time, I'd always known Marco was coming back. I didn't know that this time.

He touched my hand. 'You come with me,' he said. 'You come to Italy.'

I looked at him. 'You could always come back here.'

'I can't live in Scotland, Carole – I'd die of cold! My family, my friends are all in Rome—'

'And all mine are here.' I pulled my hand away. 'It's the same for me, Marco.'

I got up and took the plate out, trying not to be annoyed. How many times had I explained it to him? Everything I had was in Scotland. I couldn't just give all that up – not for what we had at the moment.

When I came back, he looked so glum I immediately felt bad. But he got straight up and came over to me.

'Carole – the present I promise you. You come with me tomorrow. We buy it together.'

I laughed. 'It sounds pretty big if it needs two of us to go! What is it, a duvet or something?'

Marco shook his head. 'It's a ring.'

'A ring?'

'In Italy,' he said, 'friends, they give rings to show how much they care for each other.'

I felt myself go very still inside.

'In Scotland, it's to show they want to marry each other.'

Marco's eyes were glistening. 'I know.'

'Oh Marco—'

We hugged so tightly I never wanted him to let go of me again.

We bought the ring from Ratner's in Carrick Street, just down the road from the day centre. Some of the rings were very expensive, but I knew Marco didn't earn a lot at the Turnberry so I chose a simple diamond solitaire in an eight-pointed flower setting. Marco slipped it on my finger, and the diamond sparkled and flashed in the shop light. It was the most beautiful thing I had ever owned.

'Oh Carole,' Val cooed when I showed it to her. 'So this is it, eh? The real thing. I'm so happy for you.'

But, gorgeous though it was, the ring couldn't put off the day of Marco's departure. The morning of his flight I went with him to Glasgow airport.

I hate saying goodbye in public places, but this was doubly

painful. We hugged and kissed by the departure gate. The tears were pouring down Marco's face, but I didn't dare cry in case I broke down completely. I thought I was going to die. It took all the strength I could muster to push him away, or he would have missed his flight altogether.

'I write, I call,' he cried as he went through the gate. 'We work something out. I love you, Carole!'

People smiled around me. I turned bright scarlet, but I didn't care. We waved until we couldn't see each other any more.

The weeks passed in a kind of grey fog, only brightened by a phone call or a letter from Marco. He was going to be stationed in a place called Orvieto, which sounded a long way from his family in Rome. He wasn't looking forward to it.

I told him not to pine; the sooner it was all over, the sooner we could be together again. I wanted us both to believe it with all our hearts. But, even though I prayed for that, I had my black moments, too.

It could be two years before we were together again. What if he met someone else? What if his family decided he ought to marry an Italian girl and not a foreigner? So many things could go wrong.

Then I'd hear Marco's voice on the phone and it would be like standing close to him, seeing his smile again, and I wouldn't have any doubts at all that everything would be all right.

But the letter that landed on the mat one spring morning was still a bombshell.

'Are you OK, Carole?' Gran asked, coming out of the living-room. 'You look like you've seen a ghost.'

'She's just mooning over Marco again!' Billy called from the kitchen. 'Oh Marco! Marco! Come to me! Come to me!'

'It *is* from Marco.' I ignored my brother. 'He wants me to meet his family. He wants me to go and live in Italy. Oh Gran,' I cried, 'he really does want to marry me!'

Rome

MAY 1982

Suddenly the days weren't long enough. I had my flight to arrange, my notice to hand in at the day centre, packing to do, a whole mass of shopping to get through – summer clothes, a new bikini, sun-tan lotion, new sunglasses – the list was endless. And, of course, I had a lifetime's goodbyes to say.

Val was astonished when I told her, gave me a big hug, then wailed, 'But Carole, I'll never see you again!'

'You won't get rid of me that easily!' I laughed. 'I'll be back. I just can't say when.'

'You're so lucky,' she said. 'Could you get Marco to send over a friend to take his place? I'd take good care of him.'

Lots of the old folk came up to wish me luck, as well as Essie and the others. I think I even managed to impress Billy for the first time in his life. Gran wasn't so impressed.

She didn't say much, but she didn't have to. Going out with Marco when he lived down the road was one thing; disappearing with him to a foreign country was breaking up her little family. But I knew she was leaving the big guns to Mum and, even in my excitement, I braced myself.

My flight was on Monday 31 May. Mum came down for the the weekend to help me get ready, and arranged to have the Monday off from her two cleaning jobs so she could see me on to the plane.

'You don't speak a word of the language, Carole,' she told me. 'You don't understand the money or the food—'

'Marco does,' I said. 'He'll show me all that.'

'Marco! Marco! Don't you ever think of anything else?'

I slammed a sweater into my case. We were in my bedroom on the Sunday night, putting my things together for the last time.

'I'm going, Mum,' I said. 'And that's that.'

She turned away and lit up an Embassy. 'What'll you do out there? Have you thought about that?'

'Marco says I can find work with a nanny agency. Lots of foreign girls do it. I'm used to little Sean. It'll be easy. I'll be all right, Mum.'

'I don't know how people can give over their kids to some stranger; *I* couldn't do it.' Mum pointed at the case. 'That's my sweater you've got there.'

I took it out, and pushed it into her hands. She folded it carefully, then put it back in the case.

'Good for the old ego, going shopping with you,' she said softly. 'People thinking we were sisters.'

We looked at each other. I'd always thought of Mum as such a toughie, so strong and sparky; suddenly it was a shock to see how petite she really was, how vulnerable underneath. For the first time I saw my leaving as she did.

'What can I do?' she breathed. 'I can't keep you chained up.'

I smiled. 'No, Mum.'

The last time I'd stood at the departure gate I'd thought the world was ending. The feeling came back in a rush as Mum and I had a last hug.

What if Marco changed his mind when I got to Italy? What if his family didn't like me? What would happen to me then?

'God,' I whispered, 'I hope I'm doing the right thing.'

Mum's grip tightened, then the call for the Rome flight came again and we broke apart.

'I'll ring you tomorrow evening, see you arrived OK,' Mum said. 'It's easy enough to use the Mobil Oil phones when I'm cleaning. Take care, child,' she whispered.

I picked up my bulging case, took a deep breath, and hurried.

Just after the captain announced we were about to land, the plane's nose dipped and the sunlight pouring in through the cabin windows suddenly seemed harsher, more real, even though it had been bright enough in Glasgow.

The flight had been a dead time, but at least it had given me a chance to settle my thoughts. I loved Marco. There wasn't a doubt of that in my mind. If he only loved me half as much – and I was sure he loved me much more than that – everything would be all right. Whatever problems we had, I knew I could make things work for us. I rolled my ring between my fingers as the wheels bumped on to the runway and screeched loudly.

The heat outside was like slipping on a warm coat. It rose up from the tarmac and bounced off the white-painted buildings. It was like stepping into another world.

Wishing I'd kept my sunglasses somewhere handy, I followed the other passengers through passport control, and felt a twinge of unease as the man in the booth studied my photo. Then I joined the jostling crowd by the carousel.

Someone nudged my back. I turned and nearly jumped out of my skin. A dark-uniformed policeman, who looked no older than Marco, squeezed past me. He had an enormous black sub-machine-gun slung over his shoulder. *My God*, I thought, *who are they expecting?*

The luggage began to thump on to the carousel. What if my case was lost? What if Marco had been delayed? I looked round. No one looked British; no one seemed to be speaking English. Then my case tumbled into view. Breathing in, I heaved it on to a free trolley. Through the customs gate were more police-men, more guns. And then a mass of faces under a low ceiling.

Sing-song Italian voices were all round me; men with topcoats draped over their shoulders, like old-fashioned gang-sters; pencil-thin women who looked as though they'd stepped out of snooty fashion advertisements; two nuns sweeping by; children shrieking.

Where was Marco?

Then, with a shock, I realised I was looking straight at him. He was gazing away from me, dressed in a smart, light brown uniform with shiny buttons and a peaked cap, a big bunch of roses swinging in his hand. Of course. Why hadn't I thought? He was bound to be in uniform.

My heart began to bump. I couldn't stop my grin as I moved closer, reached up and tapped him on the shoulder.

'Carole!'

His arms swept round me. Suddenly people were clapping

and laughing. I looked round in surprise.

'Carole,' Marco beamed at me, 'my mother, my father, my sister Marguerite – all the Vitulanos are here to welcome you!'

I blinked at the three smiling faces and stretched out my hand. Immediately each of them hugged me in turn, pecking me on both cheeks, gabbling brightly in Italian.

Marco burst into laughter. 'My Carole!' he cried. 'Always blushing!'

I felt my face burning as I grinned and nudged him.

'Is good,' his sister nodded. 'You show him who is *capo* – boss.'

Marco made a face at her, and Marguerite butted him with an elbow. 'See, my terrible sister!' he cried. 'Don't listen to her, Carole, she give you bad habits.'

I laughed as his mother shooh-shoohed him. Marguerite was a pretty, petite, fair-haired girl of about sixteen. She and Marco reminded me of Billy and me. I was glad she knew some English.

Mr Vitulano was pulling my case off the trolley. Marco slid his arm round my waist.

'Come on, Carole,' he said. 'Now we go home.'

Home was in the *Citta Militare* at Cecchignola, a huge barracks about half an hour's drive from Rome airport. Marco's father was a civilian worker there.

It seemed to be in the middle of open countryside. We drove past playing fields down a long, shaded entrance road. Young soldiers lounged and joked at an open barrier, waving us through as Marco's father showed his pass.

Marco's family lived in a flat overlooking a parade ground. It was cramped but homely. They had a large living-room, but only two small bedrooms; one belonged to his mother and father; the other was to be mine. I was worried about taking up so much space.

'It's OK,' said Marco, showing me two fold-up beds in the living-room. 'Marguerite and I, we sleep here. Is no problem.'

If it was, nobody seemed to show it. Marco's mother, who was small and fair, chattered away endlessly, smiling and patting my hand. She was so friendly, I felt bad that I could only nod and smile back.

After the excitement of the airport, Marco's father became quieter, more self-contained. He was short and dark, like

Marco, with a gentle way about him. Even though I couldn't understand a word they said to me, I thought they were both nice people; I felt welcome.

Over dinner they all laughed as I struggled with my first Italian spaghetti. Mr Vitulano showed me how to curl the long strings around my fork. Mrs Vitulano took my hand to have a closer look at my ring.

'What does she say?' I asked Marco.

'She says the diamond sparkles like your eyes – lovely blue eyes, *bella*, beautiful –'

I smiled, and thanked her. Mr Vitulano raised his wine glass and spoke.

'My father says he is proud to have an English daughter,' Marco translated.

'Scottish,' I reminded him.

'Ah, *scozzese* –'

'*Scozzese! Scozzese! Viva la Scozia!*' Mr Vitulano cried.

Even I could understand that. I grinned, and lifted my glass. Something jumped on to my lap and dug needles into my thigh, right through my skirt fabric.

I shrieked, splashing my wine. A tiny bundle of black fur shot across the floor and rocketed up the curtains near to Mr Vitulano.

'*Gatto matto!*' he snapped, throwing out his arm. The kitten twisted and fell back on to the carpet, eyes burning, then raced away behind the furniture. I gave a shudder.

'Are you all right, Carole?' Marco asked.

'Cats,' I said. 'I can't stand them. They give me the willies.'

His mother and father both started to talk to him, glancing at me. Marco shook his head. Mrs Vitulano dabbed at a spot of wine I'd splashed on to his shirt. Marco frowned, and shrugged her away.

'Tomorrow,' he told me, 'we go to Rome. I show you everything. We have fantastic time.'

We did. Marco wasn't due in Orvieto for a couple of weeks. Fourteen whole days to spend together! More than we'd ever had in Scotland.

Next morning we began by catching the early bus to the Coliseum. We did the whole tourist bit – joking at the awful, gawdy souvenirs outside the Vatican, throwing coins in the

Trevi fountain (even though it was boarded up for renovations), listening to the young people playing guitars and singing pop songs on the Spanish Steps.

We watched policemen in stylish red and black capes posing with tourists for photos (Marco insisted I had a go, too, even though I hate having my picture taken). We dodged scooter drivers – without helmets – weaving recklessly in and out of the traffic, and even on the pavements. We drank cappuccinos in bars, and gobbled endless pizzas and ice creams, until Marco warned me I'd explode or turn into a fat Italian mama.

Rome was bright and gawdy, gorgeous and grotty, full of mad Italians shouting at the tops of their voices, making weird gestures I didn't understand, or posing like film stars, and laughing and kissing and hugging each other – even the men – as if they didn't care what anyone thought.

I'd never seen people so stylish, so larger-than-life. Sometimes I was tempted to laugh out loud; I just couldn't believe they were being serious. Then I'd see people in traffic queues have screaming rows, leaping out of cars and waving their arms about; I'd be terrified they were going to kill each other. And Marco would just shrug, as if it were perfectly normal.

I knew Scots had a reputation for being dour and undemonstrative, but at least you knew where you were with them.

But all I really noticed was Marco, seeing him smile, feeling his arm round my waist, loving the warm kisses we shared on the stairs up to his parents' flat every night. I'd never felt so close to him before. I'd never felt this close to anyone.

'Carole,' he'd whisper, '*ti amo*—'

'*Ti amo*, Marco—'

I didn't need any more Italian.

One evening Marguerite and her boyfriend came with us to Luna Park, an enormous permanent funfair just down the road from Cecchignola.

I thought it was great; there were dozens of stalls, a big-dipper, a big-wheel, a full-sized American riverboat, a light-house, a ghost-house, a lake with pedaloes, rides through a gold mine, rides with sea monsters and a giant octopus – even a ride named after the Loch Ness monster.

'You see it?' Marguerite asked me. 'This monster, in Scotland?' We had to shout over the booming pop music.

I laughed. 'It's not real, Marguerite. It's just something for tourists.'

'But I see pictures – photos – is very famous.'

'We don't see much of it in Ayr.'

Marco laughed and squeezed my waist.

We ran into a group of his friends. They were lively and friendly, but none of them seemed to speak English.

As we came out of the Love Boat – the American riverboat – a small, dark girl came up and smiled at Marco. He said something to her in Italian. The girl took a long, careful look at me, then waved to the others and strolled away.

I asked Marguerite who she was.

'She was his *ragazza* – his girlfriend.'

'She's very pretty.'

Marguerite shrugged. 'Not nice girl, like you. Too much—' She grinned. 'I don't know word.' She put a finger under her nose and pushed it into the air.

'Stuck up? Snobbish?'

'*Snobismo, si*,' Marguerite nodded. 'They were to be – *sposati* – married. Everyone think so, but Marco say no. All finish now.'

Marco appeared, grabbing hold of my hand and dragging me off to another ride. Moments later we were whirled away into a kaleidoscope of bright colours and pounding music, his arm tight around my waist. But inside I was quite still.

Of course, I knew Marco had had other girlfriends, but I hadn't realised there had ever been talk of marriage. Had he given this girl a ring, too? Had he told her he loved her? They still seemed friendly enough.

Was it a coincidence she'd turned up tonight?

Suddenly all the closeness and warmth of the last few days felt threatened.

The next day Marco played tennis with a friend. We'd talked about going shopping in Rome with Mrs Vitulano, but I decided to stay in and catch up on my washing. When Marco came home from his game we had the flat to ourselves.

He put on his favourite Black Sabbath album at full volume – he'd always been a heavy metal freak. I told him he ought to turn it down before the neighbours started to bang on the walls.

'But it's for my English,' he protested. 'You can tell me what they are saying.'

'They're not *saying*,' I said. 'They're shouting.'

'Italians love to shout,' he grinned. 'They like a big noise.' But he reached over and turned down the volume.

I sat next to him on the sofa. He slipped his arm round my shoulder, and I snuggled up close. It was something we could hardly ever do in the flat. There were always other people around.

'I learn to speak good English,' he said. 'I go to the United States, I open hotel with good food, with swimming pool. I get 1937 Buick convertible and play Black Sabbath out of big loudspeakers. Don't laugh! Is true!'

'I'm not laughing,' I grinned.

Through the living-room window I could hear soldiers tramping on the parade ground, cars passing, people talking in the flats nearby. I wondered if it would be like this when we were married, alone in our own little flat with no one to please but ourselves.

Marco turned to me and we kissed. After a moment he brought his hand up on to my T-shirt.

I remembered a Saturday night back home when I'd seen Marco at the Turnberry. We'd walked and talked on the beach for so long I'd missed the last bus, and he'd sneaked me into his room in the staff cottage just below the hotel. If I'd been found there, he could have been sacked.

I'd spent the night in his bed, with Marco curled up uncomfortably under a blanket in an armchair. He hadn't been too happy about that, but he was a Catholic like me; he knew I wanted to save myself until I was married.

But that was a long time ago, before rings and promises and big decisions.

He looked surprised when I didn't push his hand away. We sank on to the cushions. My heart was hammering.

'Carole,' he said softly, 'is all right?'

I didn't want him to see how terrified I was.

'I will be gentle,' he whispered. 'Very gentle . . .'

Afterwards I knew we couldn't get any closer. I couldn't give him any more. If we weren't married in the eyes of the Church, we were married in every other way.

Via Margutta

JUNE 1982

Though I hated to think of it, I knew this time would come to an end and I would have to be sensible about the future.

Mr and Mrs Vitulano didn't put any pressure on me, but I knew I couldn't continue to accept their hospitality once Marco had gone. I already felt guilty about keeping Marguerite out of the bedroom I was using. She was staying on at school to retake some exams, and she needed somewhere to study.

By now I was registered with a nanny agency – nannies were called 'baby-sitters' in Italy. Quite soon a job came up, looking after a two-year-old boy at an address in the Via Margutta. Marco said it was one of the most fashionable areas in Rome; only wealthy people could afford to live there.

One afternoon Marco and Marguerite came with me to meet the little boy's mother, a Mrs Ricci. The Via Margutta turned out to be close to the Spanish Steps. It was a narrow, cobbled street with high buildings painted the dingy, orangey-brown colour that was everywhere in Rome. Behind the shop windows, though, were expensive antiques and tapestries.

We found the address and went through an archway into a tatty-looking yard, full of Vespas and the cluttered balconies of flats. On one of them was a tailor's dummy painted with bizarre colours. Paint was flaking off the walls and there were piles of rubbish in the corners. If this was how wealthy people lived in Rome, I wasn't too impressed.

Mrs Ricci's was through another archway at the far end, and up a flight of old stone steps. At the top, off a winding pathway, was a house with peeling green shutters, and a green-painted front door. There seemed an awful lot of cats about outside.

Inside, though, everything was much smarter – big, cool rooms with high ceilings and polished floors; not much furniture, but all of it obviously very expensive.

'From Scotland?' said Mrs Ricci brightly. 'Recently I had a girl from Australia. A student. She was very good. It helps me with my English.'

I smiled politely. Mrs Ricci was very attractive. She was about thirty, with a beautiful tan, and long, thick, dark hair which she constantly tossed back off her face. Her clothes were gorgeous. But she was so mannered I wondered if she was putting it on. I kept thinking of Miss Piggy in the Muppets. I tried not to look at Marco in case I laughed.

I explained all about my work with the old folk, and how much I enjoyed looking after little Sean, who was about the same age as Mrs Ricci's son.

But Marco and Marguerite did most of the talking, in Italian. Two enormous St Bernards wandered in, and were shoohed out by Mrs Ricci. Then a little blond-haired boy peered round the edge of the door.

'Emanuele!' Mrs Ricci cried. 'Come say hello, *caro. Venite*—'

The little boy ran over, and buried his head against her. 'Say hello to Carole,' she said. '*Di buongiorno a Carole.*'

The little boy turned his head to me and covered his face, looking warily through his fingers. We all chuckled.

'He's shy,' said Mrs Ricci.

'That's all right,' I said. 'So am I.'

I held up my hand and peeped round the side of it, the way I used to do with little Sean. Emanuele stared, then there was a ghost of a smile. Mrs Ricci laughed.

We left after an hour. Marco and Marguerite thought Mrs Ricci liked me. The next day the agency phoned to say I had the job.

How could I bear to say goodbye to Marco again so soon?

Talking about it was one thing – going through with it was another.

We made endless promises to write every day, to talk on the phone as often as we could. At least Orvieto wasn't as far away as I'd feared – just a couple of hours' train ride from Rome.

Marguerite and I planned to go and visit whenever I had a weekend free, and Marco would come home whenever he had two or three days' leave. We would be much closer than if I'd been stuck back in Scotland.

But none of those thoughts stopped the pain, the feeling of unfairness, as if no one had any right to keep us apart after what had happened in the last fortnight. As soon as Marco had gone there was a horrible emptiness. I was suddenly on my own in a country where I couldn't even say hello properly, let alone ask for help. I couldn't help feeling apprehensive.

I started in the Via Margutta on Monday June 14.

Mrs Ricci seemed just as flamboyant alone with me as she'd been in company, but I was grateful she was so friendly. 'Call me Emanuela,' she said at once.

She showed me the bedroom I'd be sharing with little Emanuele, introduced me to her maid, Rosa, who came in every day to look after the house, then sat down in the kitchen to write out the Italian words I'd find most useful, like 'bread' and 'drink' and 'ice cream'. It was up to me how I looked after Emanuele, as long as I kept Mrs Ricci informed. She would be in and out all the time, though she didn't give me the impression she had a job.

The only thing that didn't appeal to me was having to feed the cats I'd seen lurking outside. Mrs Ricci looked after a dozen of the local strays. I was glad her two St Bernards kept them out of the house.

When she'd finished explaining about the job, she showed me where the pushchair was kept and told me to take Emanuele for a walk so we could get to know each other. Then she opened her bag and pushed a wad of notes into my hand.

'If he cries for anything, you get it for him,' she said. 'And get yourself something, too. I have to go now.'

She smothered the little boy in kisses. As she went out of the kitchen door, his little face dropped and he burst into tears. I picked him up and cuddled him, and tried to distract him with a toy.

Rosa came in, frowning. She gave me a thin smile when she saw what I was doing.

She was a small, dark, middle-aged woman, who didn't

speak any English. Mrs Ricci had told me she had been with
the family a long time; I had the distinct feeling I was treading
on her toes.

She could be very odd, too. A few days later I was walking
down the corridor just outside the kitchen and there was a
crash right behind me. I looked round and a little religious
picture had fallen to the floor and smashed. It was a very dark
corridor; I'd probably brushed the picture without noticing.
The next thing I knew Rosa was there, looking as if she'd seen
a ghost, gabbling away at me. She made me cross myself and
say what sounded like a little prayer. I thought she was off her
rocker, but I did what she wanted just to keep her quiet.

At least Emanuele was straightforward. He was a sweet little
boy. At his age his Italian was about as good as mine. His
shyness didn't last, especially after Rosa had showed me his
favourite ice cream – peppermint-flavoured – and how to make
pasta the way he liked it. By the time I was tucking him into
bed for the night we seemed to be getting along fine.

The first evening the telephone rang, and Emanuela called
me in from the living-room. I rushed into the hall, thinking it
was Marco, but it was Mum, ringing from the offices where
she had her cleaning job.

'Are you well, Carole?'

'I'm fine, Mum. I've got a lovely little boy to look after.'

'Was that the woman you're working for?'

'Emanuela, yes; she's been great. It's a lovely house, too.
How's little Sean?'

I didn't want to say how much I missed Marco.

As soon as Mum had gone the phone rang again. 'You are a
popular girl, Carole!' Mrs Ricci laughed when she answered it.
This time it was the voice I'd been longing to hear.

'Carole, I miss you so much.'

' I miss you, too, Marco.'

I went to bed feeling things weren't so bad after all; they
would work out, we would be OK.

It didn't take very long to settle in. Emanuele had his tantrums,
like any toddler, but he wasn't a naughty boy; looking after
him was easy.

The area turned out to be nicer than I'd first realised. Most days, after I'd got Emanuele up and given him his breakfast, we'd have a walk. Just outside the archway in the Via Margutta was a furniture restorer's shop with a big window; Emanuele liked to stand outside, watching the men work. Occasionally we'd go left down the Via del Babuino or the Via del Corso and have a look at all the smart shops. Usually, though, we turned right towards the huge, open Piazza del Popolo with its pavement cafés and tall Egyptian column in the middle. At one side steps led up to the Pincio and the Borghese Gardens, which Emanuele loved.

From the parapet at the top you could see right across Rome. There was a little roundabout for children and usually a van selling ice cream nearby. Then we'd walk down the long, tree-lined paths, looking at the smartly dressed horse riders, or the ducks on the lake. It was lovely and peaceful.

When we got home again, Mrs Ricci – Emanuela – would be flitting in and out. She couldn't have been more generous. She let me phone Marco as often as I liked. She even offered to lend me some of her clothes; we were a similar size. I had the impression she was a bit miffed when I turned her down. She didn't seem to understand that her things were much too swish to wear for just messing about with a toddler, and with Marco away I didn't have anyone to dress up for.

One thing that puzzled me was that there didn't appear to be a *Mr* Ricci. Emanuela mentioned Emanuele's father – he seemed to be some kind of architect – but she didn't give the impression she was married to him. She seemed to have lots of friends, though.

One night she gave a dinner party for her brother, Enrico, and a girlfriend she said was visiting from Rio. Enrico was in his late twenties and tall, with short brown hair. He could speak a little English, but not as much as Emanuela. He was outgoing and friendly, and very good-looking.

The girl from Rio was very attractive, too. She had strawberry blonde hair and wore piles of expensive-looking jewellery. When Emanuela introduced us she looked at me as if I was something the stray cats had brought in.

Emanuela also went out a lot. The third night I was there a boyfriend called for her.

After Mum had telephoned, I went to bed early with a slight

tummy-ache. It felt like indigestion, and I thought it would go away overnight. But it got worse, and I started to feel sick. Eventually I had to get up. The pain was agonising. I could hardly walk. I literally crawled downstairs. Emanuela had mentioned that I could always ring her mother in case of emergencies, but I couldn't find the number. Eventually I collapsed on the settee in the living-room.

Emanuela, thank goodness, wasn't home late. By now all I could do was groan. My side felt as if it was on fire.

'Carole,' Emanuela cried, 'what's wrong? Have you been taking drugs?'

I told her she must be joking; I'd never done anything like that in my life.

Her boyfriend had come with her. They both looked really worried.

'We'll have to take you to the hospital', Emanuela said. 'But you must say you are on holiday with me, Carole. Do you understand? I don't have a permit so you can work for me. Just say I am a friend.'

I nodded. I didn't really care what I said as long as someone stopped the pain.

Emanuela and her boyfriend helped me to his car. Every movement seemed to drive knives through me. I thought I was going to faint. 'It's only a little way, Carole,' Emanuela said. 'You will remember what I told you won't you?'

But the last thing I remembered was the grizzled old head of a statue looming out of a wall as we drove through the hospital entrance.

I found out later I had appendicitis.

I spent just over a week in San Giacomo hospital. It was only a couple of streets away from the house, just off the Via Del Corso.

After I'd been operated on, I seemed to feel woozy for ages, drifting in and out of sleep. One evening Marco's mother came to visit me. I dozed off, and suddenly it was morning. Mrs Vitulano was still sitting beside me. It was so nice of her, and I couldn't even thank her properly.

She came back regularly with Marguerite and Mr Vitulano, and then – the best tonic of all – with Marco, who had a few days' leave.

Emanuela only visited me once, but she paid all the bills and never mentioned the money. When I got out of hospital she let me invite Marco round one evening when she was out.

I also had a frantic phone call from Mum.

'Carole, where the hell have you been? I've been ringing and ringing – I've been that worried!'

She got even more agitated as I told her what had happened. 'My God,' she said. 'My God—'

'There was nothing you could do, Mum,' I told her. 'I didn't see any point in letting you know when it was only going to upset you. And I'm fine now—'

'For God's sake, Carole,' she cried. 'I'm your mother. I'm entitled to be upset!'

I saw Marco every day he was back. We took Emanuele for long walks in the Borghese Gardens, played with him and bought him peppermint ice creams. Little old ladies used to smile at him, then smile at us, thinking he was ours.

Even though I blushed and made Marco laugh, it was a nice feeling. I wondered how long it would be before it was true.

Marco had to go back, of course, but the blow was softened when Marguerite and I took the train to Orvieto the following weekend. We spent the Sunday with Marco, wandering round the town.

Marco's barracks looked quite grim, but Orvieto was extraordinary, a cramped little town full of incredibly old, grey stone buildings and narrow, winding streets right on the top of a massive hill. Its cathedral was as beautiful as anything I'd seen in Rome.

It was a lovely break, even if leaving each other didn't get any easier. But what I didn't find out until I got back to Rome was that we were saying goodbye for much longer than I'd realised.

One morning towards the end of June I came down early to get breakfast started. The stray cats began scratching at the kitchen door, which they always did when they heard someone inside.

I took some scraps out of the fridge, opened the door a crack, threw the scraps out and slammed the door again with a shudder.

'Carole!' Emanuela cried suddenly from behind me. 'You make me jump! You're so quiet – nobody in Italy is that quiet!'

I turned with a slightly guilty smile. Emanuela was still in her nightdress. There was more scratching at the door.

'Are you sure you're feeding those cats?'

'Yes, Emanuela. They're eating fine.' I knew she wanted me to take the food outside and make sure each of them got fed, but there was no way I was going to do that.

'I have to go to Paris for a few days soon,' she said. 'I think it would be nice for Emanuele to have a little holiday, now the weather is getting so hot. My parents have a holiday home in Ortisei, near Bolzano. Enrico can drive you all up there. It'll do you good, too, Carole.'

I felt a twinge of unease. I'd got used to the Via Margutta. 'Is it far?' I asked.

'Ortisei? Not too far, no. It's in the Alto Adige – you know, the Italian Alps. It's beautiful this time of year.'

The Alps? I thought they were in Switzerland. Surely that must be hundreds of miles away.

'How long will we be away, Emanuela?'

She shrugged. 'A few weeks, I don't know. We'll see how we feel.' She gave me a quick smile. 'You and Emanuele have a good time, Carole. You'll love it there. Now, have you made the coffee?'

4

Ortisei

JULY 1982

Enrico arrived early one morning. We loaded up his car, Emanuela said her goodbyes, and I sat in the back with Emanuele on my lap. Then we set off across Rome to pick up Emanuela's mother and father.

I couldn't pretend I was happy about going. It was bad enough that Marco and I would be even further apart – too far, I was sure, for us to see each other during leaves or at weekends. Even worse was not knowing how long this would last.

On top of that Emanuela obviously wasn't going to be around. I was going to be stuck in a household full of people I didn't know at all, and who hardly spoke any English. I couldn't see Emanuela's parents letting me phone Marco as often as Emanuela had.

The mother was in her fifties and struck me as a similar character to Emanuela; the father was quite a bit older, a tall, grey-haired, stout man. Emanuela had told me he had been quite ill recently, which is why he needed a nursemaid to look after him. Her name was Nicole.

She was about ten years older than me, and she came from Mauritius. She had dusky skin and dark, waist-length hair. Her looks were stunning. The first time I saw her, helping Grandfather Ricci into the car, I thought, 'My God, are there only rich or glamorous people around here? When am I going to meet someone ordinary?'

But as the day went on Nicole did take away one worry. I found out her English was very good. At least I'd have someone to translate for me.

The drive was a long one, the worst part at the beginning crossing hot, flat countryside that seemed to go on forever, with towns perched on hills on either side of the autostrada; one of them, I realised as I saw the sign, was Orvieto. Then, suddenly, it was all long, dark tunnels or bridges strung over plunging ravines, with rivers bubbling away miles below.

Quite late in the afternoon, we saw the first of the mountains. They looked like a massive, jagged barrier that would stop everything dead in its tracks. But the motorway seemed to find a way through, with steep cliffs rearing up on either side. Finally we turned off. A little road wound upwards along the side of an enormous valley. There were tremendous drops on our right-hand side, giving me more than a few lumps in my throat as Enrico raced along. He was yodelling out of the car window and making Emanuele laugh.

The scenery was wonderful. Lush and green, almost like a park, with pretty little houses, decorated like cuckoo clocks, dotted all over the place. Everything was either up or down; I couldn't see level ground anywhere.

My ears started to pop, and we were still climbing.

Eventually, the valley flattened out and Ortisei was in view – row upon row of cuckoo-clock houses; only the fir forests and mountain peaks seemed to be higher.

Number Ten Via Meisules, the Ricci's house, was a white-painted, wooden-roofed terrace on one of the long hillside roads overlooking the village. Inside everything was neat and wooden. There were four floors, but only a garage on the ground floor. Nicole and I had a bedroom each in the attic, and I shared with Emanuele.

Ortisei was beautiful, and the house was very comfortable, but the first few days were quite hard for me. Emanuela's parents were pleasant enough, even if the grandfather tended to be a bit grumpy, but they weren't as friendly as Emanuela, and not being able to talk to them properly made things difficult.

Nicole helped, of course, but it took me a while to get to know her. Perhaps it was because she was older and more self-assured, or the fact that she was much more part of the family than I was – I don't know.

I wrote to Marco a lot, and we did manage to talk on the phone; those were precious times. But I couldn't help thinking that I'd made all this effort to come to Italy, and now we weren't seeing any more of each other than if I'd stayed at home.

Things improved after Enrico and his mother went back to Rome. Nicole and I had more time to ourselves, and I found out she wasn't as stuck-up as I feared she might be. In fact, we had a lot more in common than I realised: she told me she was planning to give up her job and move in with her boyfriend, though she didn't want the Riccis to know about it until it was all settled.

She was good company, and we spent most of our time together, either in the house or out shopping or taking Emanuele for walks in the village. We used to joke about who needed more looking after, the little boy, or his crotchety old grandpa.

After a couple of weeks there was still no sign of Emanuela arriving, and no one seemed to have any idea when we were going back to Rome.

One Sunday – it was 11 July – Nicole and Emanuele and I spent the afternoon and the early evening in the village. Nicole wanted to stay out even longer because it was her half day off, but it was getting late for Emanuele's tea. All three of us walked back to the house.

While I prepared Emanuele's pasta, Nicole chatted through the kitchen window. Next door, in the sitting-room, Grandfather Ricci was watching football on television. Apparently it was the World Cup final between Italy and Germany; Italians are soccer mad, and everyone in the village was talking about it. Nicole didn't want the grandfather to know she was around. When I laughed out loud at one point, she pressed a finger to her lips and shook her head.

'Quiet!' she hissed. 'If the old man knows I'm here he'll find a job for me – you know what he's like.'

'Don't worry,' I said. 'He can't hear a thing with the telly on.'

We went on talking while Emanuele finished his meal.

'Come for a walk,' said Nicole. 'I can't stand watching football. There's nothing else to do here.'

I cleaned up Emanuele's face and hands. 'I can't. It's

Emanuele's bedtime in a minute, and I've got to wash up.'

'Carole! Don't be mean! Give me a break from the old man—'

'OK.' I smiled. 'Just a wee walk up the hill, then.'

I helped Emanuele out of his chair, and we went out.

It was a beautiful evening, still bright and warm. We went up the road, away from the village. Not far from the Ricci's there was a gap between the houses, and a grassy bank with a path leading up to the road above. We started to climb it.

Nicole was talking about her boyfriend when, all of a sudden, she stopped. She was gazing back the way we'd come.

'What's the matter?' I asked.

'Isn't that smoke?'

I looked. There *was* smoke, drifting over the rooftops further down the road. It was odd. Ortisei seemed much too neat and tidy a place for people to have bonfires in their gardens.

'I can't see where it's coming from,' I said.

Nicole took Emanuele's hand. 'Go and have a look, Carole.'

I went back down the slope until I could get a better view of the terrace which included Number Ten.

'I think it's the house next to ours,' I cried.

Nicole was following behind me. 'No, it isn't—' she gasped.

'Oh my God.' I felt a cold stab of fear. 'Signor Ricci!'

I ran down on to the road. As I got closer I could see thick smoke pouring out of a second floor window at the front.

I rushed round to the main door at the back, calling out as I went in, 'Signor Ricci! Signor Ricci!'

The little hallway smelled strongly of smoke. I heard a crowd roar on the television. I pushed open the sitting-room door.

The air was grey with smoke haze. Billows of it were rolling down the staircase in the corner. Oblivious to it all, Grandfather Ricci sat hunched in his armchair, eyes glued to the blaring set.

'Signor Ricci!' I cried. 'Get out! *Fuori! Presto!*'

He turned and scowled at me – and turned back!

Really frightened now, I clutched at his arm and tried to pull him out of the armchair. At first he struggled and barked angrily in Italian. Then it finally dawned on him something was wrong. He lurched to his feet. I was so relieved. He was a big man. I couldn't physically have dragged him anywhere.

We went back towards the door. The old man was getting

more and more excited, shaking his head and patting his pockets.

'*Mio denaro*—!' he cried suddenly. '*Mio denaro*!' The house was on fire and he was worrying about his money!

He charged towards the staircase.

'Signor Ricci, no! We must *go*!'

He was already halfway up the stairs. The smoke was catching in my throat. I ran after him.

'*Please*, Signor Ricci—!'

He stopped on the landing, wheezing. The smoke was really thick now. I could see it streaming from under the door of the main bedroom.

Mr Ricci reached for the handle.

'Don't open it!' I cried.

He took no notice. There was a rush of hot air that made us wince and jerk back. I glimpsed a chair and a wardrobe blazing fiercely. Then he slammed the door shut again.

'Signor Ricci – *please* come down now—'

Outside I heard a siren wail. Someone was moving around downstairs, shouting out in Italian.

We went back down the staircase. We were both coughing. There was a fireman in the sitting room. He and the grandfather started to shout at each other. The grandfather still seemed to want to go back for his things.

I'd had enough. The fireman could look after the old man now. I could hardly breathe. My head was swimming.

As I went out of the front door more firemen were rushing in. Someone threw a blanket over my shoulders, and led me away.

I saw Nicole and Emanuele sitting on some steps to the side of the house. Nicole looked terrified. Emanuele just seemed fascinated by all the strange activity.

I picked him up and hugged him, and the tears came pouring out. That set Nicole off, until we realised we were frightening Emanuele, so we stopped and just sat, huddled together, and watched the fire brigade put out the fire.

The whole second floor of the house was a ruin.

Nicole talked to one of the firemen. He said that when the call had come through to the fire station they'd thought it was a hoax to keep them from watching the football on TV, and they almost hadn't turned up!

He also said they thought the fire must have been caused by an electrical fault, some wires sparking under the floorboards. Apparently there'd been a blaze in the house next door quite recently. There was so much wood in the Ortisei houses I was surprised people didn't take more care with the electrics.

Nicole and I were lucky not to lose anything of our own. But we obviously couldn't stay in the house. One of the neighbours, a Mr Moroder, offered Mr Ricci a flat in the centre of the village. It was an attic conversion on the third floor above a shop selling wooden sculptures, but it had three bedrooms so there was room for all of us. We slept there that night.

On the Monday Enrico and his mother rushed up from Rome. I could understand them being worried about the grandfather, and upset about the fire, but the grandmother was very twitchy. Early on the Tuesday morning I was still half asleep when I heard her shouting. She stuck her head into the bedroom I was sharing with Nicole and Emanuele, and started sniffing.

'Mrs Ricci thinks she smells burning,' Nicole told me.

We both got up and followed the grandmother into the kitchen. She dived into cupboards, still sniffing furiously. Nicole joined in. It seemed crazy. I wasn't sure I could smell anything. Then Mrs Ricci gave a cry.

She was rummaging through the undersink cupboard, where there was a refuse bin. She moved back to let us see. On top of the rubbish in the bin was a small paper packet, almost completely charred; a few embers still burned at one end.

Mrs Ricci glared at me, and rattled away in Italian.

'She says somebody's been having a cigarette and trying to cover it up,' said Nicole.

'Well, don't look at me,' I said. 'I don't even smoke.'

Mrs Ricci crushed the burnt paper down into the bin, and went out, muttering. Nicole looked at me then raised her eyes to the ceiling.

That afternoon Emanuela phoned. The telephone was in the living-room. I was sitting in there, writing a letter, when the grandmother took the call.

She was obviously still upset. But I noticed my name kept

coming up. Then I realised the grandmother was calling me to the phone.

'How are you, Carole?' Emanuela asked.

'I'm OK. When do you think we'll be leaving here, Emanuela?'

'It depends how long the decorators will take at the house. The Moroders are being very good about the flat.'

'Aren't we going back to Rome?'

'Oh not yet, Carole. I hadn't planned on going home until September.'

'Oh.' My heart bumped. September was nearly two *months* away. She'd talked about *weeks* before. Now it was the whole summer without Marco! I found myself saying, 'I was going to start my Italian classes in August.'

'In August?' Emanuela sounded confused. 'No classes start in August, Carole. You must have got it wrong.'

I didn't say anything. Marguerite had been finding out about them for me.

'Carole,' Emanuela said, 'my mother's quite upset, isn't she? I think the fire shook her up, *si*?'

'Yes, I think so.' I didn't really like to say anything more with her standing right next to me. 'Did she mention about this morning?'

'I told her not to be so neurotic. It's just a coincidence, a careless accident – *vero*?'

'It must have been.'

'Are you happy there, Carole?'

'Ortisei's OK, but I don't really know anyone here. It's not so easy to get out on my own.'

'Perhaps Nicole can help, give you an evening off sometimes. I'll talk to my mother. Shall I do that?'

'Oh, thanks, Emanuela. That would be great.'

The grandmother was still glaring at me as I handed back the phone. I wished I knew what she'd been telling Emanuela.

The next morning the grandparents and Nicole went out. After I'd given Emanuele his breakfast, we played in our room. I was tickling him under his arms, which he loved; he was shrieking with laughter. A door thumped loudly in the corridor, and I heard Enrico shouting, '*Al fuoco!* Carole! Fire! Fire!'

It didn't occur to me for a second that he meant it. Enrico

would joke about anything. I made Emanuele be quiet, got up and opened the door. 'Ha! Ha!' I called. 'Not very funny, Enrico.'

To my surprise, he went shooting past me. All he was wearing was a towel, and his hair was sopping wet. Then I saw smoke. It was curling out from the door of Mrs Ricci's bedroom.

'Oh my God—'

I grasped Emanuele's hand and hurried him down the corridor, past the grandmother's room. The door was ajar, the room full of smoke. Through it I could see flames leaping up from the middle of the bed.

Enrico rushed out of the kitchen, a saucepan of water in his hand.

'*La campanella?*' he cried. 'You didn't hear the door bell?'

'I didn't hear anything!'

He pushed past me. I took Emanuele into the kitchen and made him wait on the veranda which opened off it. Then I found another saucepan and filled it with water.

There was a whoosh of steam from Mrs Ricci's room. Enrico came out, coughing. I held my breath and emptied my saucepan over the burning bed.

It took three or four trips to put out the flames. They left a big, blackened circle in the middle of the mattress, surrounded by soggy bits of newspapers and magazines which had obviously been lying there before. As I stared at it, I realised how fast my heart was beating. I looked at Enrico.

'*Non senti l'ordore del fumo?*' he asked. 'You didn't smell smoke?'

'No. Emanuele and I were playing. We didn't notice anything.'

'I was – *fare la doccia* – the shower. If I hadn't come out—'

He looked as frightened as I felt.

Shortly afterwards the fire brigade arrived, though there wasn't really anything for them to do. I don't know who called them. I found out later that Grandfather Ricci had been downstairs, ringing the bell for the main door of the flats. That was what had brought Enrico out of the shower. All I'd heard was Emanuele shrieking.

After that the atmosphere changed completely. I had the

feeling that everyone in the flat was treating me with kid gloves, even Nicole, as if they all knew something they weren't telling me. It was a horrible feeling, but it was still a shock when Emanuela phoned again and asked to speak to me.

'I've decided to invite the family back to Roma, to my house, Carole, while the decorators finish here,' she said. 'All these shocks are not good for my parents. I have to think about my father – his health, his heart – he has the pacemaker, *no*?'

I told her I knew he wasn't well.

'I'm sorry, Carole,' she said, 'but it means there won't be room for all of us. I feel awful doing this—'

It finally began to dawn on me that she wanted me to leave; that was why everyone had been acting so oddly.

'You are a good girl, Carole,' Emanuela went on, 'and Emanuele loves you. I don't want to lose you. Why don't you ask your boyfriend's father if you can stay again? I'm sure he won't mind. Things will be easier after the summer, in September. Then we'll talk again. *Si*?'

'Well – OK.'

'*Bene*. My mother will pay you to the end of the week, plus a little extra for the train. Say a big goodbye to Emanuele. Don't forget, eh?'

'I'll miss him.'

'He'll miss you too, Carole.'

I arranged to go back and stay with the Vitulanos, who were very good about it. One piece of good news was that Marco had more leave coming. We could have another ten whole days together.

But on the train back to Rome I couldn't help feeling depressed. I wasn't going to miss Ortisei, and it wasn't as if Emanuela had actually sacked me, but I hated the feeling of being under suspicion for what had happened.

The best explanation I could think of was that with the last couple of fires at least, someone must have been having a quiet smoke without owning up. Someone must have been quite happy to let me take the blame.

It was a complete mystery.

5

Elba

31 JULY – 2 AUGUST 1982

Perhaps I expected too much from Marco. His first reaction, after I'd told him what had happened, was: 'September? But what are you going to do until September?'

'I thought I'd learn to be an Italian housewife,' I said. 'Learn to make a proper pizza. Your mum could teach me. Marguerite's finished her exams now – she won't need her room so much.'

'It's too cramped, Carole. You know that. And you can't live on nothing.'

I gave a sigh. It wasn't what I wanted to hear.

'Come on.' Marco put his arm round me. 'You'll get another job.'

'I don't care about another *job*. I just care about being with you. That's why I came to Italy.'

'It's not *my* fault, Carole.' Marco frowned. 'What can I do?'

I felt sorry at once. I was being unfair, but the whole situation was unfair.

'There's plenty of time,' Marco went on. 'We are not ready yet. When I finish military service, when you speak Italian, then we make plans.'

Now I frowned. 'What plans are we talking about?'

Marco shrugged. 'To travel, see the world, enjoy ourselves—'

'Marco.' I stared at him. 'Do you still want to marry me?'

He bent down and kissed me. 'I love you, Carole. More than anything. But we're young. Let's enjoy life. There's no hurry, is there? Is there?'

'No.' I summoned up a smile. 'As long as you still care about me.'

'Of course I do.'

I didn't tell him that if he'd had any doubts at all I would have gone straight back to Scotland.

Our ten days sped by. I spoke to Emanuela on the phone and explained that I couldn't afford to wait until September before I worked again. She was very good about it, said she understood and wished me luck. Marco went and picked up my things from her house. Marguerite talked to a nanny agency for me.

A few days later a Mrs Tonti got in touch. She and her husband needed a nanny for their three-year-old girl, starting at the end of July. She came round to interview me at Cecchignola.

Mrs Tonti was about Emanuela's age, but much slimmer, with long blonde hair parted down the middle and very fine, model-type features. She was much less flamboyant than Emanuela, and didn't seem to be as obviously well-off; but she was very friendly, and her English was good.

She told me she and her husband had jobs in television.

'My father used to work in the movies,' she said. 'When I was a little girl I'd see him on the set at Cinecitta with his big hat and big cigar. He used to hold out his hand and say he could feel the light.'

Mrs Vitulano, who was sitting with us, smiled politely, not understanding a word.

'It must be a really exciting job,' I said.

Mrs Tonti laughed. 'It's hard work! When we're not working, we're driving. My husband's parents have a house on Elba. We try to be there as often as we can in the summer, but so much travelling is not good for little Agnese. That's why we need help. We had another girl – a Scottish girl.'

'The best kind,' I smiled.

Mrs Tonti smiled back. 'Yes. It's a shame she had to go, but her father was ill.'

As she was talking I noticed the Vitulano's black kitten creeping about behind the furniture. I stiffened; every day it seemed to have a mad half-hour, racing around the flat and clawing the furniture and wallpaper – and me, if I got in its way.

'So,' said Mrs Tonti, 'will you teach my little girl English, Carole?'

'I'll give it a go, aye.'

Mrs Tonti looked puzzled. 'What is "go-aye"?'

'I mean, I'll try my best,' I said.

Mrs Tonti smiled. 'Carole, please try and speak correct English in front of Agnese, OK? Otherwise none of us will be able to understand you.'

I felt myself blush. Mrs Tonti laughed to show she was only joking. She spoke in Italian to Marco's mother, then got up. We shook hands. Mrs Vitulano showed her to the door.

As they reached it, Mrs Tonti pointed to the scratches in the wallpaper the kitten had made. Mrs Vitulano raised her eyebrows, and made some remark about the cat.

The animal seemed to take that as its cue. It shot up the back of the sofa where I'd been sitting and skidded across the carpet. I nearly jumped out of my skin. Mrs Vitulano shoohed it away.

'Don't you like cats, Carole?' Mrs Tonti asked.

'Some cats are OK,' I said, 'but not crazy ones like that.'

'Well,' she said, 'we have cats in Elba, but not in the house.'

When she'd gone, Mrs Vitulano smiled at me, and nodded. I knew I had the job.

Marco had gone back to Orvieto by the time I started at the new house. Mrs Tonti picked me up from Cecchignola on Saturday, 31 July. In the car with her were her daughter and her husband. His surname was Cecchini – apparently Mrs Tonti kept her maiden name for professional reasons. I was to call them Daniela and Luigi.

Luigi was tall, dark and bearded, about the same age as his wife, but he didn't speak very much English. Agnese, their little girl, was lovely; very bright and lively with fair, curly hair.

We were driving straight to Elba. All I knew about it was that it wasn't as far as Ortisei and it was very popular with Italian holidaymakers.

I'd hoped there was some chance of us staying in Rome, at least for a while. But Daniela was keen to take Agnese to the seaside as soon as possible, and Luigi would be coming back on his own to their Rome flat after the weekend because he had to go to work.

It seemed crazy to me that after the trouble in Ortisei had given me a chance to come back to Rome I was rushing off again as soon as possible – with people I didn't know at all, and with about as much chance of seeing Marco as I'd had in the Alps! But there was nothing I could do about it; I knew there was no point in getting upset.

We drove up the coast for a couple of hours and caught the car ferry at a place called Piombino. The ferry was packed to overflowing, but the weather was beautiful: a fresh breeze, brilliant blue skies, the sunlight sparkling off even bluer water. I just wished I could have shared it with Marco.

Daniela had told me the crossing would take an hour. I didn't realise at first that the rocky, blue-grey outline looming out of the sea right in front of us was Elba itself. We crossed to it in about twenty minutes, then the ferry began to follow the line of the coast.

The scenery was very rugged: steep mountain sides, covered with rich, green vegetation, sweeping down to deep coves. As we passed, we could see holidaymakers on the sandy beaches.

Daniela told me that one of the beaches was Bagnaia, where we were going, but I couldn't make out which she was pointing at.

The ferry docked at Portoferraio, and we drove off through the town. In five minutes we were in the countryside. It was almost tropical: palm trees and cactuses and bursts of brilliantly coloured flowers everywhere. It was very warm, too. I was glad I'd only put on a light skirt and my bikini top.

The main road began to climb into the hills, but after a short while we turned off down a smaller road, full of twists and turns, leading back to the sea.

Every time we went round another headland or another bend I thought we'd arrived. And then, suddenly, there it was – a broad cove with a wide beach and dozens of white-painted houses stretching back into the green hills. It looked beautiful.

We drove down a hill on to the only street – a little promenade, with a couple of restaurants and cafés, facing the beach – then sharp right at the far end.

The grandparents' house was higher up, overlooking the village. It was quite small, painted white with green shutters. There was a courtyard with a well and a big palm tree in front, and a shaded patio down one side. It wasn't anything like as smart as the Ricci's house in Ortisei, but very pleasant.

I helped Agnese out of the car while Luigi went up to the front door. As he opened it I saw a tiny little old woman getting to her feet just inside. She was wearing a kind of dark shift, and she'd obviously been scrubbing the floor.

I walked over with Agnese and Daniela, and Luigi introduced me to his mother. I smiled and went to put out my hand, but the old woman just frowned at my bikini top, and said something to Luigi.

'*Perche porti un'altra inglese? Perche non un'italiana?*'

I knew enough Italian by now to get the message. 'Why have you brought another English girl? Why not an Italian?' Luigi spoke to her, something about me being a good girl and telling her not to argue. But the old woman's eyes didn't change.

'Papa!' Luigi called. A large, white-haired man, with a big drooping moustache, appeared behind the grandmother. He greeted Luigi and Daniela with a kind of gravelly bark, scattering ash from the cigarette in his mouth. Then he and the grandmother swept up Agnese and carried her inside, cooing and beaming at her.

Luigi followed them. Daniela gave me an awkward glance. She was obviously embarrassed by the grandmother's attitude.

Then she sighed, reached out and picked up the grandfather's cigarette. He had left it dangling, still alight, on a ledge beside the door.

The house only had two bedrooms; the grandparents were in one, Daniela and Luigi had single beds in the other, with a cot for Agnese. I had a camp bed in the living-room.

It was obvious the grandparents were going to be a problem. The grandfather virtually ignored me. The grandmother would mumble in Italian whenever I was near her; I couldn't tell if she was talking to me, or to herself. But whenever I did something for Agnese, either on my own or because Daniela asked me to, the grandmother would do the same thing again in her own way.

I decided I wasn't going to let myself get annoyed – it was her house, after all – but even Daniela admitted she was difficult.

As soon as the car was unloaded, we changed into our swimming things and went down to the beach; it was only a

couple of minutes' walk away. It was fairly crowded, mainly
with families; a lot of people were in the sea.

Luigi took Agnese down to the water with a lilo and let her
ride on it. I sat down on the sand with Daniela, and we chatted.
I told her about Marco and our plans after he finished his
military service. It was she who brought up the subject of the
grandmother.

She told me her mother-in-law hadn't got on very well with
the last nanny. 'You must give her time, Carole,' she said. 'Try
and help her.'

I didn't want to be rude about the old woman, but she hadn't
exactly been polite to me. 'She doesn't seem to want my help,'
I said.

Daniela sighed. 'Luigi's mother believes in the old way. She
thinks wives should be in the house, cooking meals, looking
after their own children. It doesn't make it easy for me
sometimes – but it's just the way her generation is. She doesn't
mean any harm by it.'

I didn't know what to say.

'In Italy,' Daniela went on, 'there's a special feeling between
grandparents and grandchildren. It's even more important for
us. You know, we lost our first child. It was born dead. It was
alive inside me, but–' She looked down. 'They made us hold
it in our arms.'

'I'm really sorry,' I said.

There was a shriek from the water. I looked up and saw
Agnese's lilo bobbing about, but no sign of her. Luigi was
thrashing about in the sea next to it, then he stood up suddenly
with the little girl in his arms, her hair all wet and streaming.

People were turning round and calling to us.

'*Che cosa c'è?*' Daniela cried, jumping up. '*Cos'è successo!*'

We rushed down to the water as Luigi came out. He looked
tense and angry. Agnese had her arms round his neck. He
snapped something at me.

'He says you should be looking after the child,' said Daniela.
She was bristling. 'She could have drowned.'

'But he was right next to her–'

Luigi snapped at me again.

'That's not the point,' said Daniela. 'It's what we're paying
you for, Carole!'

Other people were staring at us. I went bright scarlet.

Luigi put down Agnese. Daniela squatted down and hugged her. Almost at once she started squirming away, tugging at her mother's arm, eager to get back in the water.

I didn't know what to say.

Nothing more was said about the bathing incident when we got back to the house, or at least not that I was aware of. Daniela and Luigi seemed quite normal and friendly again.

I was still shaken, though. They'd changed so quickly, and hadn't hesitated to blame me for the trouble. It was quite worrying if they were going to make a habit of that.

They were obviously much more nervous about Agnese than I'd realised. I wondered if it had anything to do with losing their first child. It didn't make things any easier for me.

We ate outside, at a round table by the kitchen door under an awning. The grandmother was still giving me disapproving looks, but it was something she was going to have to sort out with Daniela. I was just going to get on with my job.

That evening, after I'd helped put Agnese to bed, I started a letter to Marco, but it had been a long day, I was tired and I didn't get very far. I'd really have liked to talk to him, or to Mum, on the phone, but I couldn't see the grandmother being very pleased about me making long distance calls on my first day.

For the first time since I'd come to Italy, I really missed Scotland. I was glad to get to bed.

The next day, Sunday, 1 August, was as bright and sunny as the one before. Luigi was going back to Rome that afternoon, and he was making a special fuss of Agnese at lunchtime. She finished eating before the rest of us, and started to play with her food.

'Oh Carole,' Daniela told me, 'take her to the bathroom and wash her hands. She's messing up her clothes.'

'Come on, Agnese,' I said, getting up. '*Avanti – stanza da bagno.*'

'*Va bene,*' she said, sliding off her chair. Her parents exchanged grins with me. Agnese was a lovely little girl. The grandparents just looked at me, stony-faced.

Agnese and I went through the kitchen, round to the left,

past the grandparents' bedroom, and into the bathroom next to it. I drew Agnese up to the wash basin and turned on the tap.

'*No, no,*' she said, as I took her hands. '*Ragazza grande!*'

'Oh, you're a big girl are you?' I let her go. 'OK, you do it then.'

Pleased with herself, she fumbled with the soap, then began to rub her hands under the running water. I put the plug in, turned off the tap, and sat down on the side of the bath.

When she'd finished, she reached up to pull out the plug. I looked for her towel, then remembered I'd seen it in her parents' bedroom next door.

The grandmother's towel was hanging on the back of the bathroom door. I reached out, pulled it off and used that instead. The door swung shut.

As I finished drying Agnese's hands, a bird landed with a flutter on the window sill. Agnese's face lit up. She pointed a finger.

'*Uccello!*'

'That's a dickeybird, Agnese. Say "dickeybird".'

She grinned at me.

I heard footsteps from the kitchen, and cups chinking. Daniela called out something in Italian.

'Two little dickeybirds sitting on a wall, one named Peter, one named Paul.' Agnese's eyes fastened on my face as I sang. 'Fly away Peter, fly away Paul. Come back, Peter, come back, Paul—'

'*Aiuto! Aiuto!*'

The door burst open. Daniela was standing there. There was smoke behind her.

'Take her outside, Carole!' she cried. 'Take Agnese outside!'

I scooped Agnese up and hurried into the hall. Luigi and his father rushed past me into the grandparents' bedroom. The room was full of smoke. They began dragging the mattress off the bed.

The grandmother rushed out of the kitchen, shrieking and flapping her hands. Everyone was shouting.

Then the two men swept past me, bundling the smouldering mattress and bedding through the living room – and throwing it out of the French windows.

I carried Agnese out through the kitchen, put her down by

the dinner table and told her to stay there. Then I went back in to see if I could help.

'No!' Daniela cried when she saw me. 'Outside! Stay with Agnese!'

In the living-room Luigi was waving a cigarette packet under his father's nose and scowling. The old man was shaking his head.

I went back to Agnese and sat with her. My heart was thumping. All I could think of was Ortisei, and the thought made me go cold inside.

Oh God, don't let all that happen again here.

The mattress didn't actually seem to have caught fire, but the whole of one edge was scorched. Luigi checked the wiring and the electrical points in the bedroom and couldn't find anything wrong.

Daniela said they thought someone might have thrown a cigarette butt through the bedroom window – perhaps passing children, for a joke. I got the impression, though, she and Luigi thought it was the grandparents. Both of them smoked, and they were always putting lighted cigarettes down and forgetting them.

I was just glad they weren't blaming me.

That evening I found myself following the grandmother across the living room; we were both heading towards the French windows. Just before we got there I heard a thump. We both looked round. A little statue was lying on the floor. It had been standing on a small table next to the bed I used – a good few feet away from where we were. I'd no idea what made it fall.

The grandmother gave me a filthy look, and muttered something in Italian.

'*I* didn't touch it,' I told her.

She muttered again, and went to pick up the statue.

Later on I helped Daniela tuck Agnese up in her father's bed; now that he had gone she preferred it to her cot. We pushed the cot against the side of the bed to stop her falling out. Just before we turned off the main light, Daniela switched on a little bedside lamp as a nightlight; it was in the shape of a small, brightly coloured globe of the world with the bulb inside.

Afterwards I went back to the letter I'd been writing to Marco. I told him how nice I thought the family were, and how fond I was becoming of Agnese. I didn't mention the grand-parents, or the fire. There wasn't anything he could do about either; there didn't seem any point in worrying him.

As I was writing, Daniela came up and asked me if I was writing English or Italian. I told her my Italian wasn't good enough for letters, and Marco spoke very good English, anyway.

She was very friendly. The fire seemed forgotten.

The next morning, Monday, 2 August, a loud noise woke me. I turned away from the wall, which I'd been facing, and sat up, blinking in the light.

Daniela was in the middle of the living-room, next to the round table that stood there. She was frowning.

'Did you hear something?' she said.

'Yes, it just woke me up.'

The grandmother appeared from the hall and said something in Italian. Both women were dressed.

Then we noticed a silver cake-stand lying on its side on the floor beside Daniela. The last time I'd seen it it had been in the middle of the round table.

'What happened to this?' Daniela asked me.

'How do I know?' I said. 'I was asleep.'

Daniela grunted and put the cake-stand back where it had been. The grandmother muttered something, then they both went out.

Had Daniela knocked the thing over, and tried to blame it on me? I couldn't see why she should. Then I remembered the statue falling over for no reason the previous evening, and gave a shudder. It was weird.

I got up, went to the bathroom, washed and dressed. It was just before eight o'clock. Agnese and the grandfather were still asleep. I went into the kitchen and helped Daniela and the grandmother make breakfast. After a few minutes the grand-father got up and came into the kitchen. We started to eat.

Afterwards I went back into the living-room to make up my bed. As I was tucking in the top sheet, there was a loud crash right behind me.

I nearly jumped out of my skin. Daniela was instantly at the door. We both looked round.

A vase made of blue glass was lying in pieces on the floor, only about three feet away from me. It had been standing on a small table next to the television set, but still out of my reach.

'Honestly, Daniela,' I gasped, 'I don't know what happened.'

She just frowned and shook her head. I hurried out into the kitchen, found a dustpan and brush and came back to clear up the mess.

When I went to tip the broken glass into a wastebin in the kitchen, the grandmother snatched the dustpan from me and took the pieces out. She was muttering to Daniela, something about me having the devil on my back, and a word I hadn't heard before – *strega*.

Daniela didn't seem to be taking much notice. I told her all these weird things were giving me the shivers.

Daniela shrugged. 'Forget it, Carole. If I told my friends, they'd just laugh.'

The grandmother glared at me.

I went back into the living-room and picked up a towel and a pair of knickers I wanted to put away. Daniela had let me use a drawer in her bedroom for my things. I opened the door carefully in case I woke Agnese, but she was fast asleep on Luigi's bed. As I bent down to the drawer, Daniela suddenly hissed at me from behind.

'Carole, what are doing? On no account come in here while the child is still asleep!'

I blushed and got up. As I slipped past Daniela, she was bristling.

Feeling awkward, I went back into the kitchen and helped clear up the breakfast things. The grandfather left as I came in. The grandmother was washing up at the sink.

Daniela came in behind me, poured herself a cup of coffee and lit a cigarette. Then she took her coffee out into the courtyard. It seemed that she was deliberately not looking at me.

This was becoming silly. Everything was so tense. It had been bad enough getting black looks from the grandparents all the time; I couldn't stand it if Daniela started turning funny, too.

After a few minutes I wanted to use the toilet. I left the

kitchen, then realised the grandfather was probably in the bathroom already. He had a habit of leaving the door unlocked.

I listened at the door. Sure enough, someone was inside. I moved towards the living-room to wait, standing just by Daniela's bedroom door. Just then I heard an odd scratching, crackling sound, quite faint. I couldn't tell if it was coming from Daniela's bedroom, or the living-room. I didn't want to open the bedroom door again in case Daniela became even more annoyed.

Instead I called, 'Daniela! Will you come and listen to this?' Perhaps she couldn't hear me from the kitchen, but she didn't reply.

The toilet flushed and the bathroom door opened. I turned and was face to face with the grandfather. He frowned at me, and walked off towards the kitchen.

I could hear him talking to Daniela, asking where Agnese was; I heard the word 'baby-sitter'.

Then I heard the odd noise again. I wondered if it was cats trying to get in. There were a couple always lurking around the patio.

I moved across the living-room, wondering if I could see anything out of the French windows, but the noise seemed to stop.

I turned round just as Daniela and the grandfather were reaching Agnese's bedroom door.

'Daniela,' I said, 'I think cats are trying to get in.'

She didn't say anything. The grandfather opened the door.

Smoke billowed out.

'*Jesus*—!

I rushed up behind them. There was smoke everywhere. The edge of Luigi's bed was smouldering. Agnese lay curled up on the opposite side of the mattress, apparently still asleep.

Daniela seemed to freeze. I pushed past her and went to grab Agnese, but the grandfather elbowed me out of the way. Daniela snatched up her daughter. Startled, Agnese woke up and began to cry.

The grandfather yanked the mattress and bedding off the bed and flung it through the window. I followed Daniela as she hurried Agnese out of the room – and bumped straight into the grandmother.

The old woman's face was black with rage. She began to prod me in the chest, shrieking.

'*E tu! E tu che inizia questi fuochi! E maligna!*'

She was telling me I'd started the fires, I was *evil*. She kept on prodding me, pushing me through the kitchen. I held up my arm to fend her off.

As she chased me, I backed through the kitchen door, crashing into the dinner table. Suddenly the woman's hands were grasping me by the arms, shaking me.

'*Strega!*' I'm sure it was that odd word again. '*Strega!*'

'Get off me!' I cried. 'Leave me alone! What's the matter with you!'

I tore myself away, and ran out into the courtyard. The old woman was still shrieking at me.

'*Vacca! Parti da mia casa! Vacca!*'

She went back into the kitchen and slammed the door. I heard the key click in the lock.

I didn't know what was happening. Everything, everyone had suddenly gone mad.

I went back to the door and rattled the handle. 'Daniela!' I called. 'Please! Let me in! Tell me what's going on! Why are you doing this to me?'

The door burst open again. '*Uccisore! Assassina! E prova uccidere nostra bambina!*'

The grandmother was shouting, not just at me, but over my shoulder. I turned round. Neighbours were appearing on the other side of the courtyard, calling out. The grandmother called back. She was telling them I'd tried to *kill* Agnese.

'Daniela!' I shouted. The old woman moved towards me.

Terrified, I ran. There was a rickety wooden door on one side of the courtyard – a kind of store room where they kept wine. I pushed it open and hid inside. I was shaking. Tears were pouring down my face. Almost at once there were footsteps outside. The door was yanked open.

Scowling, the grandfather came in. '*Avanti! Avanti!*' he bellowed, clutching at my arm. '*Prima di iniziare un altro fuoco in qui!*' He wanted me out because he thought I'd start a fire there!

He pushed me through the door. The others were in the courtyard; Daniela clutching Agnese, the grandmother still having hysterics, and about a dozen neighbours, all talking at once, then looking sharply at me.

I ran to a wire fence on the opposite side of the courtyard, and leaned against it, clutching at the strands. On the other side was a vineyard. I heard a noise behind me. I looked round. Two children of about six were standing there, staring at me as if I were some kind of monster.

Their mother – one of the neighbours – shouted at them. They scurried away.

'Daniela,' I called. 'What's *happening*?'

At first I thought she wouldn't answer. Then she said: 'We've telephoned the police.'

'Why?'

'There's been a fire. We have to.'

'Can't we talk?'

The grandfather barked something. Daniela turned away. One of the neighbours shouted at me.

I shut my eyes, feeling tears squeeze down my cheeks.

Marco, why aren't you here?

The police arrived quite soon. Two young carabinieri in sunglasses and shiny boots.

One came over to me; the other spoke to Daniela and the grandparents. Then they made us all go into the living-room. One of the neighbours had Agnese. The carabinieri took statements off Daniela and the grandparents. I had to sit on my bed with one of them standing over me.

'*Passaporto?*' he said. '*Documenti?*'

'My passport's in Rome,' I said. '*Roma. Via Battaglione d'Assalto. Sono ragazza di Marco Vitulano. Signor Vitulano.*'

He looked confused, but scribbled in his notebook. His companion picked up a can of insect spray from the round table. He showed it to the first carabiniere, who took my hands, sniffed my fingers, then shrugged.

On the other side of the room the grandmother started to shout again, pointing a finger at me. The second carabiniere tried to calm her down.

'What is she saying, Daniela?' I asked.

Daniela wouldn't look at me. Instead she glanced down at her wrist. Her face fell.

'*Il mio orologio da polso! E partita!*' She snapped at the carabinieri, then stared at me, her eyes blazing. 'My watch, where is it?'

'Your *watch*?' I thought she'd gone mad. 'What are you talking about—?'

She lunged at me. I jumped back. One of the carabinieri caught her, and pulled her away. She was shouting at me.

'Don't think you can get away with this! I know you've got it! I want you to strip! Come on, now! Take off all your clothes!'

I almost laughed. 'You're crazy—'

The carabinieri were talking to each other. They both looked as confused as I was. The one holding Daniela nodded to her.

'OK – *subito.*'

He let go of her. Fuming, she jerked me to my feet. The grandmother followed as she pushed me into the bathroom. They slammed the door behind them.

'Go on,' Daniela snapped at me. '*Tutto.* Everything.'

They folded their arms and stood against the wall, glaring at me. How could the police let them do this? I felt sick and humiliated. I could feel the tears coming back.

I turned my back and took off my T-shirt and skirt.

'*Tutto!*' the grandmother rasped.

I unclipped my bra and slid down my pants.

As soon as my clothes were on the floor, Daniela and the grandmother began rifling through them. They didn't find anything.

Neither of them apologised. They just muttered to each other while they waited for me to dress again. Then we went back into the living-room. The carabinieri began to talk to Daniela.

'What are they saying, Daniela?' I asked. 'Please!'

She wouldn't meet my eyes. 'You have to go with them.'

'Why? Where are we going? I don't understand.'

'Just go with them.'

One of the carabinieri took my arm. The other picked up the can of insecticide and a small bottle of solvent Daniela had used. We went outside. They opened the rear door of their police car and told me to get in. The carabiniere who'd held my arm slid in beside me.

As the other carabiniere got into the driver's seat, Daniela came out of the house. She was waving her watch. She said she'd found it in a drawer.

We drove off, down into the village. I didn't know where I was going, or what was happening to me. All I could think of was that Daniela was sending me away, back to Rome, back to Marco's family, back to sanity.

Livorno

AUGUST 1982

When we reached the main road to Portoferraio we turned left instead of right, and started to climb into the mountains. I wondered if the *carabinieri* had made a mistake. The only ferry to the mainland I knew of was in Portoferraio.

Did *anyone* know what they were doing any more? I lifted my hands to wipe my face, and felt the damp on my cheeks. After all that sobbing, I must have looked a sight.

It was all so stupid. The police must have realised the Cecchinis were completely crazy. I just didn't know enough Italian to tell them properly. I couldn't until I found someone who spoke English.

I'd have to get in touch with Marco. Marco would explain everything. He'd sort it out.

The road began to slope down. The rocky scenery opened out and I saw the sea again, and a town below us. We must have driven right across the island. As the ground levelled out, we passed a sign that read: Rio Marina.

Just after the houses began, the car pulled up outside a carabinieri station on the ground floor of a small block of flats. We went inside. I was led into a room with a desk and a typewriter.

A woman officer came in, and one of the carabinieri who'd brought me here asked me more questions about the fires while he typed my answers. Neither he, nor the woman, understood any English; I don't know what they made of my Italian.

By now I wanted to go to the toilet. That they did understand. The woman carabiniere showed me to it. When I went to shut the door, she said, '*No! No!*' and pulled it open again. I couldn't believe it. What did they think I was going to do? Deeply embarrassed, I tried to ignore the woman.

Afterwards I went to go back to the room where I'd been, but the woman shook her head and drew me towards another door with a little opening in it at eye level. There was a key in the lock.

Inside was a tiny room with a single light bulb, a little sagging bed and a small, barred window high in the opposite wall.

'You want me to go in a cell?' The woman stared at me. 'But I haven't done anything.'

The carabiniere who'd been typing appeared behind her.

'Look,' I said, 'it's the grandmother you should be locking up, not me!'

Their faces didn't change.

'But this is crazy!'

The woman officer touched my arm. I shook my head and stepped into the cell. The door shut. I heard the key turn.

I was under arrest. I'd been so stupid – it just hadn't occurred to me before that that's what was going on.

They believed Daniela and the grandmother. They really thought I had something to do with the fires.

I sat on the bed. The springs squeaked. The mattress almost touched the floor. The only covering was a rough woollen blanket.

I looked around. The walls were bare, covered with bits of graffiti in biro, or just scraped in the plaster. There was a sour smell.

It was a joke, a big joke. It had to be!

I had to think it through. I had to make sense of it all or I'd go mad, too.

Obviously Daniela had been frightened and upset by what had happened, just like she'd been on the beach with Agnese and the lilo. She'd lashed out at me then. This time the grandmother, who had it in for me anyway, had only made it worse.

But within half an hour of the bathing incident Daniela had been fine. It had all been forgotten.

That was it. In a couple of hours Daniela would come to her senses again, realise that blaming me was all nonsense. Perhaps even the grandmother would come round, though I doubted that. All I had to do was sit tight, and wait for Daniela to call the police.

By the evening I was still sitting in the cell. They brought me a meal and let me wash my face and brush my teeth. They gave me my own toilet things. I felt a twinge of alarm. Had they fetched them from Daniela's? Or had someone from the house brought them over?

Did that mean I was going to be kept here for a long time?

'*C'e qualcuno che parla inglese?*' I asked the carabiniere who collected my plate. 'Is there anyone who speaks English?'

He shrugged and went out. The light bulb, which had been on since dusk, snapped off without warning.

I sat in the darkness and fought a feeling of panic. If Daniela *had* brought my things over she obviously hadn't changed her mind. Perhaps she wasn't going to. I wanted to cry. But what good would that do? All today's tears had brought me were swollen eyes and raw cheeks. Surely someone would let Marco's family know what had happened. The police had the Vitulanos' address. If Marco couldn't telephone, his father could.

I wrapped myself in the blanket, not wanting to touch the bare mattress. I never thought I'd sleep, but I did.

The key rattling in the lock woke me up. It was very early. After I'd washed and dressed again in yesterday's clothes – no one seemed to have brought a change – a carabiniere I hadn't seen before opened the door and beckoned me out of the cell.

At last! The Cecchinis had come to their senses after a night's sleep. It was all going to be settled.

As I went through into the main room of the station, I saw two more carabinieri standing waiting. I blinked at the sub-machine-guns slung over their shoulders – just like the ones I'd seen at Rome airport. They didn't seem any less threatening now.

Then I realised one of the policemen was carrying my toiletries bag.

The carabiniere who'd brought me out of the cell turned me round. Before I realised what he was doing, he reached down and snapped handcuffs on to my wrists. I was so surprised I didn't react. He nodded towards the two waiting officers.

'*Avanti!*' he said. They were waiting for *me*.

I stared at him. 'What do you mean? Where am I going?'

He nodded towards the officers again. '*Vacci*. You go. *Subito*.'

They took my arms. We went out into the sunlight. A car was parked by the kerb.

I couldn't believe any of this. Why did I have to wear handcuffs? Why should I run away? And why on earth did they need sub-machine-guns? This wasn't being sorted out at all; this was getting more and more ridiculous, more and more frightening.

I was put in the back of the car, between the two carabinieri. Another officer drove.

We climbed back up the mountain road, past the Bagnaia turn-off and down into Portoferraio, on to the quay. A large hydrofoil had just docked. Holidaymakers were pouring off; others were waiting to go aboard. The police car drew up near them, and the two carabinieri led me out. I could feel everyone's eyes on me. I curled up inside with embarrassment and shame.

What would these people think I was? Some kind of gaolbird? A terrorist? I just wanted to hide. But it got worse.

The carabinieri took an arm each and led me towards the hydrofoil. We walked past everyone, up the gangplank and on to the deck. Then we went to the back, and stood against the handrail.

One of the carabinieri lit a cigarette; the other began to chat to a crewman. People started to pour aboard behind us; mums, dads, grandparents, curious children, all stared at me as if I was some kind of freak. I could feel my face scalding.

How could the police do this? If they really thought I was so dangerous, why were they letting me stand in the middle of a holiday crowd?

I caught the eye of the younger carabiniere. He glanced down at my handcuffs and shrugged with a faint, apologetic smile, as if he knew exactly what I was thinking. Then he puffed at his cigarette and looked away. I turned to the rail, put my hands on it, and leaned on the handcuffs. That way, at least they might not be so obvious.

Presently the hydrofoil filled up, the gangway was pulled back, and we reversed away from the quay. The boat turned, and started to pick up speed. As we moved out of the harbour, it surged forward and rose out of the water. The engine roared. We began to skim over the waves with a loud thud-thudding sound.

I watched two lines of wake streaming behind us. There was a strong breeze whipping my hair about, but the sun was so warm it didn't feel chilly. I was in the middle of a nightmare and it was a glorious day.

We were at Piombini within half an hour. Another police car, with three more carabinieri, was waiting at the dock. I was pushed in the back again, between two of them. At least these carabinieri weren't carrying machine-guns.

We drove off through back streets I only vaguely remembered, until we reached a large main road. A sign showed Roma to the right. We turned left.

'Where are we going?' I asked. '*A Roma?*'

'Livorno,' said one of the carabiniere. 'Carcere Domenicani.'

The words didn't mean anything to me. All they made clear was that I definitely *wasn't* being taken to Rome. I sank back into my seat.

The journey seemed endless. Long, dusty, tree-lined roads, busy little towns, slow shuffling behind wheezing lorries that filled the road. The car grew hot and stuffy. Once or twice I even felt myself dozing off.

Then we began to see glimpses of the sea. The outskirts of a large town appeared. We were driving down a kind of long promenade with huge houses on one side and the beach on the other. Traffic increased. The road narrowed and twisted. Suddenly we were in the middle of busy city streets. It was hot and noisy and dirty, like the muckiest parts of Rome.

I glimpsed giant harbour cranes looming behind a high wall, then a row of ocean-going ships, butting up almost to the edge of the road, then – across a strip of water – ancient, crumbling ramparts that looked as if they belonged to a castle. Then we were in darker, narrower streets where the buildings seemed almost as old.

We crossed a bridge, drove down a narrow, shadowy street and over a second bridge. Facing the end of it was an enormous church. We turned in front of it. Now we were driving alongside a canal with steep, grey walls. Suddenly we stopped.

There was a tall, orangey-brown building on our right, joined on to the church and almost as massive. It looked ancient. Paint was falling off the walls leaving big grey patches.

But at one end it had a very modern glass booth built into the wall. A man, wearing what looked like an army uniform, stood in front of it, with a sub-machine-gun on his shoulder. He came over as the carabinieri took me out of the car.

The building was five storeys high with thick iron bars on all the windows. It looked more like a prison than another police station. But that didn't make sense. Surely you had to have a trial before they put you away, or at least go to some kind of court?

The carabinieri showed papers to the guard. I looked round. On the opposite side of the canal were blocks of run-down flats with washing strung from the windows like flags. Young children were playing noisily in front of them.

Something prickled in my nostrils. I frowned. There was a foul smell coming from somewhere. I could see down into the canal where it curved away. The water was still and murky, dotted with pieces of floating rubbish. Were people using it as a dustbin? No wonder it ponged in this summer heat.

The guard handed back the papers, and went back to his booth. The carabinieri led me up to a large, grey metal door, which swung open. We went up some steps into a room with a counter. A man in a white, short-sleeved shirt and dark trousers stood behind it. One of the carabinieri talked to him, while he scribbled on a pad. The other took off my handcuffs. I heard my name a couple of times. A woman in a dark skirt and white shirt came in behind me. The carabinieri left.

The man behind the counter picked up a large brown envelope and gestured towards a little silver crucifix I was wearing on a chain round my neck.

'You want me to take it off?'

He nodded and snapped his fingers. I didn't want to take it off; it was a present from my father. But I did what he said and put the crucifix on the counter. He began to scribble again. Then he pointed to my wristwatch. When I'd taken that off, he motioned to the pockets of my skirt. I turned them out. All I had there was a handkerchief. He scribbled again, and pushed the handkerchief back to me.

Next I had to lift my arms while the woman patted all over my body. Then the man nodded towards the door, and started to put my things in the brown envelope. The woman led me up some more stairs. She had keys jangling from her waist. We went into a smaller room. There was a waist-high screen in the corner. The woman gestured to me to go behind it, then pointed at my clothes.

'Take them off?'

'*Tutto.*'

I stared at her. It was just like the grandmother and Daniela all over again.

'*Subito!*'

I turned my back. As I undressed there was a snicking sound. I turned round and the woman was pulling on some white rubber gloves. She motioned me to bend over.

I was trembling as I put my things back on. Not even the Cecchinis had prepared me for *that*.

The woman led me down the corridor into another room. I had to stand against another screen, this time white and blank. A man took my picture. Then I was led out into the corridor, and into another room to have my fingerprints taken.

Blank, white-painted walls, wide, dim corridors, dingy stairs, steel doors clanging, keys jingling, and everywhere the sour, musty smell of old, old building – I felt I was living in a mad dream where everything I was was gradually being taken away from me: my name, my clothes, my bodily privacy, even the words I spoke.

Marco, when are you going to make them stop all this?

'I want to telephone my boyfriend.'

I was in a room that was bare but for a long table and half a dozen chairs. I had been made to sit at one end. A guard in a dark blue uniform stood behind me.

'*Posso telefonare?*'

The guard shook his head, barely glancing at me.

I sighed and folded my arms. I was hot and sticky and I was starting to feel hungry. My clothes felt grubby. I'd have done almost anything for a shower and a change.

Footsteps echoed outside. High up in the building someone was yelling their head off. The door opened. Two men and a woman came in. They were in everyday clothes; both men were carrying briefcases. One was small, dark and dumpy, in his forties; the other was about ten years younger, but his face was very stern behind steel-rimmed glasses. The woman was about the same age.

All three sat down opposite me as the guard went out. The man in glasses took some papers out of his case and started to speak to me. His Italian was much too fast and formal for me.

'I'm sorry, I don't understand. I don't speak Italian that well. I just want to know what's going on. No one'll tell me! And why can't I phone my boyfriend?'

The man in glasses looked at the woman.

'Signorina Compton,' she said, 'these things will be explained to you.' I almost sobbed with relief. Her accent was very thick, but at last someone was speaking English!

She nodded towards the man in glasses. 'This is Dottore Cindolo. He is public prosecutor for the city of Livorno. Under Italian law it is his responsibility to consider the allegations made against you.'

I frowned. 'You mean the fires? But I told the police in Elba all about them. They're nothing to do with me.'

The man in glasses shook his head and muttered something.

'No,' said the woman, 'you do not understand. Dottore Cindolo is a magistrate. You have to answer his questions.'

'Can't I speak to my boyfriend? It's really important.'

The woman looked blank. I suddenly had a horrible feeling that she didn't understand a word I'd said. Then the older man leaned forward and spoke to her. The woman nodded.

'You are advised that you do not have to respond to the interrogation. You can keep silent. It's your choice.'

All three looked at me.

'Why would I want to keep silent? I've already tried to explain everything.'

The woman nodded. 'Do you have someone to represent you? Do you have a lawyer?'

I stared at her. How could I have a lawyer when I hadn't been allowed to talk to anybody? I shook my head.

The woman glanced at the older man. 'This gentleman, Avvocato Mori, has been appointed to act on your behalf, if you wish it.'

I could feel the tears stinging my eyes again. I'd thought that if I could only talk to someone in English all of this would make sense; it would come right. But this woman wasn't saying anything I understood.

'What I *wish*,' I cried, 'is that someone would tell me what to do!'

'The British Consul will be formally notified in the next twenty-four hours,' said the woman. 'For now it is very important you tell Dottore Cindolo everything that happened on Elba.'

I shut my eyes. I could feel the tears pouring down my cheeks.

'Marco. I have to phone Marco. When can I phone Marco?'

'You can make a telephone call later,' said the woman. 'Now – please – answer the questions.'

The telephone rang and rang. Why wasn't anybody answering? Someone should have been at the Vitulanos' flat. But I didn't have my watch. I didn't know the time.

The guard standing next to me gave a sigh. We were in a dim corridor, using a coin phone.

'*Basta*,' he said, taking the receiver from me. He listened, shook his head and put it back. He went to lead me away.

'Can I call again later? *Piu tardi?*'

The guard shrugged and tugged at my arm.

'Paper? Something to write on?' I motioned with my hand. 'I have to get in touch with someone!'

The guard grunted. I let him lead me away.

I was put in a cell even smaller than the one on Elba. It was just as bare, and smelled older. In the corner was a stained, battered pail.

I sat on the bed and felt it give. I didn't know how long I'd been here. I didn't know how long I'd have to stay. I couldn't count on anything making sense any more.

All I *could* count on was Marco.

I went to lie down, then the door rattled and opened. The guard who'd taken me to the phone leaned in and pushed a notepad and a pencil towards me. I took it, and was writing before the door shut again.

Dear Marco . . .

*

The next morning, after breakfast, I was taken back to the room where I'd seen Cindolo, Mori and the woman interpreter. They appeared after a few minutes.

Cindolo, the man in glasses, was as formal and serious-faced as he'd been the day before. I still didn't understand a word he said. He took some papers out of his briefcase and gave them to me. I could see my name and my address in Scotland at the top of the first sheet, but the rest was in Italian.

'You must study these papers, and then discuss them with Signor Mori,' said the woman interpreter. All three looked at me as if they expected a reply. 'Do you understand?' asked the woman.

I couldn't help but laugh. 'I haven't understood a thing since this all started—'

The woman turned to Cindolo and spoke in Italian. He grunted, and said something, then stood up. The others got up, too.

'Is that it?' I said.

Later I was moved from the little cell. A male guard gestured for me to pick up my things along with the blanket on my bed, and then led me to the stairs. As we climbed I could hear shouting from above.

We didn't stop until we reached the very top. The guard unlocked a steel door, and we walked down another narrow corridor. There were more doors on either side with small, barred openings in them. They were cells, but they had men inside. I glimpsed faces at the openings.

They started to whistle and call out; some stuck their arms through the bars. The guard shouted, and banged at the doors with a dark stick he carried.

My stomach was suddenly in knots. Surely they weren't going to put me in with them?

But we moved straight to the end of the corridor and stopped in front of another steel door. The guard pressed a button in the wall next to it, and a bell sounded. There was a pause, then a key rattled in the lock and the door opened.

A woman guard in her forties stood just inside. The male guard nodded me forward. I waited while the woman locked the door again behind me. We were in a kind of small lobby.

To one side was what looked like a bathroom. Straight ahead
was a long room with a table in the middle. Another female
guard was sitting at it, reading a magazine.

The guard beside me turned from the door and drew me
forward into the room. Two or three other women were there,
too. They looked up as I came in. They were young, but dark
and scruffy-looking. They stared at me.

On one side of the room were four doors, all open. I could
hear pop music playing somewhere, and what sounded like a
game of ping pong.

The guard at the table glanced up, then carried on reading.
The other woman nodded towards one of the open doors. It
was another cell, but larger than any I'd seen before. It had four
single beds in it. Facing the door was a brick cubicle with
shoulder-high walls and a toilet bowl inside. Behind it was a
large, barred window which didn't seem to have any glass in
it. I caught a whiff of the canal.

Next to the door was a television set, turned on. A girl lay
on the bed in the opposite corner, watching it.

The guard pointed to a bed just to the left of the door.

'This is mine?'

'*Si.*'

I put down everything I was holding. The guard said
something I didn't understand, but she didn't seem to expect
an answer and turned and left. I sat on the bed.

There was a small cupboard beside it. I reached down and
opened it. It was empty. At least I'd have somewhere to put my
notepad and pencil.

I looked at the television set. It seemed to be showing some
kind of quiz show. Now that was an improvement on a slop
bucket and a bare wall. I glanced at the girl on the other side
of the room.

She was pale and heavily-built with short dark hair. She
looked about thirty, and thoroughly bored. She wasn't taking
any notice of me at all.

I picked up the papers Cindolo had given me. They were a
joke. The odd word looked vaguely familiar, but I'd only ever
spoken crude Italian, I'd never tried to read it properly. The
words might as well be Chinese.

If the guard had posted my letter to Marco, he should get in touch within a day or two. I couldn't do anything before then.

'English?' said the girl across the room.

I looked up in surprise. 'Yes. I mean, Scottish. Do you speak English?'

'*Non.*' She shook her head, her eyes still fixed on the TV. 'Hello . . . goodbye . . . how are you . . .' She shrugged.

'Oh.'

Another girl came in. She was very tall and thin with long, blonde hair, younger than the dark girl. She glanced at me, then went over to another one of the beds, sat down and started to talk to the other girl. I heard the word '*inglese*' a couple of times.

Who were these women? Were they real criminals, or just locked up like me? I felt a twinge of real fear. They could be anyone – murderers, maniacs –

Someone jumped on to the mattress next to me. The dark-haired girl held out her hand.

'*Posso vedere?*'

For a second I thought she was trying to shake hands, then I realised she meant the papers I was holding. I gave them to her. There was a line of unhealthy-looking scars along the inside of her elbow. She began to read, calling out to the blonde girl.

I watched them uneasily, not knowing what to think. Was I meant to let anyone else see the papers? What if they ripped them up? The dark-haired girl answered by putting them back on the bed. She stared at me without any expression.

'Do you know what it means?' I said.

'Don't you know?' asked the blonde girl. Her accent was as thick as the interpreter's but, at last, it was English!

'No one'll tell me!' I cried. 'I can't understand a word of this! It's just crazy!'

The blonde girl frowned. 'Speak more slowly,' she said. 'I can't understand you.'

'I just want to know what it says. I want to know why I'm here.'

'It says you made two fires and you tried to kill a little girl.'

'*Kill* –'

My mind went blank. Daniela couldn't have believed I'd

deliberately tried to hurt Agnese—? She couldn't have made the police believe *that*—?

But they'd put me in handcuffs, they'd taken me away with sub-machine-guns, they'd locked me up in a foul, crumbling gaol—

I went cold all over.

I'd never felt so lost, so frightened, so completely alone.

7

Minervini

AUGUST 1982

The woman interpreter said: 'Signor Mori advises you that a plea is possible in Italian law related to crimes committed in a state of "incapability" of the mind—'

She paused. Mori was watching me. We were in the same room I'd met him in before, but this time without the man in glasses.

All I was aware of was my head throbbing; I'd hardly closed my eyes the previous night. I felt drained and short-tempered. Then it dawned on me what the woman was saying.

'You mean say I'm mentally incapable? Mad? I'd have to be mad to set fire to a child's bed, wouldn't I?'

The interpreter talked to Mori. He spoke again.

'You must understand,' the woman said, 'the sentence for attempted murder can be between seven and twenty-one years. But this way it is possible to get you perhaps only two years—'

'Two years?' I laughed. 'If I plead insanity? I'm not insane – you are! You're the ones that are crazy!'

The interpreter muttered a few words to Mori. He sighed and looked glum.

Why didn't Marco reply to my letter?

He'd had a day to send a letter himself, though I knew he hated writing. But he could have phoned. I'd written to his barracks. Could he have been moved somewhere else?

Back in the cell I began another letter. This time I would send it via Marco's mother and father.

Three of the girls were standing up at the window, shouting

to someone outside, and laughing. They were making so much noise I eventually got up to look.

Just outside the window, only ten or twelve feet away, was a block of flats. A middle-aged woman was standing at the window opposite. Behind her I could see right into her living-room. She was arguing with the girls, shouting and waving her arms about. They were laughing at her and making rude signs. Suddenly one of them threw something. It pinged off the woman's window glass. She swore, and slammed her shutters. The girls roared.

Was everyone mad in this city? How could anyone live so close to a place like this? How could they stand it?

Bored now the woman had gone, the girls moved away from the window. One of them was the dark-haired girl who'd talked to me yesterday. I'd heard someone call her Lori. She barely glanced at me as she walked past.

No one seemed to take any notice of me. I didn't know whether it was because I didn't speak Italian, or because they all thought I'd tried to kill a child. If they thought that, I'd rather they left me alone.

There were about a dozen women altogether, most of them young and Italian, three or four to a cell. I shared with Lori, a German girl and another Italian.

The tall, blonde girl who knew English hadn't spoken to me again. I didn't like to talk to her first. I wasn't sure about talking to any of them. God, if I was supposed to be a murderess, what awful things could *they* have done?

We ate at the table in the main room. I noticed a lot of the girls had food of their own; I'd even seen them cooking on little camping-gas-stoves they kept in their lockers. I'd no idea how they got the stoves or the food.

The food the guards brought was dreadful: soggy pasta and hard lumps of awful smelling cheese. Even if I'd been hungry I couldn't have eaten much of it.

When I sat down, the girl nearest me got up and moved further down the table. No one looked my way, but I could feel their eyes on me. I couldn't swallow the food in my mouth.

Two years . . . Twenty-one years . . .

I couldn't stand two more *hours* of this. I could feel panic rising in me. I didn't want to break down in front of everyone, but I couldn't help myself.

'Who is your lawyer?'

I looked up. The tall, blonde girl was sitting at the far end of the table, gazing at me as she ate.

I had to think before answering. 'Someone called Mori.'

'I don't know him, but a lot of the lawyers are not very good. They never come to see you. They don't do anything. Doris has a good one.' She was looking at a girl across the table. '*Chi è?*'

The other girl said something. 'His name is Minervini,' said the blonde girl.

'Minervini?'

'He comes often, he talks, he listens, he's good. You should ask for Minervini.'

'Thank you. I will.'

I was just grateful someone had spoken to me.

That night I wept. I wanted to go to sleep, then wake up and find it had all been a nightmare, and over. But the tears kept trickling out. I didn't think I was making a noise until someone shouted something in Italian. I pushed my face into the blanket.

Through the window I could hear cars swishing by, footsteps in the street, people talking in the flats. It seemed incredible there could be ordinary lives so close. Lives like Marco and I had been living just a few days ago; a life he was still living now. But, in here, in this horrible place, I might as well be dead.

The next day I was taken downstairs to a room I hadn't seen before. It looked like somebody's office. There were filing cabinets and a big desk with a telephone. Mr Mori was there with a tall, slim man in his forties; he had frizzy, greying hair, and was wearing an English sports jacket.

'I am Enzo Masi, British deputy consul in Florence,' he said, shaking my hand. 'May I call you Carole?'

Though he was obviously Italian, his English was perfect. All three of us sat round the desk. Mr Masi asked me if I knew what a consul was. I asked if he was anything to do with the Italian authorities.

'No,' Mr Masi smiled. 'A lot of people are confused about the consulate's role. Our job is to look after the British government's interests in this party of Italy – Tuscany, as a matter of fact. If British citizens get into trouble, then the authorities notify us.'

'You mean you can help me!' I couldn't believe someone was finally offering to do something.

'Of course, I'll do whatever I can. But you must realise you're accused of attempted murder. The Italian authorities are bound to take it very seriously.'

'I keep telling them the truth. Why don't they believe me? Why do they believe Daniella and not me? How can they lock me up when I'm not guilty!' I could feel the tears stinging my eyes again.

'Carole, no one says you're guilty,' said Mr Masi. 'Under the Italian system you can be held under suspicion while the public prosecutor investigates the allegations against you. Sometimes that can take quite some time. But it gives your lawyer the opportunity to make a case on your behalf. That's Mr Mori's job.'

He glanced towards Mori, who hadn't said a word. I shut my eyes. It was like making two steps forward, three back.

'He wants me to say I'm mad, that I made the fires when I didn't know what I was doing. I can't do that!'

Mr Masi nodded. 'You know Mr Mori is here to represent your interests.'

'Well, it's not in my interest to be locked up with mad people for two years!'

'You're not happy with him?'

'Not if he thinks I'm mad!'

Mr Masi paused. He spoke to Mori. They both got up and began to talk at one end of the room. Mori looked even glummer than when I'd last seen him. Then he shrugged, picked up his briefcase and left the room. Mr Masi sat down again.

'I said he didn't have your confidence,' he told me. 'That's right, isn't it?'

'It certainly is!'

'But you're going to need someone, Carole. You have to have a legal representative.'

I nodded. 'One of the girls mentioned a man called Minervini. He's supposed to be very good.'

Mr Masi frowned. 'I know most of the lawyers in Livorno. That name's not familiar. Let me check.'

'Livorno? Is that where I am?'

Mr Masi looked astonished. 'You mean they haven't told

you? But that's appalling! Elba is in the Livorno judicial region, which is why you were brought here. This is Livorno prison – the Carcere Domenicani. It means "prison of the Dominicans". It used to be a monastery. It's very old.'

I grimaced. 'It's very smelly.'

Mr Masi shrugged. 'Old buildings often are, and prisons are never very pleasant, anyway. There's nothing I can do about that, I'm afraid.'

I suddenly felt a spark of hope.

'Could you get in touch with my fiancé?'

He nodded, and reached for a notepad. 'Is he in Scotland?'

'No, he's Italian. He's doing his national service.'

I began to tell him about Marco. We talked for a long time. He was very sympathetic. For the first time since leaving Rome I felt I could unburden myself; the relief was enormous.

When he got up to go I couldn't help hugging him. He laughed, and blushed.

'No, you embarrass me. I am only doing my job. Is there anything I can get you?'

'I just want to talk to Marco,' I told him. 'That's all I really want.'

That night was the easiest I'd had since I'd arrived. In the morning I didn't even mind the showers. They always seemed to be grubby and had tiny white insects crawling between the tiles.

At first I'd thought they were lice; I didn't even want to step in the tray. But it was so hot and my clothes still hadn't been sent on, so I didn't have much choice. I washed my underclothes with the hard, white soap the prison provided, draping them over my little cupboard to dry overnight, though it was almost impossible to get a lather. I always felt uncomfortable.

After breakfast, the post arrived. Still nothing from Marco. I began to feel low again.

During the morning the cell doors were left open. We could go into the long room, or a cell which had been turned into a games room. It had a ping-pong table and a rickety exercise bike.

The hour before lunch a door at the far end of the long room was unlocked. There were stairs which led up past a small room

which was used as a chapel, and into an exercise yard on the
roof.

The walls were too high to look over, and the whole area
was caged over with wire. But at least there was fresh air and
I could see the sky.

After lunch we were locked up again. I spent my time writing
to Marco, flicking through Italian magazines and watching
television. In the middle of the afternoon a guard called me out
of the cell.

I went downstairs to a small room with a table and two
chairs. A short, dark-haired man of about fifty was waiting for
me. He had a long chin, yellowy skin and the tiredest eyes I'd
ever seen. He stuck out his hand.

'Carole Compton?' His voice was deep and gruff, as if he
smoked a lot. He had a gap between his front teeth.

'Yes. *Si*.'

'*Mi chiamo Sergio Minervini*.'

He showed me a chair. We sat down.

'*Parla italiano?*'

'No.' I shook my head. 'Not really.'

He nodded, took a pad and a pen out of his briefcase and
pushed them along the table towards me.

'*Scrive*—' He made a writing motion with his hand.

'What do you want me to write?'

'*Tutto che e successo in Elba – i fuoci – la famiglia – tutto*.'
He shrugged, lifting both his hands.

'Everything that happened in Elba—?'

'*Si – si*.'

I began to write. Mr Minervini sat back and took a packet
of chewing-gum from his jacket pocket. He offered me one.

'Thank you.'

'*Prego*.'

It was the first time anyone from outside – even Mr Masi –
had given me anything since I'd arrived.

The next day Mr Minervini was back again. There was a tall,
dark woman of about thirty with him.

I shook hands with both of them.

'Hello, Carole,' said the woman. 'I'm Joyce. I'm going to
interpret for Mr Minervini.'

I stared at her, and almost burst into tears. Her accent was Glaswegian.

'You're Scottish!'

'I'm from Glasgow, but my husband's Italian. I do secretarial work for Mr Minervini.'

'I never thought I'd hear a Scottish accent again!'

She laughed as we all sat down. 'Well, you'll have to make do with me for the time being.' Mr Minervini spoke to her. She nodded.

'Mr Minervini has gone through your case, and he thinks there is a lot of room for doubt. He'd be happy to represent you.'

'That's great.' Mr Minervini smiled as I nodded at him. He spoke again.

'But now, I'm afraid, more questions,' said Joyce.

When we'd finished, Mr Minervini opened his briefcase and took out a bar of soap, a small book and a couple of magazines.

'*Li prenda – è la vostra.*'

'They're for you,' said Joyce.

I looked closer. The book was an English-Italian dictionary; the soap was much better than anything I'd seen in here. Mr Minervini said something.

'He asks if you have any money,' said Joyce. 'Did you know you can send out for things you need – toiletries, food? He knows the meals here are pretty bad.'

I looked at him. 'I don't know what to say. I can't pay you back. Daniela never gave me any money–'

Mr Minervini shook his head dismissively. He reached into his jacket, took some notes out of his wallet and pushed them into my hand.

I could feel myself beginning to cry.

'*Eh–.*' Mr Minervini put a full packet of chewing-gum next to the magazines and motioned me to have one, twisting his mouth around as if he was chewing. I found myself grinning. He spoke again.

Joyce chuckled. 'He says that's better – no more crying. Pretty girls should never cry. You should listen to him. He knows what he's talking about. No more worries, eh?'

They were both smiling at me. I tried to smile back.

'That would be nice, yes.'

*

I should have been easier in my mind, but I wasn't. No one seemed able to deal with my biggest worry which got worse day by day: why hadn't I heard from Marco?

I couldn't believe he hadn't received any messages. I'd written letters every day. I'd used the money Mr Minervini had given me to send telegrams to his home and to his barracks.

But there'd been nothing – and it was already the weekend.

Something must have happened to him. Something so dreadful he couldn't even reach a phone.

Monday passed, Tuesday – I'd been here a whole *week* now! Then, as I dozed on my bed early Wednesday evening, half an eye on the television, a guard came and fetched me.

'What is it? *Cosa c'é?*'

'*Non lo so. Una telefonata.*'

'A telephone call! Who from? *Chi?*'

She shrugged.

My heart was thumping as a male guard took me downstairs. We went into an office. There was a phone on a desk with the receiver off. I snatched it up.

'Hello?'

'Carole? It's me. It's Marco.'

I could feel the tears welling up inside me, everything I'd held back, everything I'd been too frightened or too embarrassed to say for so long threatening to burst out at once.

'Oh Marco – Marco, I've been praying so long just to hear your voice–'

'It's been difficult, Carole–'

'Did you read my letters? Do you know what they're doing to me?'

'I know. The carabinieri went to see my parents – to ask questions–'

'*Eight days*, Marco. Eight whole days, and I haven't heard from you. I haven't had a letter, a phone call–'

'I try–'

'I *need* you, Marco–' Now the tears spilled out on their own. 'Don't let them do this to me. Do you know what it's *like* for me in here–?'

I heard him sigh. 'What do I do, Carole? What am I supposed to do?'

'Just come. Just see me. Be here. Please.'

'You mustn't cry. I hate you cry.'

I shut my eyes. 'Just speak to them. Tell them what they're saying about me is rubbish—'

The line went quiet. For a second I thought we'd been cut off. 'Marco?'

'This is hard for me, Carole. I think — we must finish.'

I felt a pit open in my stomach — a cold, dark pit.

'Oh no, Marco. Not now — not here. Not like this—'

'Is best now. They will deport you. You'll go back to Scotland. It will be — all over.'

'Scotland? What are you talking about? Scotland? I'm here, I'm in prison! I'm not going anywhere! Marco, you're upset. I know, I understand. You don't mean it. Marco, talk to me—'

There was silence.

'Marco—'

The phone buzzed. He'd gone.

When I didn't move, the guard took the receiver out of my hand, listened and put it down.

I don't remember being taken back upstairs. I was aware of the cell door shutting, the key turning in the lock. I sat on my bed. The guards called out. The television went off; the other girls groaned. Then the cell light went dark, too.

In the flats opposite music was playing; I could hear people laughing. There was a roaring in my head. I began to shake. My arms and legs had lives of their own; my teeth rattled.

'Carole?' Lori, the dark-haired girl, stood over me. 'Carolina?' She touched my shoulder.

Something snapped. I started screaming. I couldn't stop. I wanted to break down the walls, I wanted to smash through the bars. My arms were flailing, tearing things from the walls. The girls were shouting. I didn't hear the door burst open.

Someone caught me from behind. They dragged me to the floor. A guard straddled me, tugging at my arm. I glimpsed a needle, blood all over my hand. There was a sharp pain, then a great wave of drowsiness, rolling over me, drowning me . . .

The man was tall, middle-aged and very English. He said, stiffly, 'I'm Roger Eilbeck, Miss Compton. I'm the British consul in Florence.'

'Couldn't Mr Masi come?'

We were sitting in the office where I'd talked to Mr Masi.

'I'm afraid not. This did seem an urgent matter. We heard that you'd tried to harm yourself.'

'Harm myself?' I glanced at the bandage on my hand. 'I got a bit upset, that's all. I caught my hand on a nail on the wall. I didn't see it was there.'

'Well, the prison authorities seem to think otherwise. You do realise we're doing as much as we can. We can't change the legal system, and you really aren't being treated any differently from an Italian subject under the same circumstances. There's no obvious miscarriage of justice—'

'Even though I'm not guilty!'

'You have to prove that, I'm afraid. Which brings me to your lawyer – Mr Minervini? He's been in touch with the consulate with regard to legal aid. We had to tell him it's not available for UK citizens abroad. What are your financial circumstances?'

I shrugged. 'I don't have any.'

'Is there no one at home who can help you?'

'Only my mother, but she's hard-pushed as it is. I don't want to worry her.'

Mr Eilbeck sighed. 'I don't think you've much choice, Miss Compton.'

I didn't know if I cared any more. Every waking minute – day and night – I went over my last conversation with Marco.

I couldn't believe he'd meant what he said. The more I thought about it, the more stupid I realised I'd been. Things had always been so easy and comfortable between us. That's why it had been so good – Marco had never liked pressure.

Suddenly, here I was, bombarding him with frantic letters and telegrams, hysterical on the phone, making demands – it must have been a terrible shock for him. No wonder he'd panicked. And perhaps breaking up hadn't been his idea at all. Hadn't he said the police had talked to his parents? Perhaps they'd insisted on it. Marco had always done what his mother said.

We couldn't throw away in a moment all the time we'd spent together, all the feelings, all the promises. That didn't make sense at all. I'd write again; I'd explain. He had to listen. And

I had to be calm, like Mr Minervini said; above all, I had to try and stop crying.

But first I sat down and wrote out the telegram I'd hoped I'd never have to send: MUM: IN GAOL LIVORNO ITALY. SUPPOSED TO HAVE SET FIRE TO CHILD'S COT INTENDING TO KILL HER. TELEPHONE MARCO VERY QUICKLY.

'So does Mr Minervini still want to be my lawyer?'

Joyce told him what I'd said. He threw his arms up in the air, and rattled away for so long I thought I'd made him angry.

'He says you're not to worry about money – it's not a problem for now. He thinks you're a nice girl, a good girl, who wouldn't deliberately hurt anybody. He wants to help you. He also had a phone call.'

'A phone call?'

Joyce talked to Mr Minervini again.

'A call from Rome. Some woman told Mr Minervini you were evil, and he shouldn't defend you. It made him very suspicious.'

'*Evil?*' That old feeling of craziness came back. Was it Daniela? Was she *still* trying to hurt me? 'God, isn't gaol enough? What else do the Cecchinis want?'

'Mr Minervini doesn't think it was Mrs Tonti. What about this other lady you worked for in Rome?'

'Emanuela?' That threw me. 'She wouldn't do anything like that. I left her on good terms. She wanted me to go back and work for her. It was Marco who said I ought to get a new job.'

'You also mentioned fires that happened with this other family. When you were staying near Bolzano?'

'Yes, but Emanuela never thought I had anything to do with any of them.'

Mr Minervini was staring at me, his chin resting on his hands. His eyes suddenly seemed hard. As he spoke, Joyce translated.

'How do you explain these other fires, then?'

'I can't. Apart from the big one in Ortisei. They said that was an electrical fault. I don't know about the other two.'

'So that's five fires in twenty-three days? And you're the only common factor. That's a pretty big coincidence, isn't it?'

'Yes, I don't know – I suppose so –'

'Can you really blame people for being suspicious? From the outside it looks pretty bad.'

I could feel panic rising, tears approaching. These people were supposed to be *helping* me.

'I can't help that! I don't know what caused the fires. I'd be lying if I said I did. All I know is it wasn't *me*—'

Mr Minervini paused, then smiled and touched my hand, speaking.

'Mr Minervini says he's sorry,' said Joyce, 'but these are questions the prosecution are asking, and he must be sure of your answers.'

I gave a sigh. 'I'm glad he's on my side.' When Joyce translated, he laughed. Then he began to rifle through his papers, talking as he went.

Joyce explained: 'The prosecution have a theory that you were so crazy to get back to Rome to see Marco that you were prepared to do anything.'

I laughed. 'That *is* crazy! Marco wasn't even in Rome. I couldn't have seen him even if I had gone back.'

'Did you miss him?'

'Of course I missed him, but not enough to make me set fire to anything! We'd been apart enough times before. We knew we were going to be together eventually.'

Mr Minervini nodded, and spoke.

'Dr Cindolo, the prosecutor, has decided your case needs further investigation,' said Joyce. 'He's passed it on to what we call an examining magistrate – a judge – who will carry out further investigations. This man is called De Franco.

'It would be a good idea if we had some character references from home. People you've worked for, some of the old folks, perhaps, or a priest. That would all help to impress the judge.'

I wasn't sure. I could imagine Mum's state of mind after she'd got my telegram. I didn't want to burden her with anything else.

'You mean that might make the judge release me?'

Mr Minervini shrugged broadly. 'It's a possibility,' Joyce told me, 'but really it depends on many things. Mr Minervini has found out that the Cecchinis may have had more than one nanny in the fortnight before you started.'

'Really?' Daniela had only told me about the Scottish nanny before me.

Mr Minervini nodded. 'He's trying to trace them,' said Joyce. 'He thinks they may have some very interesting things to say about the Cecchini household.'

I smiled as Mr Minervini spoke again. 'Dr De Franco has ordered two reports on your case. One is a forensic report on the causes of the Elba fires. That should clear up some important questions.'

'But that'll prove I didn't start them!'

Mr Minervini gave a quick smile. 'That's what we're hoping for,' said Joyce. She paused. 'The other report the magistrate wants is a psychiatric one.'

'Why do they need that?' I glanced at Mr Minervini.

'Basically,' Joyce explained for him, 'it's to test out the prosecution's theory about your motives. The magistrate wants to know if you can be held responsible for your actions.'

'You mean if I'm crazy or not?' I was getting alarmed again. 'What if they decide I am! The first lawyer wanted me locked up for two years!'

Mr Minervini was shaking his head. '*No, no—*' he said, and spoke again.

'Mr Minervini is sure you're perfectly sane, Carole,' said Joyce. 'What does concern him is that the psychiatrists may be inclined to support the prosecution's case. Perhaps they will, perhaps they won't. But we really ought to have our own psychiatrist. We want to be able to prove the prosecution's theories are all nonsense.

'And ideally our psychiatrist should be British, or English-speaking, so they can properly understand a Scottish temperament – and also what you're saying, Carole.'

'God,' I said, 'I had enough trouble with Cindolo's interpreter.'

'There you are,' said Joyce.

'But can't we get our own psychiatrist, then?' I asked.

When Joyce translated, Mr Minervini looked embarrassed.

'Unfortunately, cash is a problem,' Joyce explained. 'Flying a psychiatrist in from Britain would be extremely expensive.'

'Oh.'

When he saw my expression, Mr Minervini leaned forward and spoke quickly.

'Mr Minervini says not to worry about this. Nothing is settled. He's sure we can get round this problem.'

'How long will all these reports take?'

Mr Minervini gave a very broad shrug; he pursed his lips and moved his head from side to side.

'He says the expert has been given sixty days. It could be sooner. He hopes it'll be very soon.'

Two more months.

A few days later a priest came to visit me. His name was Father Henry Nolan. He was in his seventies, tall, open-faced and soft-spoken. He said he was Irish, originally, but he'd been in Florence for years looking after the English-speaking community. Now he called himself a citizen of the world.

The consulate had asked him to get in touch with me.

He was a kind man, and a good listener.

'There is a difference between the justice of God, Carole, and the justice of man,' he told me. 'When you're tempted to despair or to become bitter you should think of that.'

He gave me a rosary, and some religious books in English, and promised he'd ask some of the younger members of his congregation to write to me to keep my spirits up. Finally he suggested we say some prayers together.

I appreciated his visit, even though I had to admit I hadn't been to church for ages. When he'd gone, I wondered if praying was the only thing I had left to do.

Nisbet

AUGUST – SEPTEMBER 1982

We filed down the steps towards the visiting room. From the bottom I could hear a babble of voices, men and women and children.

A guard held me back at the barred entrance gate. Beyond him was a long room with a table running all the way down the middle; prisoners on one side, visitors on the other. The prisoners were all mixed up, men and women, young and old. Some people were crying; children were running about. The room was packed to bursting, the din tremendous.

I was near the end of the line. I couldn't see any room left for me on the table, let alone any faces I recognised. Then the guard let me pass.

I saw Mum at once. She was sitting at the far end of the table, her little face pinched and anxious, eyes darting up and down the row of prisoners. Then she caught sight of me.

I'd steeled myself for this moment, promised myself I'd be calm and low-key, as much for my sake as hers. But the second our eyes met all that flew out the window. Suddenly I was a little girl again, lost and afraid, and the tears came pouring out. I had to turn my head away.

'God love you, hen—' Mum clutched me across the table. I clung on to her for a long moment, not able to speak. 'Come on and sit down here,' she whispered.

She began to pull me round the end of the table. A female guard, standing just behind me, stepped forward. Mum's face hardened.

'Don't you put one finger on my daughter! Don't you dare! If that cow takes one step closer, I'll lay her out, I swear!'

The guard hesitated – as well she might; Mum had bested tougher characters than her. Mum pulled up a chair, and I sat up close to her.

'Oh Mum,' I said, 'I'm that embarrassed you finding me in here.'

She shook her head. 'Don't be silly, Carole.'

'I just don't want you to tell me that you were right in saying don't come.'

'You won't hear that from me, hen.'

We hugged each other again.

'God,' she said, 'there's a niffy smell about this place. That canal out there *reeks*.' She pushed me back to look at me, frowning. 'You're in a state, too, girl. Don't they look after you?'

That started the tears again. 'Mum, I've been in the same clothes for *three weeks* now—'

'You what? What about your things in Elba?'

'They're still there, I suppose.'

'I don't believe it – didn't you ask for them?' I felt myself redden. 'Oh, Carole, you're too shy for your own good. But what's this Minervini character been doing all this time? And the consul people? My God, they'll hear from me—'

I asked her what she thought about Mr Minervini. Her frown got deeper.

'He's got a poky wee office – hasn't seen a duster in weeks. He's got half his family working for him, too. It's like the Walton's up there. You know he's only been practising for about six years? He was a colonel in the Italian paratroopers before that. He's got medals all over his walls! I hope to God he doesn't think this is another military campaign.'

'He's been very good to me, Mum.'

'Good or not, he'll want paying some time. You know he's talking about hiring an English psychiatrist to take a look at you. That's two hundred pounds!' She looked at me and her face softened. 'But that's not for you to bother your head about, right? I'll take care of all that. You concentrate on keeping yourself cheerful and well.'

'I just keep thinking about Marco.'

'Marco! Marco!' Mum's eyes blazed. 'Listen, girl, stop worrying about Marco and start worrying about yourself!'

I couldn't believe how soon the visit was over. I was OK until I saw Mum going out of the door. Suddenly the thought that I could have so much of home dangled in front of me and still be dragged back to that cell was too much. I couldn't help it. I just screamed.

'Mum! Mum, don't leave me! Please! Don't go! *Don't go!*'

Two guards took my arms and pulled me towards the steps. I could see more of them behind Mum, ready to jump if she tried to get near me. There was so much pain in her face.

'Hang on, Carole!' she called. 'I'm going to get you out of here! Within the week – you mark my words!'

I wanted to believe her so much. If anyone could do it, my mother could. After all, she'd managed to get all the way to Italy on nothing at all.

She told me she'd been knocked flat by my telegram, first wondering if it was some kind of weird hoax and then, when she decided it wasn't, not knowing where to turn. She'd phoned up my Uncle Ronnie, who was her oldest brother, in Ayr; but he'd been just as flummoxed.

Finally she'd broken down at her morning cleaning job at the local Fishermen's Mission, and told the director there all about it. He'd rung up the Italian embassy in London and confirmed that it was all true; by then I'd been in prison for ten days.

Mum had no money for trips to Italy, let alone legal expenses, and neither did the rest of the family. She'd decided her only chance of getting any help was to appeal to the media. A friend at the Mission telephoned the *Sun* newspaper for her, and they ran a story about me.

Then she'd approached North Sound, Aberdeen's local radio station. They had interviewed her, too, and, as a result of the broadcast, the local branch of Intasun had phoned the station offering Mum a free return flight to Italy. All she had to find was her living expenses.

On top of all that she'd also organised the petition Mr Minervini had asked for, and had hundreds of signatures from the Carrick Street Day Centre. Now she was stretching what little cash she had in the cheapest hotel she could find in

Livorno. She'd even brought along a reporter from North
Sound, who knew Italian and could translate for her.

This was all from someone who'd never been out of Scotland
before in her life. I didn't know anyone else who could have
done so much.

Ever since my phone conversation with Marco, my cellmate
Lori had been more friendly to me. Part of it, I'm sure, was
because I was getting sleeping tablets for her. I'd been given
them after getting so upset over Marco, though I'd never taken
any myself.

Lori had wanted me to keep on asking for them, and to buy
wine for her as well. After lights out the girls would swallow
lots of the tablets at once and get high. In return Lori let me
use her tape recorder to play music cassettes Father Nolan
brought in for me.

I now knew Lori and several of the others were heroine
addicts. If they didn't take something they'd start to moan and
scream, and tear at their hair. Some of them would touch
themselves in disgusting ways. I'd never seen anyone behave
like that before. Sometimes I just didn't believe my eyes.

The nights were always the worst. There were taunts, and I'd
wake up and find things of mine had gone missing. During the
days I was usually left to myself, but I never felt safe.

The next morning, as I finished my shower, I was so busy
avoiding the little beasties on the shower walls I didn't notice
one of the scruffier Italian girls right behind me. As I stepped
back, I butted her hip. Before I could apologise, she jerked
forward sharply, knocking me off balance. My head smacked
against the side of the cubicle.

'*Scusi, signorina*,' she said, sneeringly, and went out.

Mum was allowed to visit again that morning. By the time I
saw her I had a vivid black eye.

'What's this business?' she cried, touching my face. 'Who did
this to you?'

'I slipped on a bar of soap,' I said.

'Oh yes?' She obviously didn't believe a word. 'What are they
doing to you in there?'

I could feel myself redden. 'Nothing, Mum.'

'Carole?'

'Mum, they think I'm a child-killer! You don't know what it's like – I'm terrified being up there—!'

I was crying. 'Oh, hen.' Mum held me tight. 'It'll be all right. Don't let those bastards get you down. You've just got to be tough.'

I nodded and sat up, wiping my eyes.

Mum told me she'd talked to Minervini and my clothes had been sent for from Elba. She'd also seen Mr Eilbeck from the consulate.

'It's a crazy system over here, Carole,' she said. 'You're guilty until you're proved innocent. Eilbeck says they won't do anything until there's been an appeal against your arrest.'

'Well, when's that?'

Mum's face drooped. 'They're talking about November. I'm sorry, Carole—' She squeezed my hand.

'I'll never last, Mum—!'

'You will!' Her grip tightened. 'You're a Scot, and you're my daughter – and don't you forget it!'

Usually prisoners were allowed only two visits a month but, because of the distance Mum had come, we could meet every day. She was soon shopping for me in the local markets, bringing me in decent food, new toiletries and magazines to read.

It made all the difference in the world just knowing she was there. But that also made it even harder when, after just eight days, she had to take up her return flight.

'I'll be back in November, Carole,' she promised. 'I'm going to get all the money Mr Minervini needs – for doctors, translators, everything. Don't give any of that a thought. All you have to do is be strong. Do you promise me?'

Through my tears, I did.

It was September the second. I'd been in gaol exactly a month.

I still didn't know when I was going to be released, or even if I was going to be charged. After all the endless questions about Elba and the Cecchinis, all the efforts of Mr Minervini and Mr Masi and Mr Eilbeck, I didn't know any more about my fate than when I'd first walked through the doors of this terrible place. I wasn't at all sure I could keep my promise to Mum.

Then, just after she'd left, Mr Minervini came to see me. He was in very good spirits.

'There's a Scottish lawyer coming to Italy on holiday very soon,' he told me through Joyce. 'He's very experienced in securing bail. He's read all about your case and he's offering his help – free of charge. This is very good news, Carole!'

I'm not sure what I expected a Scottish lawyer to look like, but it probably wouldn't have been anything like this man.

He was round and chunky and surprisingly young. He breezed into the little interrogation room with a smile on his big, round, smooth face; his hair was long and fair, and he was wearing shorts with a bright, stripey, short-sleeved shirt.

Mr Minervini was with him. He introduced us.

'Carole, Lawrence Nisbet; Mr Nisbet, Carole Compton.'

We shook hands and sat down.

'Now the important thing, love,' Mr Nisbet said briskly, 'is to get you out of this hole. It's scandalous you were ever put in here in the first place. Mr Minervini and I plan to go to the examining magistrate and get you released on the basis of lack of evidence. We think he'll be sympathetic.'

I found myself staring at him in disbelief. He was like a breath of fresh air.

'Will the magistrate really do that?'

'I can't see he'll have any choice,' said Mr Nisbet. 'Look at the evidence. There are no witnesses: all they have is a hysterical accusation from the mother of the child, and the ravings of this grandmother, who sounds a complete nutter to me. Now she's talking about bowls and statues flying about whenever you were near! What did she call you? *Strega*? Witch?' He laughed loudly. 'It's practically medieval! Back home it'd be laughed out of court.'

I was grinning. I couldn't help myself.

'That would be just great.' I looked at Mr Minervini who nodded and smiled back at me.

'We're aiming to have you home for Hogmanay, young lady,' Mr Nisbet beamed.

More good news followed. Back in Scotland an appeal had been started to raise money for my case. A lawyer called Nicol Hosie of C and P H Chalmers in Aberdeen was to administer it.

There had already been a collection at my mother's work, and more had been collected by my father and friends in Ayr. Uncle Ronnie had gone round pubs, leaving bottles to fill with donations, and he was organising a fund-raising disco.

But what really astonished me was that people who'd only read about me in the newspapers – total strangers – were sending in money, too. One oil worker in Aberdeen had actually given five hundred pounds. And two old-age pensioners had come up to Mum in the street and handed her a twenty-pound note.

When I heard about it I burst into tears. After all that had happened to me here, I couldn't believe how generous people could be. All that, and the arrival of Mr Nisbet, cheered me a lot. He seemed a real live wire, and visited me as often as he could.

He told me that he and Mr Minervini had had a quiet word with Dr Cindolo. If I passed the psychiatric tests the court had ordered there was every chance I'd be set free. Either the case would be dismissed, or I'd be released on bail – in Italy it was called 'provisional liberty'.

If that happened, Father Nolan could arrange for me to stay in a convent on the outskirts of Livorno. Mr Nisbet went to see it, and said it was quiet and peaceful; I'd have my own room, and bathroom, and Father Nolan would visit me once a week. After the Domenicani it sounded like heaven!

The only problem was the tests themselves. Both Mr Nisbet and Mr Minervini still wanted me to be examined by an English psychiatrist, or at least have one present. Mr Nisbet was convinced it was the only way of being sure that the prosecution's theory – about my starting the fires so that I could get back to Marco – were nonsense. That still didn't seem to have been sorted out. I just hoped that the money people were sending in at home could pay for it.

It seemed odd to me I'd once been so embarrassed by my imprisonment I hadn't wanted anyone to know. I hadn't known how many friends I had.

One day Mr Minervini came to see me with Joyce. He showed me a British newspaper. I looked at it in amazement. My picture was on the front page, next to a headline that read: THE GIRL THEY CALL A WITCH.

The story quoted Mr Nisbet, who said that my psychiatric examination would include tests to see if I had 'witch-like' powers. There was even a quote from my mother saying how normal I was.

I burst out laughing. It seemed so stupid. I joked to Joyce: 'Tell Mr Minervini that if he's not careful I'll turn him into a frog!'

But Mr Minervini wasn't smiling.

'He feels he may have to apologise to you,' said Joyce. 'When he was talking to Mr Nisbet he made a joke about the grandmother saying you were a witch. He said Scotland was supposed to be the land of witches. You know, *Macbeth*, and all that? Mr Nisbet mentioned it at a press conference. Mr Minervini had no idea this would happen.'

I couldn't see what the fuss was about.

'No one'll take it seriously, surely?' I said. 'It's just rubbish.'

Mr Minervini gave one of his big shrugs.

'Sometimes too much publicity can harm a case,' Joyce said for him. 'We'll just have to see.'

With Mum gone, it wasn't so easy getting my own food, so I was back to the prison menu of soggy, lukewarm spaghetti and stringy meat. One lunchtime, shortly after I'd seen Mr Minervini, I collected my meal and went to sit at the long table.

The girl next to me immediately got up and moved away. So did the girl opposite, and the girl next to her.

I stared at them. They hadn't been like this since my first few weeks here. Why were they being like this again?

As I ate, I felt everyone's eyes on me. When I'd finished, I carried my tray back to the woman who brought in the food. She picked up my cup and plate, then, to my horror, deliberately threw them on to the stone floor, smashing them to bits. She stared at me as she did it, as if I'd done something disgusting.

No one said a word. Not even the guards.

I ran into my cell. An Italian magazine was lying on my bed. There was a black and white photograph of me on the front cover, the word STREGA! printed across it. It had been slashed three or four times with something sharp.

I was nearly sick with fright.

That evening the guards made me wait until everyone else had finished before I could have dinner. The food was even colder than usual, but I couldn't eat a thing. Even Lori wasn't talking to me.

I dreaded lights-out, and the night to follow.

There were two new girls in my cell. They were swarthy and rough-looking; one had tattoos on her arms. As soon as it was dark I heard them moving about, whispering. There was a popping sound and a sharp hiss. I turned and looked.

They were huddled in the middle of the floor with Lori. The cell was dim, but there was enough light from the window and the flats opposite. I could see they were putting tablets and pills together. One of the new girls was holding a canister from the little butane gas cookers. She held it up to her nose, moved her finger and there was another hiss. She took a deep breath and held it. Her eyes began to flicker as she passed the cylinder carefully to her friend.

Lori was popping pills into her mouth, swigging them down with gulps from a wine bottle. The swarthy girls began to giggle. The one with the tattoos snatched the wine off Lori and took a swig. Then she looked up, and saw I was watching. She waved the bottle, called 'Carolina!' and something else I didn't understand. Her friend laughed.

Then she got up and stumbled over to me. I lay there, frozen. Behind her Lori had flopped on to her bed. The other girl was curled up on the floor, sniffing at the canister again.

The tattooed girl sat on my bed. 'Carolina,' she whispered. Suddenly she leaned down and pushed the wine bottle into my mouth. I pushed it away, spitting out the wine. She grabbed hold of me, forcing the bottle back between my teeth.

She was very strong. When I'd swallowed some, she put the bottle down, but she still wouldn't let go of me. She started to stroke my hair, grinning at me, talking softly. I could smell the gas on her breath and see sweat on her face, but her hands were icy cold.

Then she stopped stroking my hair and moved her hand down my body, between my legs. I jerked away in horror, and disgust. Someone else dropped on to the bed behind me.

It was Lori. She snapped at the tattooed girl, and pushed her away. The tattooed girl grunted, then smirked at us, and got down on the floor with her friend.

They curled up together, laughing. I heard the canister hiss again. Then they began to kiss each other, rubbing their bodies together.

I turned to the wall. Lori was a dead weight against my back. I was shivering so much my teeth rattled.

'You've got to have me put in solitary confinement, Mr Nisbet! Please, I can't stand another night in there!'

He looked shocked as I told him what was happening.

'Carole, it's appalling you've been put in with people like that,' he said. 'I'm going to see the consul straightaway. We've got to do something about it.'

'They really seem to think I'm a witch!' I was crying now. 'I offered a girl a Coca-Cola this morning, and she wouldn't drink it. She was afraid it was a potion or something! It was bad enough before, but this is really crazy!'

Mr Nisbet sighed. 'Italy is a very superstitious country, Carole. The Italians love this kind of thing. Do you know what book's at the top of the Italian best-seller list at the moment?'

I shook my head.

'*Firestarter* by Stephen King. It's about a girl who sets fire to things with her mind.'

'Oh Jesus,' I said.

'It might not be as bad as it looks, Carole. It could actually work to our advantage.'

I blinked at him. 'What do you mean?'

'Firstly, as another line of defence. Ever since this witch thing started, Mr Minervini's been bombarded with offers of help: parapsychologists, pyrokinetic experts, experts on the paranormal – you name it. There are plenty of perfectly respectable scientists who actually believe you can start a fire simply by thinking about it, whether you're conscious of doing it or not.'

'But that's rubbish! I don't believe any of that – it's like saying I *am* a witch!'

Mr Nisbet laughed. 'You don't have to tell me love! Of course it's rubbish, but if the judge believes it and it helps get you out of here, don't knock it.'

'I won't say I'm guilty when I'm innocent. I won't do that.'

Mr Nisbet nodded. 'OK, but remember the more we read

about you in the papers, the more pressure it puts on the prosecution to settle this thing – not to mention the consulate, and the British government; they seem quite happy to sit on their arses while you languish in this pit!'

I sighed. 'I just want to go home.'

'So you will, love,' Mr Nisbet smiled. 'So you will.'

I didn't get a cell of my own, but the two swarthy girls were moved.

Mr Nisbet launched an appeal for more money in the papers, reckoning that between fifteen hundred and two thousand pounds would be needed for my bail.

My psychiatric examination was set to start on 17 September. That was good enough news in itself, but there was better. I was to be examined by two English-speaking psychiatrists, and one of them had actually done some of her training in Scotland. That meant we wouldn't have to find the money for a British psychiatrist to fly over, and could save more for my bail.

Meanwhile the stories in the press got wilder and wilder. The Italian papers were the worst. Somehow they got in touch with the Riccis. There were interviews with Rosa, Emanuela's maid, saying that pictures of the Madonna had spun round and fallen off the wall when I came near, and that a hot water boiler, which had been turned off, had started to bubble for no reason.

I knew Rosa and I hadn't hit it off when I first started working for Emanuela, but I couldn't understand why she was saying these things.

But the most wounding thing was an interview with Emanuela herself, even though she wasn't mentioned by name. She claimed that she'd suspected me of fire-raising after the first fire in Ortisei, and that the third fire had almost killed Enrico.

According to her, the corridor in the flat had been blocked by flames with Enrico trapped on one side, and me on the other, carrying two bags and ready to escape. The only reason she hadn't reported me to the police was that no one had been hurt.

She also said that whenever I picked up little Emanuele he had cried, and said, 'Mummy, she's burning,' and that he couldn't stand me.

'I *loved* Emanuele!' I told Mr Minervini. 'Emanuela *knew* that! She must have.'

Mr Minervini gave one of his broad shrugs.

'He says you shouldn't take what the papers say so seriously,' Joyce translated for him. 'They are just sensation-seekers.'

'She says she only left me alone once with Emanuele. But I remember often taking him for walks in the Pincio on my own.'

Mr Minervini spoke. 'He says there's no point in getting upset,' said Joyce. 'You should make yourself calm for the psychiatric tests. They're all that count now.'

'I thought the Cecchinis were the only crazy ones,' I said. 'I thought Emanuela was my friend. Why is she *doing* this?'

9

Inquisition

SEPTEMBER – NOVEMBER 1982

As I walked into the examination room my hands were sticky with sweat. The two psychiatrists who were going to examine me were wearing white coats, just like in all the jokes. The man was tall and middle-aged and balding with a bushy moustache; the woman dark and petite with thick, black glasses.

Mr Minervini introduced us. '*Carole, la dottoressa Bertocchini e il professore Inghirami.*'

'Hello, Carole,' said the woman. 'How are you feeling?'

'A wee bit nervous.'

'There's no need to be nervous. This will be very straightforward. Will you sit down, please?'

She turned to a chair in the middle of the room. I sat, resting my hands on my knees. Mr Minervini had settled on another chair in a corner. He gave me a reassuring smile as the male doctor stepped in front of me.

'Look up, please,' he said. I did, and he leaned over me and flashed a little pencil light into one eye. 'Try not to blink.'

I kept still while he moved to the other eye. 'Now cross your knees.'

He tapped my knee with a little hammer, and made my leg twitch. Then he took hold of my hand and felt my wrist. He said something to the woman doctor. Then he turned to me.

'Your hands are perspiring quite heavily, aren't they?'

'They're always a bit like that,' I said. He nodded.

After the physical examination, they sat me in front of a small table and got me to do a series of puzzles and games – a small jigsaw, simple sums, matching shapes, looking at cards with strange blotches on them and saying what they reminded me of. Some of it seemed childish; some plain daft. All the time one of the doctors was scribbling something on a notepad.

Then they gave me a plain pad and some crayons and asked me to draw myself, which was impossible – I couldn't draw to save my life. So they asked me to do a picture of my house in Ayr instead. As I went to pick up a crayon the woman doctor seemed to hover over me. I asked if there was anything wrong.

'I just want to see which crayon you choose,' she said. I picked a blue one. She scribbled again.

Then I had to draw something fierce. I tried a lion, but it came out more like a weird kind of dog with a ruffle collar.

Next they rubbed vaseline on my forehead and my wrists and attached small pads with wires leading off to a machine.

'This tests what we call galvanic skin responses,' the woman doctor explained. 'There's no need to worry. It can't give you a shock or anything.'

The machine had a small TV screen and a drum covered with paper. When the male doctor turned it on the drum began to turn slowly, and a pen on a holder scratched a line along the paper.

'We want to ask you a few questions now,' he said. 'Please answer as truthfully as you can.'

I nodded. Some of their questions struck me as very odd.

'Do you remember when you had your first menstruation?'

I shrugged, surprised. 'Fifteen or sixteen, I suppose. Whatever's normal.'

'Are your periods particularly heavy?' asked the woman doctor. 'Do you find they're accompanied by fluctuating emotions?'

I started to blush. Why were they so keen on my periods? It not only didn't make sense, it was embarrassing.

'They're not too bad normally,' I said. 'They don't bother me too much.'

They began to ask about my childhood, who had brought me up, what I thought of my mother and my father, had I ever seen arguments or violence between them.

Then they asked if I had a phobia about cats.

'I don't have a phobia, I just don't like them very much. I'm more of a dog person.'

We went over the fires in Ortisei and in Elba. Did I have an explanation?

'No, I don't.'

What did I think of the Cecchini grandmother's accusations?

'I think they're crazy. I just don't understand why she's saying things like that.'

Had anything strange ever happened to me before?

'Nothing strange happened before I came here.'

'Carole,' the woman doctor asked, 'do you believe in the devil?'

I couldn't help laughing. They were supposed to be *doctors*. I glanced at Mr Minervini. Was this a serious question?

Then I looked back at the woman. Her face was perfectly straight.

Mr Nisbet was smiling as he came into the room. I knew the news was good.

'You're fine,' he said. 'Clean bill of health. You even passed their lie detector tests.'

I shut my eyes. 'Thank God for that.'

'On Wednesday Mr Minervini and I are making a bail application at the Palace of Justice, just down the road. It's looking very good, Carole. You could have seen the last of this place in a day or two.'

I took a deep breath. Now release was so close it seemed an impossible dream. 'I'm praying for it.'

'Fingers crossed.'

That night I managed to call Mum. We were crying over the phone. 'I can't believe it, Carole. I daren't let myself believe it.'

'It's true, Mum. Mr Nisbet is very confident. If anyone can do it he can.

'I hope so, hen. I hope so.'

Wednesday 6 October came, and went. I heard nothing.

I'd bundled my things together next to my bed. Lori and I had shared some wine, and had a bop with my disco tapes.

On Thursday Mr Nisbet came to see me. He wasn't smiling.

'Oh no,' I said.

'I'm sorry, Carole.' He looked pale. 'The magistrate changed his mind.'

'But you *said*—'

'Look, don't blame me, love. I feel as badly about it as you do. It's this bizarre legal system. A magistrate can do what he damn well likes! Do you know, on Wednesday, according to Minervini, the guy was so incensed by all this press coverage he was talking about postponing a hearing indefinitely!'

I gasped.

'No, don't worry. I went back and saw him on my own and smoothed things over. He's decided he has to see the forensic reports before he can make a decision. I'm afraid that won't be till November, Carole.'

I breathed out slowly. That old twist of panic was there again in the pit of my stomach. I was almost getting used to it.

'You shouldn't have *said*. I packed my things—'

Mr Nisbet looked very glum. 'Carole, I'm truly sorry. I only told you what I believed to be true. But you mustn't think it's all over. If we keep up the pressure, there's no doubt in my mind that you *will* be released.'

'Yes, but *when*?'

'Soon, Carole. Soon – I'm sure of it.'

The weather changed. The sticky heat of the summer went and with it, thank God, the stink of the canal. But the nights began to get chilly. The broken plastic in the cell window hadn't been replaced, and the floor was stone. There was central heating, but it never seemed to be warm enough.

Yet, in spite of all that, or perhaps because I was just becoming used to my situation, things actually felt better.

Lori was a good friend now, and the other girls finally seemed to accept me. Thanks to the money I got from Mr Minervini, I was able to get my own food sent in, and the others started to share theirs with me. My Italian was improving, too.

One of the guards, a woman called Anna, even asked me to help her with her son's English homework. I did, and he got good marks!

The biggest surprise was a bunch of flowers sent by one of the male prisoners, a man called Bruno. I wasn't sure who he was – and even less sure if I wanted to find out – but it was a great boost to my morale.

I was getting more and more letters from people all over the world who'd read about my case – people wishing me luck, telling me to keep my spirits up, even offering to be my boyfriend. I spent most of my time replying to them, and writing to relatives and friends.

I still wrote to Marco, but the only replies I had were from Marguerite. Once she told me Marco had been to Livorno, but he hadn't been able to get a pass to visit me. I didn't know whether to believe her or not. Mr Masi said that if Marco had come to him he could have arranged a visit quite easily.

Then a letter arrived with completely unexpected news. Mum had got together the cash for a fifteen-day visit. She arrived in the last week of September, with a bag full of heavy woollen jumpers.

'My God,' she said, after we'd hugged, 'you're looking better, Carole. You've got some colour back in your cheeks.'

I grinned. 'They let me go up on the roof for a couple of hours every day. I've been doing a bit of sunbathing.'

'You've put a bit of weight on, too. Didn't I tell you it was no good moping? You have to fight for yourself in this world, girl.'

I smiled. Mum had brought someone with her – a girl about my own age, very pretty and slim, with long, blonde hair down to her waist.

'This is Kay Gordon, Carole,' Mum explained. 'She's from North Sound. She came with me last time, but we couldn't get her in here. She knows Italian; she's been a great help.'

We shook hands. 'Hello, Carole. There are lots of people back in Scotland following your story. They're all on your side.'

I smiled, and thanked her for her help. She seemed very nice.

Mum leaned forward. 'If anyone should ask,' she said quietly, 'Kay's your cousin, OK? We had to say that to get her into the prison.'

Now I had a good look at her, Mum seemed low to me.

'It's the strain,' she said. 'The phone's going all the time at home. It's either Nisbet with some new date for the hearing, or the bloody press. They're even chasing me round the streets here! No one'll give me a straight answer about anything.

'We've just been to see Minervini – all he does is shrug, or talk about Mussolini! He's got his picture on the wall – the fellow's got a fixation with him! I told him, "Bugger Mussolini!

Mussolini's dead. My Carole's still alive and she's stuck in that gaol. When are *you* going to get her out?"'

'He's doing what he can, Mum,' I said. 'It's up to the magistrate.'

'So everyone keeps telling me,' she grunted.

But Mum's visit brought me luck. Within a couple of days I had my best news in a long time. After an item about me on the TV at home, the Scottish nanny who had been working for the Cecchinis came forward.

Apparently she had been on holiday in the Lake District, which is why she hadn't responded earlier.

'Her name is Teresa Hunter, she's twenty-one, and she comes from Lanarkshire,' Mr Minervini told me through Joyce; he was very excited.

'Mr Nisbet has taken a statement from her. She was employed by the Cecchinis from 14 July to 25 July. She says they worked her terribly hard, and she felt that the grandmother, in particular, disliked strangers in the house and resented her having anything to do with the child.

'In the end she was so unhappy she invented a story about problems at home as an excuse to leave.

'Both grandparents smoked all the time, and Mrs Tonti scolded the grandmother at least twice for leaving lighted cigarettes lying about.

'The first day she was there the lamp in the child's bedroom stopped working and had to be replaced. According to this girl, the electricity supply system in Elba becomes very overloaded in the summer because of all the holidaymakers and it was well known that there were frequent fires.'

Mr Minervini was beaming as he read from a sheet of paper.

'Miss Hunter says that if she had been there when the fires occurred,' Joyce translated, 'she thinks she would have been blamed, and would be where Carole is now.'

'But that's great!' I cried. 'They'll *have* to believe me now!'

Mr Minervini nodded and smiled.

Perhaps I should have realised things were going too well.

I was summoned on the first Tuesday in November. In the interrogation room Dr De Franco – a stern-looking man of about thirty – and a woman interpreter sat waiting. Mr Minervini was with them.

'Dr De Franco would like to ask you some more questions,' said the interpreter.

'Is it about what the other nanny said?' I asked.

The interpreter spoke to the magistrate. She turned to me.

'No. These questions are about certain fires in Ortisei.'

Suddenly everything was on hold. On 12 November Dr De Franco wanted to see me again. There were more questions about Ortisei.

'They've asked for further reports,' Mr Minervini told me afterwards. Joyce, as usual, translated for us. 'It should take about a month.'

'*Another* month!' I couldn't believe it. 'But they've got the psychiatrist reports and the forensic tests by now.'

Mr Minervini nodded. 'And, from what I've seen of them, there's no evidence to suggest the Elba fires were started deliberately. The Cecchinis are so fed up with the whole business they're even talking about dropping the charges—'

'That's fantastic!'

'No, Carole. These new investigations aren't about Elba; they're about Ortisei.'

I didn't understand. 'I explained all about those before.'

Mr Minervini sighed. 'The Riccis have made statements to the police, Carole. After all the press interest, and this *war* going on between the British and Italian newspapers, the magistrate can't ignore the Ortisei fires. He *has* to investigate them.'

The implications of it took a moment to sink in.

'Emanuela's story is worse than the Cecchinis – all that rubbish written by the magazines—!'

Mr Minervini shrugged. 'Under Italian law an investigating magistrate can act on any new information brought to him, from whatever source – police investigations, witness statements, newspaper reports—' He paused. 'Carole, you should know that these reports are to let the magistrate decide if investigations should go further. If he decides more investigations are necessary, you may have to be examined by another magistrate in Bolzano. You may have to go there.'

The dread was back. I was settled in Livorno. I could cope here. I didn't even know where Bolzano was.

'Will I be able to see you there?' I asked.

'Perhaps not so often. But I have an excellent colleague in Bolzano. His name is Alberto Valenti. He's already given me some help on your case. He'll look after you very well.'

My expression must have worried him. He reached over and squeezed my hand. 'Don't be too concerned for now, Carole. I'm just letting you know what's going on. It may never happen.'

I tried to return his smile.

In the middle of November Mr Nisbet arrived back in Italy with Teresa Hunter's statement – and my father.

I hadn't seen my dad for quite a time. Despite Mum's feelings, we'd always stayed on good terms. He'd raised money for my fund, and was asking the Ayr MP, George Younger, to take up my case with the Foreign Office.

But he was obviously not well – I knew he had cancer. It was a tearful reunion.

When it was over, Mr Nisbet became very angry about the new investigation.

'It's punishment, Carole, that's what it is! The Italian authorities are so embarrassed by all the exposure, they're taking it out on you! They know they haven't a leg to stand on.'

'Yes,' I said, 'but Mr Minervini's very worried about all these newspaper stories about me. And so is Mum – she had to get out of her hotel because the reporters wouldn't leave her alone.'

'They're doing the same to me, love. I've even had the Australian press badgering me in the middle of the night!'

Mr Nisbet leaned closer. 'The press are your friends, Carole. They guarantee you won't be forgotten. For God's sake, love, under this ridiculous system people can stay in gaol for *years* without being charged. There's no hundred and ten day rule here.'

I must have looked blank. 'In Scotland, when you're accused of a crime, you *have* to be brought to trial within a hundred and ten days, or you're released. Defendants have gone free because the authorities haven't got their act together. Here there's no pressure on *anyone* to do *anything*.

'Did they tell you little Agnese's mattress had been left in the Cecchini's back yard for *five weeks* before they got round to their forensic tests! It's unbelievable!

'The press are giving these people the kick up the bum they need, Carole. No one else is going to do it.'

I gave a sigh. I didn't know who to believe any more. The door opened. The guard appeared. It was time to go back to my cell.

A few days later Mum visited me with a parcel of my favourite food – prosciutto ham and a kind of soft cheese she'd found in a market nearby. Her eyes were blazing with anger.

'Do you know what that Nisbet's saying now?' she snapped. 'That you're going to be charged with attempted murder in Bolzano! It's all over the papers. No one's said a word about it here. Minervini's furious!

'I tell you, Carole, I've had it with that man. I don't think he's doing you any good. He attracts too much publicity. How do you think this whole witch thing started – it's the press making up stupid stories.'

'Mum,' I said, 'Mr Nisbet's been helping me for nothing—'

Mum took a deep breath. 'I had it out with him yesterday, Carole. I gave him his marching orders. He says I can't sack him. He has to hear it from you.'

'Oh Mum—'

'Now you'll probably say it's nothing to do with me—'

'I don't say that.'

'Well—' Mum sighed. 'Even Mr Masi says all this publicity is doing no good. You can't slag off the judges one minute and expect them to be lenient the next. It's not human nature, is it?'

She took my hand. 'I expect Nisbet's coming to see you this morning. I wouldn't have said a thing if I hadn't thought it was in your interest, love.'

Just after I'd got back to my cell a call came up, saying that Mr Nisbet was waiting to see me. I sat on my bed. The temptation to bawl was almost overwhelming. I didn't want squabbling; I didn't want arguments. I just wanted everyone to get together and get me out of this place.

The guard was still on the phone; she was getting impatient. I was too upset to think so I sent down a message to Mr Nisbet saying I couldn't see him.

I didn't sleep that night. In the morning there was a note from

Mr Nisbet. He said he had always done his best to help me, and he wished me good luck for the future and hoped I'd be home soon, but, in view of all the recent difficulties, he had decided to withdraw from the case. As I read the words my stomach lurched. Had I done the right thing? Should I have seen him? Mr Nisbet had done so much to help me. Who would look after me now?

'Mr Minervini thinks it's for the best,' Joyce told me at our next meeting. 'His approach and Mr Nisbet's weren't the same. Lawyers who are working together should be able to agree.'

I said nothing. I didn't really want to talk about it any more. I thought Mr Minervini was looking unhappy because of what had happened, but it was something else.

'We've heard from Bolzano,' he said. 'I'm afraid the magistrate there wants to interview you about the Ortisei fires.'

My heart started thumping.

'So I *am* going to be charged with attempted murder up there? Mr Nisbet *was* right!'

Mr Minervini shook his head. 'No, it's simply an investigation to see if you will be charged. Of course, if the Bolzano magistrate decides the offences in Ortisei are more serious than the Elba fires then your trial will take place up there.'

I was totally confused again. All I could see were things getting more and more complicated.

'But how long will that take?'

Mr Minervini's shrug told it all. 'A short time – we hope.'

'When do I go?'

'It's being organised. Quite soon. You'll actually be going to Trento. Bolzano doesn't have a women's prison. Trento is about thirty kilometres from Bolzano.'

It could be on the other side of the moon for all I cared.

'You've learned to be tough before, Carole,' Mum told me. 'It's time to be tough again.'

I could see she was as worried as I was, but I couldn't put a brave face on it. I was quaking inside.

'Lori says Trento is a place for real hard cases – murderers, terrorists, Red Brigade people – Livorno's like a holiday camp in comparison—'

'Oh, so this drug addict's the great expert, is she?' Mum snorted. 'She's just trying to make herself look big. Don't take any notice, Carole.' She paused. 'I just wish I knew when you were going. No one's saying anything as usual. I think they're afraid I'll try and bust you out the police van or something.'

'It might not be a bad idea.'

'That's better!' she grinned. 'A smile at last!' She touched my hand. 'I'll have to go home soon, Carole. I've no money left. But I'll be back – don't you fear. I'll see you in this Trento place, even if I have to walk all the way. And you know I'll do it, don't you?'

This time I managed to grin. 'Yes, Mum.'

It was the start of the second week in December. On the Sunday night I heard I was leaving the next day.

I cried when I said goodbye to the girls in my cell. Lori gave me her scarf. Guiliana, the head guard, and the guard called Anna both wished me luck. I never dreamed I'd become close to these people. So much had changed in my life in the four months I'd been here. Sometimes I wondered if Marco would think I was the same person.

The guard came for me first thing in the morning. There was no chance to let Mum know when I was going. Naturally I wasn't happy about that, but I didn't find out till much later what it had cost Mum to stay on as long as she had.

There had been ludicrous stories in the newspapers back home, saying she was having a wild time in Italy and neglecting little Sean, who was actually being well looked after by my Gran. As a result Mum lost her two cleaning jobs.

Far from living it up, she'd been left literally penniless, with no way of getting home. The consulate couldn't help her, and there wasn't the money in the appeal fund to pay for another flight. In the end she'd had to go to Mr Minervini.

He'd turned straight to his office safe, taken out all the money she needed and handed it straight over, no questions asked. 'I think he was getting sick of the sight of me!' Mum joked later.

It was just another part of the enormous debt I owed him.

10

Trento

DECEMBER 1982 — MARCH 1983

The door of the police car slammed shut. I sat in the back between two blue-uniformed guards, handcuffed to the one on my right. We were parked outside the Domenicani's main door, beside the guard's glass box.

After one hundred and twenty-eight days behind bars, I'd had just half a minute in the real world – the time it had taken me to walk from the prison door to the car.

But, as we lurched off, all I could think of was what I was leaving behind: friends like Lori and Joyce, Mr Minervini, Father Nolan and Mr Masi, even the male prisoner who'd sent me flowers.

They'd made me strong; they'd kept me going. Now all I had was a sick, empty feeling in the pit of my stomach. The thought of Trento terrified me.

We drove out through the narrow streets of Livorno – past shops and offices and factories, then into the scrubby country-side. It was a dull morning, chilly enough to need a winter coat. As we reached the autostrada it began to rain.

The car was noisy and stuffy, the journey long and boring. In spite of my nervousness, I found myself nodding off, then snapping awake again. After three or four hours, I saw mountains ahead. They were misty and covered with snow. They looked utterly bleak. The last time I'd travelled this way the sun had been shining, I'd had little Emanuele on my knee and Enrico had been singing his head off. It seemed like a whole lifetime away.

Around lunchtime we turned off the autostrada and went

down a ramp into a busy town of slushy streets and dark buildings. The mountains seemed to be all around.

The car threaded its way through the centre, and came into a quieter, more residential area. We turned into a broad side-street lined with leafless trees and parked cars. A high, sandy-coloured wall ran the length of one side. Behind it I could see a large, squarish building about three storeys high and painted a dull orange.

The car pulled up beside a pair of wooden double doors set in the wall. The driver got out and went into a smaller door to one side. When he came back, the wooden doors opened and we drove into a yard. The doors shut quickly behind us.

It was exactly like my first time in Livorno. I was stripped and searched; everything I'd brought from the Domenicani was taken away. I was allowed to keep only my cross and neck chain.

There were the same bleak, white-painted rooms, the same endless jingling of keys and slamming of doors, the same smell of disinfectant and bodies. The only difference was that the musty smell of the Domenicani was missing, because this was a more modern building.

I was shown into a large, L-shaped cell. There were eight beds round the walls, a big table in one corner and a TV set. Through two small windows I could see the mountains.

The women in the cell stared at me. They were scruffier and tougher-looking than the Livorno girls; one or two didn't look like women at all. A couple were obviously gypsies. But they all had the expression I knew of old: a mixture of curiosity and wariness and disgust, perhaps even hatred. My heart was thumping before the cell door had shut.

'*Buon giorno, Carole. Come sta?*'

'Mr Minervini would like to know how you are feeling—'

'Yes,' I interrupted, 'I understand that much.'

The interpreter was a woman I hadn't seen before. Apparently Joyce hadn't been able to come to Trento.

'Tell Mr Minervini I'm not so bad. No one here seems to speak any English, but I'm coping. Tell him I'm glad to see him.'

Mr Minervini's sad eyes lit up as he heard the translation. He spoke.

'Today,' said the interpreter, 'you will be questioned by the Bolzano prosecutor, Dr Cerqua.'

'Will he decide if there are to be any charges?'

'He will present a report to the principal magistrate, Dr Paparella.'

'Will that be before Christmas?'

Mr Minervini sighed. '*Mi dispiace, Carole. Non lo so.*' The interpreter didn't need to translate that. I felt my throat catch.

'That's a great prospect for my twenty-first.'

'Carole—' Mr Minervini touched my hand and spoke softly.

'He says you look pale,' said the interpreter. 'Are you eating well?'

I shrugged. 'The food's a bit better than the Domenicani. Not that that's saying much. I'm OK.'

'He says be strong, be patient, he is working as hard as he can for you.'

'I know.'

Mr Minervini lifted his hand. I looked down. There was a packet of chewing-gum on the table in front of me.

I smiled.

Dr Cerqua was a small, dapper man with a neat black beard and glasses. He brought along another interpreter. The questions seemed to go on for ever.

When I got back to the cell a meal had just arrived. I took my tray from the trolley and went to join the others round the big table in the corner. One of the mannish-looking women glared at me.

'*Non!*' she snapped, and nodded toward my bed. '*Vacci tu.*'

'*Come?*' I lifted up my plate. '*Voglio mangiare.* I want to eat.'

'*Vacci tu!*' She practically spat out the words. The others watched me. They weren't going to let me sit with them.

My heart was galloping. I knew now that Livorno was a prison for relatively minor offenders – drug addicts, prostitutes, petty thieves. But Lori had been right about this place; the women in here could have done literally anything.

I went back to my bed. Someone said scornfully, '*La piccola strega!*' There was laughter. When I looked up one of the gypsy woman spat on the floor, looking straight at me as she did it.

*

I'd once thought the Domenicani was a terrible place, but this was worse. Unlike in Livorno, the cell doors were kept locked all the time. We were only allowed out for the odd hour in a roof-top exercise yard.

The yard was much bigger here, but the walls were higher. I could just see the tops of the mountains if I jumped up. Sometimes it snowed; sometimes fierce winds swirled between the walls; sometimes both. It was always freezing.

The mannish-looking woman went out of her way to be unpleasant to me. I thought of complaining to the guards, but they seemed much stricter and less friendly than those at Livorno. The whole atmosphere was more tense.

Once, one of the girls was taken out and came back with a black eye and bruises. The guards said she'd had withdrawal symptoms from drugs she'd taken and had hurt herself. The others didn't believe them and started to kick the cell door and shout.

One night there was a terrible screaming in the corridor outside. It sounded like someone had gone mad. Through the little window in the cell door I saw two guards trying to strap a prisoner on to a trolley. They were hitting her with truncheons, but it didn't make any difference. She was going berserk.

Everyone in the cells nearby banged on the walls in protest. The racket was deafening, but it still didn't drown the woman's screaming. I crawled into bed and pulled the blankets round my head. I remember thinking, *This is what Hell must sound like.'*

I tried to keep myself to myself, writing letters, listening to music, watching TV. But I dared not relax. There were still stories about me in the newspapers, and the other prisoners were always wary, as if they expected odd things to happen. I was terrified something would and I'd get the blame.

One day, as we all watched television, the picture began to flicker and roll. Everyone glanced in my direction.

'*I* didn't do it!' I cried. 'Don't look at *me!*'

I jumped up, went over to the set and thumped it hard. The picture went back to normal straightaway.

Another day one of the gypsy women brought out some odd-looking cards she called Tarots, and began to tell the others'

fortunes. I was surprised when she asked me if I wanted a go.
I wondered if she was just testing to see how much supernatural
power I might have. But I went along with it, anyway.

'You have a boyfriend,' she said. '*Cos'e chiamato?* What's
his name?'

'Marco,' I said. She nodded and turned over some cards.

'You love him very much. You will get married and have
many *bambini.*'

She got quite upset when I started to laugh.

The nearer Christmas came, the lower I felt. The magistrate
interviewed me again. Officials from the British consulate at
Milan came to see how I was.

They told me my father had been trying to get the British
government to take up my case with the Italian government,
but it had been decided they could only do that when there was
a clear miscarriage of justice. What was happening to me might
be very distressing personally but, in Italian terms, it was
perfectly fair. I didn't want to imagine what 'unfair' treatment
might be like.

By now my birthday was just four days away. The only
bright spot was the cards I was receiving, not just from my
family and friends, but from all over the world, literally dozens,
all wishing me well. My cellmates were astonished.

24 December finally arrived. I'd managed to send out for
three cans of lager and a small chocolate cake. I'd have liked
to ask the others to share it with me, but I was too frightened
of them. When they went out for their exercise, I stayed behind.
Alone in the cell, I sat on my bed, ate half the cake and drank
all the beer. A thought popped into my head: wasn't this the
time when they were supposed to give you the key of the door?

I was twenty-one years old, and I'd never felt so miserable in
my life.

The room was small and bare, with just a table and two chairs.
I sat on one while the guard stood behind me. A moment later
I heard footsteps. The door opened.

'Carole?'

Mum appeared in the doorway. Her face was eager but wary,
as if she wasn't sure what she'd find. I got up.

'Hello, Mum.'

She started towards me, then hesitated as she saw the guard. Without a word, the guard walked past her and went out, shutting the door.

Mum and I hugged.

'Well, Mum,' I said, 'here I am in a different prison.'

'You know how to handle the situation, Carole.' We broke apart. 'Didn't I tell you I'd get here?' she said. 'Took some stranger sending me the money out the blue, but I did it!' We smiled at each other. 'And no one breathing down our necks for a change!'

'Yes, but we only get fifteen minutes, Mum,' I said. 'They're very strict here.'

'Never mind them – let me take a look at you.' She held me back, then frowned. 'Carole, aren't you sleeping? You're that pale. You've got to take care of yourself.' She glanced down. 'You haven't even tied up your trainers!'

I looked down at the trailing laces. 'I must have forgotten.'

'Carole–' Mum held my hand as we sat down. She was still frowning at me. 'Has no one been to visit you?'

I nodded. 'People from the consulate in Milan, a Mr Cole, and a Mr Pirie came to see me on New Year's Day – Mr Pirie was from Aberdeen. And Mr Minervini came just before. But I wrote to you about all that.'

Mum shook her head. 'We haven't had a thing since Christmas, love. Are you telling me you've been sending letters?'

'Three or four at least. But I've had nothing from you since Christmas, either.'

Mum's mouth tightened. 'I'm taking this up with Mr Masi. If they're stopping your letters I want to know why! They've no right to do that, no right at all–' She paused. 'How was your Christmas?'

I shrugged. 'Same as every other day. We had a mass in the chapel.'

'I went to midnight mass on Christmas Eve – first time in God knows how many years without you, Carole. It wasn't like Christmas at all. You did get my card, didn't you?'

I nodded. 'Thanks Mum. It was lovely. Did the consulate people tell you anything?'

'Things are "progressing normally" – whatever that bloody means!'

'Mr Minervini said we're going to see one of the magistrates in a few days,' I said. 'This one's called Paparella. Mum, I'm really worried about the translators. I saw my written statements after Christmas – they'd just put everything in any old order. If they didn't understand something, they didn't ask me, they just made it up. I had to write out *four* double sheets of corrections! Mum, if I don't get decent translators I'm going to be in real trouble!'

'Carole—' Mum squeezed my hand. 'Don't get so het up, love. We'll sort it out.'

I shook my head. 'You don't understand, Mum. The people they're getting are doing it for free, and they're rubbish. I need *professional* interpreters – properly registered ones. The money's going to have to come out of the fund. It can't be for just legal expenses.'

'I'll talk to Mr Hosie about it,' Mum said. 'I'm sure he'll be reasonable.'

'You've got to *make* him, Mum!'

She gazed at me and there was pain in her eyes. I hadn't meant to give her that.

'Carole,' she said, 'tell me the truth. Is it that much worse in here than Livorno?'

I dropped my head and nodded. I'd promised myself I wouldn't cry, and I wouldn't. But I couldn't lie, either. 'I'm scared, Mum,' I said. 'I'm really scared.'

A lady in Aberdeen had given the money anonymously for Mum's trip. It was that kind of generosity, along with the cards I'd had at Christmas, which cheered me on my down days; I was having plenty of those lately.

What I never realised at the time, of course, was how bad things were for Mum. She'd had phone calls, two or three apparently from Italy, telling her I'd never get out of gaol. For three nights, at two in the morning, a drunk had shouted outside her back door that I was a witch and he was glad I was in gaol. Everywhere there had been whispers that she was 'the witch's mother'.

Just before Christmas it had got too much when a woman

she'd worked with 'in the fish' had cut her dead in the street one night.

'Don't you know me?' Mum asked.

'Oh aye,' said the woman. 'You're the witch's mother.' Then she'd walked into a club.

Mum told John to stay where he was, marched through the doors of the club and tapped the woman on the shoulder.

'Don't you know my name?' Mum said.

'Oh, it's Pamela,' the woman said, suddenly all friendly.

'Don't you ever forget it!' Mum snapped, and floored the woman. Two enormous bouncers had lifted her bodily under the arms and swept her straight back into the street.

But the biggest boost for both of us, of course, was seeing each other again. Mum had flown to Milan on 17 January, and the British vice consul there had brought her on the train to Trento the next day, a Tuesday. She had to leave again on the Saturday, but Trento wasn't like the Domenicani – the enormous distance she'd come didn't seem to impress anyone; she was only allowed to see me twice, for just fifteen minutes each time.

When the guard re-appeared on the last visit, Mum tried to squeeze in another couple of minutes. The guard simply grabbed the back of my hair and yanked me to my feet.

I thought for a second Mum would kill the woman; I could see it in her eyes. Even the guard hesitated. 'It's OK, Mum,' I said quickly. 'I'll be all right.' The guard took hold of my arm instead.

I didn't know when I'd see Mum again. Just after she'd gone a great bundle of letters arrived for me, including several from Mum; I never did find out why they'd been held up.

A few days later Mr Minervini came to see me with Alberto Valenti, the lawyer from Bolzano who was helping him here. Mr Valenti was a tall, slim man in his forties with dark, thinning hair.

We all had a meeting with the investigating magistrate Dr Paparella. He was nearer Mr Minervini's age, grim-faced and wearing heavy, dark-rimmed glasses. They all spoke in Italian. Mr Minervini had brought an interpreter, but she didn't try to translate what was being said. I did not understand a word of the complicated legal language.

Dr Paparella was as stony-faced as every other magistrate I'd seen, but I had the feeling he didn't approve of me. Mr Minervini told me as much afterwards, through the interpreter.

'He's a hard man, Carole, and he regards attempted murder very seriously. That's his right, of course, but personally I find Cindolo easier to deal with. He's also annoyed by the continuing reports in the British press. You know there was a story that the Mafia would be willing to break you out for a price?'

I had to laugh. 'Perhaps we should get in touch!'

Mr Minervini wasn't laughing. 'This sort of thing doesn't help, Carole. Any suggestion that Italian justice can be intimidated or bribed is deeply resented.'

He told me that the magistrate had asked for forensic reports on the two larger fires in Ortisei.

'I objected,' he said, 'because the Ricci's house has been re-decorated since. It's like Elba all over again. But they have parts of the mattress in the Moroder flat and some other material to look at, so the examination is going ahead. It may do us some good; we'll have to see.'

'How long will that be?'

'A week, perhaps two.' Mr Minervini glanced into his briefcase. 'I've also been approached by two British experts on the paranormal: Guy Lyon Playfair and Dr Hugh Pincott. They say your experiences remind them of certain poltergeist cases they've investigated. They've offered to fly out to Italy at their own expense.'

'Poltergeists?' I frowned. 'You mean ghosties and ghoulies? I told you I don't believe in any of that. *I* didn't have anything to do with any of this.'

'*Bene.*' Mr Minervini nodded, and shut his case again. 'I'll deal with it.'

He had one piece of good news. Mr Masi had offered to act as my interpreter if I came to trial in Livorno.

January passed into February. To my surprise the forensic report was completed quickly, but apparently substances that might have come from petrol or other inflammable liquids were detected. Dr Paparella ordered further tests.

Mr Minervini said we needed our own forensic expert to do

the same tests. All I knew was that the longer the investigation went on, the less chance I had of a trial taking place in the spring session.

If I missed the spring, the courts closed for the whole of the summer. That would mean having to wait for the autumn session – another six months in gaol.

The days crawled by. It got easier to cope with the other girls. I was eating with them now, and even sharing the food their relatives and friends brought in for them. It made me feel guilty, because I couldn't repay them. But there was no one like Lori who I could trust; I could never relax. The worst part, though, was the boredom, and not knowing what was happening.

In Livorno I'd had visitors all the time – Mr Minervini, Father Nolan, Mr Masi; they hadn't just brought me things to make life more comfortable, they'd been able to find out things for me, get questions answered.

In Trento there was no one like that. I had visits from the consulate people in Milan, but Milan was about three times as far away from here as Florence had been from Livorno; they couldn't just nip back and forth the way Mr Masi and Mr Eilbeck had been able to do.

Mr Minervini couldn't afford to come more than once a month, if I was lucky. In a way, I almost didn't want him to because it would mean taking even more money out of my appeal fund; I kept reading newspaper stories from home that it was nearly all gone.

Newspapers and letters were my main source of news. The people who wrote to me didn't know any more than I did, and the newspaper stories all seemed to contradict each other, or say the same things over and over again.

March arrived. The forensic experts finished their new tests, and Mr Minervini's expert presented his. Apparently neither of them could tell if the items they'd examined had ever had inflammable liquid on them or not!

Mr Minervini came to see me. 'The papers have all gone to the public prosecutor,' he told me. 'All we can do now is wait for a decision.'

He still spoke through an interpreter, but my Italian was good enough now to get the gist of what he was saying.

'What do you think the decision will be?'

He took a deep breath before answering. 'I must be honest with you, Carole. There will be charges – almost certainly arson; I can't say about attempted murder. Dr Paparella seems more reasonable than I thought. I don't think he believes the fires involving Grandfather Ricci or Enrico Ricci were attempts at murder.'

I breathed out. 'Thank God for that!'

Mr Minervini shrugged. 'Unfortunately Dr Cerqua is of a different opinion. He's concerned that no one has really explained your motives for these alleged offences. He's asking for more psychiatric examinations, which would also look into the paranormal aspects.'

'They already know I'm not crazy!'

Mr Minervini's shrug was even broader than before. 'I'm just telling you what they tell me, Carole. These differences of opinion have to be sorted out.'

'But who does that? Who makes the decision?'

'Dr Paparella. He's the examining magistrate. But Dr Cerqua can lodge an appeal against the decision, if he chooses.'

I closed my eyes. 'I don't understand any of this! It just seems to go round and round, and no one *does* anything! And I'm still stuck in here!' I shook my head. 'I'm sorry, Mr Minervini – I know you're trying hard – I don't mean to criticise you–'

He touched my hand. '*Capisco – capisco – non importa* – it doesn't matter, Carole. You leave it all to me. All you have to do is be strong, like your mother says. *Si?*'

He was nodding, giving his funny, gap-toothed smile. I nodded back, but a smile was too hard to manage.

11

Return To Livorno

Easter arrived with a big parcel from Mum, including a chocolate egg. It was a lovely surprise, even though the egg was broken up by the prison authorities because anything coming into the prison had to be searched thoroughly.

The magistrates still hadn't come to a decision, but at least I had something else to occupy me. We began to make soft toys. I remembered the one I'd made for my little brother Sean back home in Ayr, around my twentieth birthday – just before Marco and I had got engaged. It all seemed another world away, as if that life had been lived by someone else, not the person I was now.

I still thought of Marco all the time. Ever since that telephone call in Livorno I hadn't heard a word from him. I think I accepted now that he didn't love me any more, though after all that had happened between us it still didn't make sense to me. My feelings for him hadn't changed a bit.

Another month passed. The weather was warm now. I looked forward to my stints in the exercise yard. And then I heard from Mr Minervini that a hearing had been fixed for 11 May in Bolzano. Dr Paparella would be announcing his decision.

The news woke me up. I realised I'd just been drifting through my days, half asleep, wishing them away. Now there was a date to look forward to, and a real chance I'd come to trial this spring. After all that the Cecchinis and the Riccis had been saying, all the absurd things written by the newspapers, I'd finally have my opportunity to give my story. I couldn't wait!

Mr Minervini was smiling as he came in to see me. I hardly needed the interpreter to translate for me.

'The two attempted murder charges have been dropped,' he said. 'The case goes back to Livorno.'

I breathed a giant sigh of relief. 'I've been praying every night.'

'Sometimes that's the best thing to do.'

We grinned at each other.

'But it's not all good news, Carole,' Mr Minervini went on. 'There are still five accusations of fire-raising, three in Ortisei, two in Elba, and the alleged attempted murder of Agnese Cecchini. Dr Paparella believes you should stand trial for those.'

'I want to,' I said. 'I want to get into a court room and prove I'm innocent.'

Mr Minervini frowned. 'I'd prefer to have the case dismissed. That's what I'll be trying to do in Livorno. If two accusations have been dropped, why not more? Remember, you still haven't been formally charged.'

'But if Dr Paparella wants me to go to trial, surely the Livorno magistrates will, too?'

'It seems likely, I agree. But there may be other grounds for hope in Dr Cerqua's opinion. He wanted you to have another psychiatric examination. Remember last year we wanted to hire our own psychiatrist, but there wasn't the money? If we produced an expert now who said you weren't responsible for your actions – for whatever reason—'

'There aren't any reasons,' I said. 'There *couldn't* be, because I didn't do anything! And if they said I wasn't responsible they might lock me up anyway!'

'There's an element of risk, yes, but I'm just exploring possibilities, Carole. Both of us know this witchcraft thing is nonsense, but if some kind of defence, based on the paranormal, is possible—'

I stared at him. 'You sound like Mr Nisbet! That's what he was saying. I get off if I say I *am* a witch!'

'Carole,' Mr Minervini said, 'it's different now. It's Dr Cerqua who is raising this possibility – not me! I must at least take a look at it. I have to explore any avenue that might help you. I would fail you if I didn't. You understand?'

I shook my head. 'I know you're doing all you can, Mr Minervini, but really I just want to get out of here and back to Livorno.'

May plodded on.

I couldn't understand why I wasn't being moved. Every day that passed meant that the Livorno authorities weren't making a decision; the likelihood of a spring trial was becoming more and more remote.

The weather got hotter. It was starting to affect everyone. There were arguments in the cell; and at least one fight. I felt myself slipping back into apathy, only now, having had my spirits raised, I seemed to sink deeper than ever before.

I was tired all the time. I felt I was swimming through treacle. Everything took too much effort. Nothing seemed quite real any more.

I didn't take a conscious decision to stop eating.

My appetite simply faded. I started to give my prison meals to the other girls. When I did feel peckish – which wasn't often – I just nibbled at an apple or some other fruit.

Somehow I stopped caring. It seemed that however much I tried to get out of this situation, however hard other people worked to free me, it didn't make any difference – there was always another decision to be made, another legal argument, another locked door.

Wouldn't it be so much easier to give in? Say, 'Yes, I did start those fires! I put the evil eye on the mattresses and the Ricci's bedroom and the wastebin in the Moroder's flat – it's an old *witchcraft* trick I picked up in Scotland! Didn't you know Scotland was the land of witches? It's bred into all us Scottish girls!'

Wouldn't they just love that!

I could see Emanuela's mouth opening in a big 'O' of surprise, and the Cecchini grandmother screaming and crossing herself, and all those Italian reporters looking up from their typewriters in astonishment, saying, 'My God, we thought we were only telling sensational stories, but it's all *true!* Perhaps she'll put the evil eye on *us!*'

Sometimes I wished to God I could.

But then, when I wasn't angry, I could imagine doing the

opposite – just letting it all go. None of the guards had noticed I wasn't eating. What if I gave up altogether, simply lay down and let myself drift away? That would be even easier.

I knew these thoughts were mad, even while I was having them, but I couldn't stop myself. I was still writing letters, though I only mentioned what I was really thinking to a friend in Livorno.

Her name was Yvonne Wolfgang. She was from New Zealand and a neighbour of Mr Minervini's. She had put Mum up when the reporters had hounded her out of her hotel, and she and Mum had become good friends. Yvonne had come to see me in Livorno, and written lots of letters trying to keep my spirits up. I was very grateful to her.

I wrote: 'I haven't eaten for twelve days. I just feel dead. I have also started to think of crazy things, but I don't want to end my life, as I am innocent. How much longer must I wait, Yvonne, serving this long time for nothing?'

A few days after I'd sent the letter, Mr Cyril Cole from the consulate in Milan came to visit me and ask how I was. I didn't find out till later that Yvonne had sent my letters on to Mum, who had been so worried she had telephoned Mr Masi. Mr Masi had asked Mr Cole to see me, and apparently he reported that I was a bit depressed but otherwise fine.

When Mum heard, she didn't believe it, and she sent the letters to Mr Masi to judge for himself. Up till then the British authorities had still been saying that there was nothing they could do about my case, and there was no point in taking it up at a high level. If that was true, I'm sure in my own mind their attitude changed now.

On the first Wednesday of June I was told to pack up my things and get ready to leave. The next morning, very early, I was taken downstairs. Two guards were waiting and there was a police car in the yard. I was handcuffed and put in the back.

I wouldn't let myself believe I'd seen the last of Trento until we were on the autostrada, heading south. When the last exit signs flashed past, all my doubts finally vanished. I dared to ask the guard on my right: 'Livorno?'

He gave a brief nod. '*Si.*'

I closed my eyes. For the first time in over seven months, I felt I could relax.

Relax because I was going from one prison to another, to an older, more decrepit prison with an open sewer on its doorstep? It seemed crazy. It *was* crazy. But, in this topsy-turvy world where I found myself, Livorno was the nearest thing I had to 'home'.

Livorno had taught me that crying was a waste of time. Trento had taught me that despairing was even more useless.

What had Mr Minervini said? Be patient, be strong.

He'd been right. Patience and strength were the only answers.

Patience was easy; you just let one day plod on from the next. Strength was the hard part. You had to dig for it, even when you were sure it wasn't there. But it was, deep down. And, when you found it, you came face to face with your real self — that solid, rock-bottom part of yourself which would always be there, no matter what.

I'd lived all my life till now without realising that. If all this hadn't happened to me, perhaps I never would have.

I knew now that I was going to get by — no matter how many more decisions were delayed, or things said against me — even if they locked me up for for another eleven months it almost didn't matter, I *was* going to win through.

Just watch me!

The Alps disappeared behind us. The land became flatter and broader, and much hotter. I'd forgotten how high Trento must be; it was bound to be cooler in the mountains.

Now the sky was blistering and there was a kind of scummy heat haze over the autostrada. It was even worse by the time we reached Livorno. The narrow, crowded streets and the tall, old buildings seemed to attract the heat and trap it. As we drove over the canal bridge and I caught my first glimpse of the Domenicani, the car window was open and I had my first whiff of the canal, too. I'd forgotten how bad the smell had got last August and September, and this was only June.

But, as the car pulled up and I was taken back through those familiar grey steel doors, I didn't mind. I had friends here.

Why the guards needed to strip and search me again, I don't know — I was hardly going to bring something *out* of prison — but they did. Afterwards I was taken upstairs.

This time, as I passed the men's cells, I didn't feel in the least apprehensive. There were the usual faces bobbing up behind the little barred windows, but when they saw me there were sudden smiles, calls of '*Eh! Carolina! Ciao! . . . Ecco Carolina! Carolina e tornata! . . . Carolina, è Bruno! I love-a you!*'

By the time I reached the door of the women's section I was blushing like a fourteen-year-old and grinning all over my face. The male guard grunted, obviously unimpressed, and rapped on the grey steel.

Giuliana, the head guard, opened the door. She gave me a brief smile. In the background pop music was playing. I could hear the wheezy rattle of the exercise bike. Giuliana re-locked and nodded me inside. I walked past the entrance to the showers, and the familiar damp, musty smell. The whole building, in fact, smelled as bad as ever.

The guard Anna was sitting at the long table. She smiled, and stood up as I came in.

'*Ciao, Carolina.*'

'Hello, Anna.'

A head popped round the door of my old cell. It was Lori, her big brown eyes widening as she saw me.

'*Carolina!*'

Grinning, she held out her arms, and we hugged.

'*Benvenuta, Carolina.*' Doris was behind her, and another friend called Sonia. We all hugged.

'Eh—' Giuliana beckoned me towards my old cell, breaking up the reunion.

'*La stessa cella?*' I asked. 'The same cell?'

Giuliana nodded. I followed her inside. The others followed me. There were a couple of new pictures on the walls, but the same crucifix was fixed over Lori's bed, the same chipped pocket mirror was hanging up next to it. The window still hadn't been repaired. I could even hear familiar voices arguing in the flats opposite.

'The same bed, too?' I said.

'We keep it specially for you,' Lori grinned. We both laughed. I couldn't see anyone else choosing a full frontal view of the toilet if they could possibly avoid it!

'OK?' said Guiliana. I nodded.

'*Benvenuta,*' she said.

'*Si,*' said Lori. 'Welcome home.'

*

'Just like old times, eh?' said Mr Minervini. We smiled at each other. We were in an interrogation room we both knew very well.

With Mr Minervini was his daughter Valeria, a pretty girl my own age. She worked in his office and spoke good English. She'd translated for us a few times before.

'Dr Cindolo has recommended you go to trial,' Mr Minervini told me. 'You're charged with five offences of arson – three in Ortisei, two in Elba – and the attempted murder of Agnese Cecchini.'

I nodded. I hadn't really expected anything else.

'When will the trial start?'

Mr Minervini paused. 'I'm hoping for November. But I have to say it could be as long as next April.'

My heart sank, but not too far; I wasn't going to fall into that trap again.

'*Two* birthdays in gaol?'

'The battle isn't over yet, Carole, not by any means. I have a couple of weeks to submit the defence's answer to the prosecution's arguments. I will try very hard to have the attempted murder charge dismissed. I will also make another request for provisional liberty. And I believe we should think seriously about getting another psychiatric opinion.'

I frowned at him. 'Didn't we settle all that?'

'Not satisfactorily, no, Carole,' said Mr Minervini. 'Dr Cindolo still believes your motive for the offences was what he calls "pathological nostalgia". In other words, you were so desperate to get back to Marco you were prepared to do anything to force your employers to go back to Rome—'

'But he knows I could have left the Ricci's or the Cecchini's any time—'

'Exactly!' Mr Minervini nodded briskly. 'And I will make that point *very* forcefully. But – according to forensic psychology – this state of mind can make the most gentle of people act in a kind of trance where they literally don't realise what they are doing. If we could get another expert opinion it might settle that question once and for all. That's all I'm saying.'

I shook my head. 'I think I'd know if I'd been in a trance or not! All I really want is to get the chance to tell the truth. I just want people to know what really happened.'

Mr Minervini smiled. '*Certamente*. I would also like to see you out of gaol.'

Valeria turned to me. 'My father knows what he's doing, Carole. He's a very good lawyer.'

Mr Minervini asked her what she'd said. When she told him, he roared with laugher. '*Mia figlia percettiva!* A clever girl, eh?'

'Pappa—' She blushed as Mr Minervini pinched her cheek. I smiled.

It *was* just like old times. Some faces had changed, of course – Anna, the cellmate who could speak English, had been transferred to another prison – but the daily routine was the same. I slipped back into it as if nothing had changed.

The eight o'clock call, when the cell doors were unlocked and the guard came in, banging a heavy stick against the window bars and making enough noise to wake the dead. Then weak coffee with a slice of bread, and perhaps a stale *panino* – bread roll – or even a *cornetto* – a thin pastry with a jam or custard filling – which you might have bought the day before, and managed to save. Then the showers, and the morning would begin. I usually spent it reading, or writing letters in the cell.

At eleven thirty we were allowed to go along the little corridor beside the showers, up the stairs and on to the roof exercise yard. Now, I was sometimes allowed on to an even higher part, where I could see over the walls and out across the rooftops of Livorno. Generally, though, I sat and chatted or watched the others play games.

Then it was back for lunch. The food hadn't improved in my absence; I had to drink a kind of tea with lumps of bread floating in it, which was supposed to fatten me up after eating so little in Trento. Unfortunately it worked very well!

From one to four we were in the cells again. At four we could go back to the roof. Six o'clock was tea-time. Afterwards we could watch TV. The cell doors were locked any time from seven until past eight o'clock, depending on who was on duty; Anna was reasonable, Guiliana quite strict.

Then the TV and the lights would be turned off, and we would lie in the thick, sticky heat and try to sleep, listening to the radios and TVs and rows of the people in the flats across the way.

The feud with the middle-aged woman opposite was still going strong. Sometimes I felt quite sorry for her. If Lori and the others weren't swapping insults with her, they were pelting the poor woman with eggs or bits of old fruit! At least one window had been broken with plum stones.

The girls could also talk to the male prisoners whose cell windows were on the same side of the building as ours. The guards weren't very happy about that, but they couldn't stop it. Messages somehow managed to get backwards and forwards. A few girls decided they'd found boyfriends. I *didn't* regard the one called Bruno as mine!

I had my regular visitors back, too. It was good to see Father Nolan again, and Mr Masi, and letters still streamed in from all over the place.

The media obviously hadn't forgotten me, either. Mum regularly sent me cuttings from the British newspapers, and there were stories in the Italian newspapers and magazines. I was even mentioned on Italian TV – as the 'witch of Isola Elba', which really annoyed me. In Italy there didn't even seem to be a hint that I might actually be innocent.

June became July. Mr Minervini's attempt to get me provisional liberty came to nothing, which I'd more or less expected. If they hadn't given it to me last year, they weren't likely to do it now, with another three charges against me.

Patience and strength, I reminded myself every day; that would get me through this. My patience, at least, was rewarded. Towards the end of the month Mr Minervini came to see me.

'It looks like we have a trial date, Carole,' he told me. 'The twelfth to the fifteenth of December.'

'*Four months* away?'

Mr Minervini sighed. He obviously wasn't very happy. 'I'd still hoped for a dismissal, but I couldn't persuade the examining magistrate. I'm sorry, Carole.'

'Don't be,' I said. 'I *want* to go to trial. I want to confront these two families. I want to make them sorry for what they said about me! You see, I've *been* on trial for the past year. Now it's their turn!'

12

Trial Run

AUGUST – DECEMBER 1983

In many ways setting the trial date was a godsend. If I'd passed the anniversary of my imprisonment with everything still undecided, I'm sure that would have undermined even my new-found strength.

Now I had something real to aim for – not just another hearing, or another magistrate's decision. This was the chance I'd prayed for, a chance to stand up for my rights at last, a chance to be free. All I had to do was to stay calm, strong and alert.

I wished away the August days – the heat was so exhausting I was almost glad I had nothing else to do. Towards the end of the month Mr Minervini paid me a visit. He brought an interpreter I hadn't seen before.

'My name's Serena Macbeth, Carole,' she told me. 'I have some friends who would like to do a television programme on you.'

'Macbeth?' For a second the name tickled me. Hadn't I had enough to do with witches already?

But she was quite serious. She was British; a slim, dark-haired girl, not that much older than me, but obviously very bright, and quite forceful, too. She spoke Italian fluently with Mr Minervini.

'It would be for Channel Four back home,' she explained. 'It would be an opportunity for you to give your side of the story.'

'That makes a change,' I said. 'No one in the media seems to have been that keen so far!'

We talked some more. She told me she was half Italian, and

she'd been on holiday in Italy when she became interested in my case. She'd offered to do some translating work for Mr Minervini, and the programme makers wanted to interview him too. They might also want to talk to my mother. Mr Minervini seemed to think the programme would be a good idea. I was certainly happy to give my point of view for a change. I agreed to do it.

Serena said they expected problems with the authorities, who would probably need to know in advance what questions the TV people would ask me, but she thought that could be sorted out. It obviously was, because a few days later I heard it was going ahead. One morning in the first week of September I was taken down to one of the interrogation rooms.

It was full of people. Serena was there, with a blonde girl about the same age called Claire Lasko, a man with a camera, and another one with a big tape recorder. So was the prison governor, and the woman interpreter who'd translated my first interview with Dr Cindolo so badly. When the camera lights were switched on the room got very hot.

Claire Lasko was in charge of the filming. She sat me on a chair next to a radiator while the camera was set up. I'd put on the nicest dress I had with me, just a plain shift with mauve and black horizontal stripes, and tidied myself up as best I could. I was still very nervous. I'd been on TV before – at least I'd been glimpsed through the barred windows of the gaol. Mum had told me all about my pictures which had been shown on the news at home. But this was my first interview.

Serena asked the questions. She asked me about the Riccis and the Cecchinis, and I said how well I'd got on with both of them at first, and how Daniella had warned me that the grandmother was a difficult person to get to know. I also got a chance to say what I thought of the way the press, Italian and British, had treated me. Finally Serena asked what I thought had caused the fires. I said what I'd been saying all along. I just didn't know.

By the time we finished my nervousness had almost gone, and I was quite enjoying myself. Serena and Claire Lasko said it had gone very well. They were hoping to do two programmes on my case, if they could persuade the TV company.

In fact, there was only the one. It was shown in a series called

Twenty/Twenty Vision on 19 October. Mum wrote and told me about it, and sent me newspaper cuttings of reviews. She was annoyed by the programme because it cut out what I'd said about getting on well with the families before the fires happened. It also suggested that Mr Minervini might have to use the idea that I had supernatural powers as my defence.

Apparently they got an expert on fires to set light to two mattresses, like the ones on the grandparents' bed in the first Elba fire. According to the forensic reports, all the burning had been along one side.

The expert found it took twenty minutes for the fire to travel from one end of the mattress to the other. I'd only been out of the family's sight for five minutes at the most. There wouldn't have been the time for me to do that amount of burning, which is what I'd been saying all along.

There was also a report about a sixteen-year-old Italian boy called Benedetto Supino who was supposed to make fuse boxes explode and newspapers catch fire whenever he was near. No one, I noticed, had locked *him* up for fourteen months.

What surprised me most, though, was that the programme makers actually interviewed Marco. According to the newspaper reviews, he'd said that *I* had asked him to get married, but he'd told me he was too young. It certainly wasn't the way I remembered it! *And* I had his ring to prove it. But he had also said that we had loved each other very much.

Not long after I gave the interview, Marco gave me another shock, though this time it wasn't his fault. One Monday morning, at about half past eleven, Anna came into my cell and said, 'You're having a visit from your boyfriend Marco at one o'clock.'

I felt my tummy jump. Then I thought she must be joking. I'd recently had a letter from Marguerite, saying Marco was going to Amsterdam on holiday. Monday wasn't even a visiting day.

'No, it's true,' Anna said. 'I've just heard.'

I asked her to phone down to the office and ask if it was really Marco Vitulano. She said she would, and she came back in a few minutes.

'*Mi dispiace, Carole*,' she said. 'They heard it wrong. It's Paulo, not Marco.'

I suddenly realised I was trembling. My legs felt like jelly. The thought that he could just walk back into my life after so long, after so much pain, and everything would be all right again was almost too much.

'Are you OK?' Anna asked. 'Shall I send this man away?'

I shook my head.

My visitor was a boy called Paulo Lantel who had started to write to me when I'd first been put in prison. He was in his twenties, and he came from Turin.

He spoke very good English, and over the past year we'd exchanged dozens of letters. He had sent me poems he'd written and a photograph of himself. He was one of the best, most helpful new friends I'd made as a result of my ordeal but, although he'd tried to see me in Trento, we had never actually met.

I went down to see him, and we were allowed to talk for two hours, all in English. By the end I'd almost forgotten my shock over Marco. Seeing Paulo at last was a lovely surprise. He promised to come to my trial.

I had another unexpected visitor at the beginning of September. Mr Minervini told me to expect someone from Germany who would be asking me questions, and it would help my case to try to answer them.

He came to see me one Thursday morning. His name was Dr Hans Bender. He was a tall, stooping, elderly man with white, straggly hair. He said he was a psychiatrist who had offered his services to Mr Minervini. I told him about the tests I'd already had, which he knew about. These were new ones, he said, which Mr Minervini was keen to have done.

Dr Bender was a pleasant man, who seemed very kind, but his questions were very similar to those the first two psychiatrists had asked me. Towards the end he started to ask me about ghosts and witches and poltergeists. I told him what I'd told everyone else from the beginning: so far as I was concerned, all that was nonsense.

Throughout September the heat was still sweltering. I kept busy with a little job in the prison, making soft toys, just like in Trento. They were mainly small animals, like hedgehogs, though I did manage a bagpiper in a kilt. There was no money paid for them, but it helped to kill the time.

Meanwhile, Mr Minervini had given me copies of the statements by the two families, and I asked Mr Masi to get them translated at the consulate. When I read what they'd said I was shocked.

Luigi Cecchini said he'd asked Agnese what happened before the fire in the grandparent's bedroom. According to her I'd left her alone in the bathroom and gone to look for a piece of thread so that we could play with a cat. I was also supposed to have been holding something orange in my hand, and there was an orange cigarette lighter in the house.

What cat? Agnese and I had been looking at a *bird*. And I hadn't left her at all, let alone had a lighter in my hand.

Reading that sent a cold shiver through me. If the authorities were going to believe what a father *thought* his three-year-old daughter was saying to him, what chance did I have?

By October the summer heat had finally begun to fade. My father wrote to tell me he'd written to the Queen to intervene for me, and sent a petition to Mrs Thatcher. I was grateful, but I honestly didn't expect much to come of it. Mum, being Mum, had already gone one step further and written to the Pope shortly after I'd been arrested. She was still waiting for a reply.

At the beginning of the month yet another psychiatrist came to see me – this time an Englishman but with a German name, a Dr Karle. He was from Guy's Hospital in London. From what I gathered from Mr Minervini, he would be the British psychiatrist we should have hired last year, when I was first arrested. Apparently Dr Karle had already spoken about me with both my parents.

We went through all the familiar questions and tests, and I was wired up again the way I'd been with the first psychiatrists. I didn't mind going over it all again, but I knew I was giving the same answers. I hoped someone was getting some benefit from them.

Mr Minervini gave me details of the trial. It was to be held in the Court of Assizes in the Palazzo di Giustizia, which was just across the canal from the prison. I could probably see its roof from the upper part of the exercise yard.

Like the Domenicani, it was a converted religious house, actually a convent; the courtroom itself had once been a chapel.

With all this talk about the supernatural, it seemed a bizarre coincidence.

Mr Minervini would defend the charges relating to Elba, and Alberto Valenti would do the same for the Ortisei fires. There would be no jury as in Scotland. The case would be heard by two judges and six jurors, who were more like British magistrates than ordinary members of the public.

'There is one thing I should warn you about,' said Mr Minervini. 'In the courtroom the defendant usually has to stand behind steel bars. These were put in a few years ago for a terrorist trial. All the courtrooms have them now.'

I had to smile. 'Are they afraid I'm going to fly out of the room on my broomstick?'

Mr Minervini grinned. 'I don't think so. But don't worry about it. I'll appeal to the court and get you taken out straightaway.'

'I don't mind where I stand as long I get a chance to have my say,' I told him.

I was more worried about the state of my appeal fund. Money had been trickling in, and it had helped to cover Mr Minervini's expenses, but the trial was going to cost a lot. Mr Minervini was very anxious that there might not be enough to pay for witnesses to fly to Italy, especially Teresa Hunter, the nanny who'd worked for the Cecchinis just before me. He was sure her evidence would be crucial.

After I'd seen Mr Minervini some of the girls mentioned the bars in the court room. Apparently they were more like a cage. The thought of being locked up in public, like something in a zoo, didn't appeal to me at all.

A few days later Mr Masi visited me. It was a particularly hot day. I felt sticky and uncomfortable; I couldn't face visitors in that state. I had a quick shower before I went down to see him.

'Carole,' Mr Masi cried, 'you don't need to make yourself beautiful for me. You are beautiful already. Please don't keep me waiting again.'

He looked quite exasperated; it was the nearest I'd ever seen him to losing his temper.

The talk came round to the courtroom cage. Mr Masi nodded as I told him my fears.

'I'll go to see the president of the Court of Assizes,' he said. 'Even if you have to go into the cage to start with, I'm sure we can get you released very quickly.'

When he left he gave me a couple of packets of English cigarettes – I'd never smoked, but the other girls did all the time. I could swap the cigarettes for food and other things. The gift made me feel quite guilty I'd kept Mr Masi waiting.

October turned into November. The days were drawing in now. The Domenicani's stone floors were starting to feel chilly again. I thought of the trial all the time.

It would be the first time I'd ever spoken in public. Even the Channel Four TV interview had been to only half a dozen people in a tiny room. The courtroom would be vast.

I could see myself shrivelling up in sheer fright, my voice turning into a tiny squeak. What if even the interpreter couldn't hear me?

Patience and strength: I mustn't forget. But I still prayed every night.

Halfway through November there was good news about the witnesses. Teresa Hunter would be able to attend the trial, and nothing would keep Mum away. Unless Mr Minervini decided to call Dr Bender or Dr Karle, they would be my only witnesses. The prosecution would be calling fourteen.

I knew my father wanted to come too, but I also knew he wouldn't be able to afford it. Mum wrote, promising to bring me a set of smart clothes for the trial. I wrote back telling her that I was desperate for a new pair of shoes, preferably black, patent leather. The only footwear I had with me was too old or too casual.

As November went on the days seemed to accelerate. There were more and more stories in the papers. Mr Masi told me there was so much press interest now that journalists would be flying in from all over the world – including one from Argentina. To deal with all the press enquiries Gordon Pirie, the Aberdonian who'd visited me in Trento on New Year's Day, was being sent down from Milan.

'It's a very big story now, Carole,' Mr Masi said. 'It's more than the consulate in Florence can handle on its own.'

After the fuss there'd been last year with so many newspaper stories about me, I wasn't sure if I was happy about that.

'It'll certainly increase the pressure on the judges,' Mr Masi agreed. 'But it's difficult to say what effect it'll have. Anyway, we can't do anything about it now.'

December arrived. I'm sure I didn't show it on the outside, but inside I had a kind of permanent bubbling feeling. It was just knowing that in two short weeks this would all be over and done with – one way or the other. The worst part of the last seventeen months hadn't been the loss of my liberty, or even the things that had happened to me in prison, however bad – it was not knowing what was happening. By 15 December I wouldn't have that problem any more.

Mr Minervini was confident.

'I am one hundred per cent certain the attempted murder charge will be thrown out,' he told me through Valeria. 'I cannot see the judges finding you guilty of that. It's the other charges that aren't so clear cut.'

'Do you mean they're going to convict me of them?'

Mr Minervini shook his head. 'I didn't say that, Carole. I'm only talking about the worst possible case. It's best to be prepared, *si?*'

I nodded. '*Si.*'

'The minimum sentence for arson is three years in prison. With more than one charge that might well be increased to four. But–' Mr Minervini raised his hand. 'you were under twenty-one when the alleged offences took place so you will be entitled to remission. And, of course, you've already been in prison for seventeen months. That will be taken as part of your sentence.'

'So what does all that add up to?'

Mr Minervini gave his familiar shrug. 'I think there is a good chance they will release you at the end of the trial.'

'My God—'

For a second my mind seemed to go blank. Thinking about my release, dreaming about it, praying for it for so long was one thing; actually hearing someone like Mr Minervini talk about it as if it might actually happen was something else.

'Please remember this is just my opinion, Carole,' he went on. 'Anything may happen in court. And, of course, I will demand an acquittal on all the charges. But I thought it would help you to know my view.'

I found myself smiling. 'It does. Thank you.' Then I stopped. 'I still want to prove I'm innocent.'

Mr Minervini's shrug was massive. '*Certamente!*' Why else have I come this far? And for very little money, I might add. You must still be strong, Carole. This is no time to be over-confident of anything.'

'I'll be strong,' I promised.

Mr Minervini reached into his jacket pocket, took something out and put it on the table between us. 'A little gift.'

I looked down, then smiled. It was a packet of chewing-gum.

13

Caged

DECEMBER 1983

As I came down the steps, I thought the visiting room was empty. The long central table stretched away with no one in sight.

But, when I reached the gate at the bottom and the guard unlocked it and let me through, I saw the single figure at the far end of the room. Mum was sitting where she'd been the first time she'd come to the Domenicani.

'Carole, love—'

We hugged for ages. It had been eleven long months since I'd seen her in Trento. We were both tearful when we finally let go of each other and sat down.

'I can't believe we've finally got this far,' Mum said.

I grinned. 'I'll be home for Christmas, Mum. I know I will.'

'So you said in your letters,' she frowned. 'Don't you be so sure of yourself, Carole. I've had enough disappointments in this game not to count on anything – and neither should you. Have you seen the papers this morning?'

I shook my head.

'Headlines full of *La strega* and *incendiaria – piromane scozzese!* I've picked up enough Italian to know no one's talking about letting you off easy.'

I looked down at Mum's clothes. 'I like your outfit.' She was wearing a new two-piece suit in a navy-blue pinstripe, with a fitted jacket and knickerbockers tucked into boots. 'I've never seen you looking so smart.'

She smiled. 'You like it, do you?'

She stood up and gave me a twirl. 'You and I are going to

be on show on Monday, Carole. We don't want anyone thinking we're rubbish. Let me show you what I've brought you.'

She bent down and picked a bag off the floor, then glanced up at the guard who was standing behind me. I turned round.

'*Posso vedere?* Can I see?'

The guard nodded.

'They've already been through it with a fine-tooth comb,' Mum grunted. 'I don't know where they think I put the hacksaw.'

She took clothes out of the bag. There was a skirt and jumper, a white Fair Isle sweater and some fresh jeans; there was also a new pair of black patent leather shoes. I snatched them up.

'Oh Mum, that's great – just what I wanted.'

'Size four, that's OK, isn't it?'

'Four?' I made a face. 'I take a five.'

'Oh no.'

'It'll be OK. They look fine.'

'Oh Carole, I didn't have time to check.'

'It doesn't matter, Mum.' I asked her about everyone at home. They were all on tenterhooks about the trial, of course.

'Your gran's upset as well. Snowy was run over the other day – right outside her house. Poor cat didn't have a chance.'

'Oh no.' Snowy had been Gran's favourite, the family pet, the one cat I'd actually been quite fond of.

It struck me as an odd kind of coincidence. The mad kitten at Marco's flat, the scratching noise I'd thought was a cat just before Agnese's cot caught fire, and now this.

'What's the matter?' Mum asked. 'You don't think it means bad luck, do you? It wasn't very lucky for the cat. I wouldn't have said anything if I'd thought you'd think that.'

'No, Mum, course not. You know I don't believe in any of that.'

We were allowed a full hour to talk, and there was no pressure to finish quickly.

The following day – Sunday 11 December – I went to mass in the little chapel next to the showers. I prayed to be calm, strong and alert, and not to be nervous. I didn't need patience any more.

As I lay in bed that night, doing my best to rest, I wondered if Marco would turn up for the trial.

I woke early. The other girls were still asleep. I felt a little light-headed, but not tired.

I had my clothes laid out in a neat pile on the bed – clean, neatly pressed jeans, Fair Isle sweater, new leather shoes – when Giuliana unlocked the door.

'*Agitata?*' she asked.

'*Un po,*' I said.

She nodded and banged against the window bars. The others stirred with the usual groans and grunts.

The trial started at nine o'clock. Because I had to be in the Palazzo di Giustizia before then I was allowed to go to the showers straightaway.

I dressed, slipped my cross and chain round my neck and brushed my hair in Lori's scrap of a mirror. My hair hadn't been cut while I'd been in prison. Now it was hanging over my shoulders. Looking clean and freshly brushed would have to do.

I could feel the others watching me as I sipped my coffee. But not in the hostile way they once had. They all knew what a special day this was for me.

The bell rang at the door to the men's section. Giuliana went to open it.

'*Carolina!*' she called.

I was already on my feet. I touched hands with Lori and my other cellmates.

'*Buona fortuna.*'

'*Grazie.*'

Lori and I grinned at each other. I made a face.

'When they let you out,' Lori said, 'will you promise to give me your suede boots?'

'Give me a chance!' I laughed. 'It hasn't happened yet.'

Giuliana's keys rattled impatiently. I hurried towards the door. Mr Minervini's chewing-gum was in my pocket. I popped a slab into my mouth as I went out.

Two policemen were waiting for me downstairs. A police van had been backed up to the main entrance with its rear doors open. I stepped out of the Domenicani straight into the back.

The two policemen settled on either side of me.

The doors slammed and we drew away. Down the side of the canal, right over the bridge, left on the opposite side. Stop. The doors rattled open again. It had hardly been a minute.

The two policemen led me out. I glimpsed the Domenicani about a hundred yards away. It was a cold, clear morning. Then we were walking through a door into a dark corridor.

Inside there were more police. There was a high ceiling, a cold, stone floor. The passageway echoed, my heels clicking, as we hurried along. The new shoes dug into my toes.

We turned, turned again, and stopped suddenly by a tall, wooden door. I could hear the rumble of a crowd from the other side. We waited. I looked round. The corridor seemed like a storage area. Chairs were stacked up against the wall. There were cabinets and piles of boxes.

The door cracked open. A tubby-looking policeman in glasses poked his head through and rattled off something to the others. I caught sight of a huge, domed ceiling – people bustling about. There seemed to be hundreds! The door shut. My heart was thumping. I took a deep breath as we waited again.

Patience and strength. Patience and strength. My hands felt sticky.

The door opened again – wider this time. The same policeman appeared. He nodded quickly at the others. They held my arms, one on each side. Before I could take another deep breath, we were moving forwards, through the doorway, into the courtroom.

The noise was suddenly all around me. It was a huge room, packed with people. To my left was a wide, semi-circular platform with tall desks and big, leather-backed chairs behind them. That end of the room was empty.

Everyone was crowded into the rest of the room. They were sitting behind three or four long tables facing the front, or on three or four rows of seats rising in tiers against the opposite wall. There were even people jammed into a balcony that went round the walls just above the doors.

I caught sight of Mr Minervini, dressed in long, black robes, talking to someone, and Mum just behind him, with Father Nolan. As I went to wave, one of the policemen drew me round.

Then I saw the cage.

It was against the wall to my right. It was enormous – it looked half the size of my cell. The steel bars sat on top of a thick wooden barrier that on its own was as high as my chest. They went up another good ten feet, and more bars went back into the wall, sealing off the top.

A full-grown tiger would have had room to spare in it.

The policeman who'd let us in unlocked a door in the side. As he held it open for me I saw one chair on its own, in the middle of the huge empty space. Then someone behind me shouted, 'Carole!'

I turned, thinking it was Mum. Everyone in the courtroom seemed to notice me at once. I picked out Mum's bright, anxious face, and lifted my hand.

Then the whole room went mad.

There was a great roar. Half the people in the room suddenly seemed to surge towards me. They were shouting, elbowing the police and each other out of the way, clambering on to the tables – chairs went crashing over, flash bulbs were exploding everywhere.

The policeman quickly pushed me into the cage, twisting the key in the lock. For one terrifying moment I thought the whole room had turned against me – they wanted to get the 'witch'.

I sat down, blinking. There was a sea of faces against the bars. They jostled each other, waving cameras and little cassette recorders and notebooks. I covered my eyes as a fierce light swept over me. There were TV cameras at the back.

'Carole!' they called. 'Look this way, Carole!' . . . 'Carole, are you innocent?' . . . 'Carole, do you believe in witches?' . . . 'What do you think of the cage?' . . . '*This* way, Carole . . .!'

English voices, Italian voices. I couldn't hear myself think. And then Mum's face was below me. She had squeezed her way to the front. With a gasp of relief I bent forward. We kissed through the bars; she grasped my hand.

'You look lovely, Carole – you look so well.' She had to shout above the hubbub. 'You're not scared, are you? I've waited a long time for this and so have you. Get up there and show them what for!'

I smiled, and felt tears squeeze from my eyes.

'Have you got a tissue?'

Mum pulled one out of her jacket pocket and handed it to
me. 'Do you want anything else, love?'

I wiped my eyes. 'I just wish I had some perfume.'

Someone pushed a cassette recorder through the bars.
'Carole, how do you feel?'

'Fine,' I said. 'I'm really glad the trial's starting at last. It's
been a long wait, but I'm well and happy.'

Everyone shouted at once. I heard, 'Carole, what about this
witch thing?'

Mum answered. 'My Carole is no criminal or witch,' she said
flatly. People were scribbling in notebooks.

'Are you nervous?' and 'How were you treated in prison?'
came at once.

'I'm not nervous,' I said. 'I've no complaints about the way
I was treated in gaol.'

'How many of you in one cell?'

Behind the crush police were shouting, trying to push people
back into their seats. But the questions went on. I began to
understand what Mum must have been putting up with.

'I'm happy and ready for my freedom,' I told them. 'I'm
ready to get up and fight.'

I held my fist in the air. The cameras clicked and flashed like
crazy. There was a flurry at the back of the crowd. Heads
turned. Over the top of them I could see the tubby-looking
policeman who'd locked me in the cage lining up with half a
dozen others. Suddenly they charged at the reporters.

There was a stampede. The press people scattered in every
direction. It was chaos.

'My God!' I saw the tubby policeman wheezing after two
reporters and burst into laughter. 'I don't believe it!'

'You want to see the public part at the back,' Mum said.
'People have brought in bottles of wine and sandwiches –
they're making a day of it.'

I looked at her. 'Mum, I wanted to tell you I loved you when
I came into the court, but I couldn't with all those television
cameras and people there.'

She smiled at me and squeezed my hand. There was some
movement at the front of the court. One of the wooden panels
behind the desk had opened. I could see people inside.

'Remember to hold your head up, Carole,' Mum hissed at

me. 'Keep a nice smile on your face.'

She scurried away and back to her seat. The police were calling for silence. Everyone was quietening down. The press were crammed on to the tiered seats opposite me. Then everyone got to their feet.

The judges came out. There were two, wearing long, dark velvet robes with gold braiding and curious white bibs round their necks. Another eight people in ordinary clothes but with broad, green, white and red sashes across their fronts followed them out. They took their places at the big, leather-backed chairs – the presiding judge in the middle. He was in his fifties, wearing glasses and a very grim expression.

A few cameras were still flashing. The presiding judge pointed at the press bench, then snapped something. There was a microphone on the desktop in front of him. But the sound boomed so much against the high ceiling I couldn't tell what he'd said. Then he and the others got up again and walked back through the door.

I'd no idea what was going on, but the police obviously did. They started to move the photographers and the cameramen off the benches, pushing them towards the door. There were grumbles and protests, but they went. In a few minutes it was over. The judges and the jurors filed back in. Everyone sat down.

The presiding judge – I found out later his name was Galligani – read out the charges. I was pleased by how much I understood; not every word, of course, but the gist, even though the sound from the microphone wasn't much better than the first time. I saw several of the reporters frowning, and leaning forwards.

When the judge had finished he checked that everyone was present. Mr Minervini and Mr Valenti, right at the front of the court, stood up and sat down again. I recognised Dr Cindolo, sitting on the opposite end of the same table, as he did the same. All of them were in dark robes. Behind them I saw Mr Masi, Mr Eilbeck and Mr Pirie from the Milan consulate, sitting with Father Nolan.

Then the judge asked about the witnesses. As he went through the names I had a chance to look round the court-room. Sitting next to Mum was a girl my own age with short, dark hair and an open, pretty face. I wondered if it was Teresa Hunter, the Cecchini's other nanny. Further back I glimpsed Emanuela, and Daniela and Luigi Cecchini. Next to the Cecchinis was a tiny little figure in a dark green coat with a woolly cap pulled down over her head. I suddenly realised it was the grandmother. Of course, I knew they would all have to be here, but to actually see them in the flesh after so long, all gathered together in this strange place, was an odd feeling.

I couldn't help looking for Marco. I didn't really expect to see him but, as I glanced up at the gallery, I had a surprise anyway. Near the front I was sure I saw Mrs Vitulano.

After the names had been called, the witnesses were told to leave. Mum waved with her fingers as she got up. Two of the prosecution witnesses were missing. One was Grandfather Ricci; he couldn't make the journey because of his heart condition. The other was his maid, Nicole. No one seemed to know why she hadn't turned up. The judge ordered enquiries to be made about her, and then got up a second time. As everyone on the bench trooped out, another flash bulb went off.

The judge stopped, pointed at the photographer and shouted angrily at the police: 'Why do *I* have to deal with photographers? It's your job!'

He didn't need the microphone for that. I felt my chest tighten. This man was obviously as strict as he looked – and not particularly even-tempered, either.

Ten minutes passed. When the judge came back, he was still fussed about the photographer. He told the police to give the man's name to the clerk of the court, and to take away the film in his camera. Then he decided that he wasn't going to allow as evidence a statement from my old boss, Mrs Paterson, at the Carrick Street Day Centre. That was supposed to be part of my character evidence. He handed it back to Mr Minervini who did not look very happy. It didn't strike me as a good start.

Then Mr Minervini stood up and spoke.

'My client is not a dangerous criminal,' he said. 'She is not about to run away. In the interest of humanity, if not as a gesture to the world's press, can the court show compassion enough not to compound the misery of her seventeen months' confinement and grant her the simple decency of the open court!'

He pounded out the words. I looked at him in surprise. I'd never heard him sound so passionate before. I half expected the judge to explode. Instead he simply nodded and spoke to the police. The tubby one came over, and unlocked the cage. As I stepped out of the door, there was a little cheer from the press seats.

Mr Minervini gave me a smile. Behind him I saw Mr Masi nodding.

I stood between the two policemen who had brought me in, while three chairs were found. Then the three of us sat down close to Mr Minervini.

'Now,' said the judge, 'we can begin.'

I glanced at my wristwatch. It was eleven o'clock.

The second judge – his name was De Pasquale – started by going over the details of the case, beginning with Elba. I found it very frustrating.

It was all based on the families' statements. When Agnese had fallen off her lilo at the beach apparently I hadn't done anything to help her. After the first fire I was supposed to have told Daniela, 'Strange things are happening in this house.'

I just shook my head. For the moment there was nothing else I could do. But as soon as the second judge had finished, the presiding judge called for me. I felt my knees wobbling as I stood up. Everyone in the room was staring at me. A court official led me to a chair right in front of the presiding judge. There was a microphone in front of it. Another chair was brought up as an interpreter sat down next to me. It was the woman Dr Cindolo had used when he'd first interviewed me. That wasn't a very good sign – as I soon found out.

Judge Galligani began to ask me questions. The interpreter translated what he'd said, then translated my replies. I'd answered the same questions so many times before they weren't a problem.

But the sound in the courtroom was. The microphone didn't seem to make any difference; my voice echoed and boomed, or just faded away. Mr Minervini and Mr Valenti were only a few feet away, but several times they jumped up, complaining they couldn't hear properly.

The interpreter was just as bad. Sometimes she didn't

understand me. Once I had to say the same thing five times. Other times she got words wrong. I was talking about Agnese's cot and she translated it as 'coat'. When I mentioned the electrical fault that was supposed to have started the first Ortisei fire, she translated 'short circuit' as 'light bulb'. When I described making little Emanuele's tea, meaning his evening meal, the interpreter said I'd been making 'a cup of tea'.

Of course, Mr Minervini and Mr Valenti were both complaining about this all the time. Two or three times I gave up trying to make myself understood, and talked in Italian straight to the judge.

Finally the judge asked the interpreter to translate one phrase at a time. Everyone in the courtroom laughed. The poor woman was almost in tears. I felt sorry for her, but having all these language problems wasn't helping me at all.

By lunchtime I'd been answering questions for nearly two hours. I'd no idea how I was doing. As the judges and jurors went out, Mr Minervini leaned towards me. 'You're doing fine, Carole. *Eccellente*. Just speak up and keep on as you are.'

At the back of the room people were pointing at something over the bench, calling out and shaking their heads. I turned to look. There was a sign in gold letters in the panelling above the presiding judge's chair. It read: *La legge e uguale per tutti*.

'Everyone should be treated the same way under the law,' said Mr Minervini. 'They're saying it hasn't been true for you. See, the people of Livorno want you to be free, Carole. That's good!'

He smiled as my two guards took my arms and led me away.

 14

The Lady in Black

DECEMBER 1983

Over lunch I changed my shoes for an older, white leather pair. I hoped Mum didn't notice, but the new ones had been killing me.

When the court started up again the judge called one of the expert witnesses. His name was Teodoro Comploi. He was the chief fire officer from Ortisei who had investigated the fires there.

'The fact that there were three fires involving one family made me suspicious,' he said. 'One of the fires happened on a bed, and started on a pile of newspapers and blankets lying on the mattress. Normally flames start at the bottom and work upwards, but in this case the flames had travelled downwards. It was very strange.'

He said that in the Ricci's house the fire seemed to have started on a stool in the main bedroom, but had then gone out. Then it had begun again inside a wardrobe a couple of feet away. There was no wiring nearby which could have caused it. There were no signs of inflammable liquids found at either fire.

'I've been a fireman for thirty-eight years,' he said, 'but I've never seen fires like those before.'

By the time the judge had finished questioning him it was getting late. The court was adjourned until the next day.

'The fireman was good for us,' Mr Minervini told me. 'It's going well, Carole.'

Then I was taken out to the prison van.

Back in the cell I told the girls everything that had happened.

During the day they had got hold of some newspapers. The local one, *Il Terreno*, had the headline '*La Strega Si Difende* – The Witch Defends Herself'. A national one, *La Nazione*, had 'Witch, Fire-raiser or Just a Baby-sitter in Love? Who Knows the Real Carole Compton?'

'They'll have to let you go,' said Lori. 'With all these reporters here they wouldn't dare put you back in prison.'

I wanted to believe she was right.

As we were talking I suddenly heard someone calling my name. It was a minute before I realised it was coming from outside. I went to the window.

'Carole! Carole, can you hear me?'

It was Mum. She was shouting up from the street at the back of the prison! Even stretching up on tiptoe I couldn't see far enough down to catch sight of her, but I could shout back through the bars.

'*E Mamma!*' Lori and the others piped up, laughing. '*Ciao, Mamma!*'

I shushed them quiet.

'I tried to bring you some flowers and fruit and your favourite cheese but they wouldn't let me leave it!' Mum called. 'I'll try to give them to you in court tomorrow!'

'Thanks, Mum! That's lovely!'

'Isn't this great, Carole? I wish I'd thought of this last time! People going past look at me as if I was mad!'

We both burst out laughing. She told me she was staying in the same hotel as Teresa Hunter.

'She's a great wee lass, Carole. You'll like her.'

Then she told me she thought she'd blown my chances with the judge that morning.

'They've got all the witnesses jammed together into this freezing cold dungeon,' she called. 'Teresa and I looked in. There were the Cecchinis and the Riccis. I said to Teresa, "This is wrong. We can't be in here." So we went to this other room down the corridor. It's warm, and it's got these nice leather chairs. So I'm sitting at this big polished desk, smoking a fag, and Teresa's away at the other end, yapping. Whose room was it?'

'Who?'

'The bloody judge's! If you'd seen his face when he came in, me sitting up in his chair, smoking a fag! He took one look and yelled for the guard.'

'Oh *Mum*—' I laughed. There was silence. 'Mum, are you still there?'

'Sorry, love,' she called. 'There's a guard just poked his head round the corner. I think he's gone away. No, he's not – Oh Christ, he's got a friend. *Carole, I have to go!*'

I heard high heels clicking away up the street – fast. Then heavier steps, speeding up, too.

'Mum—!'

There was no reply.

The next morning I saw Mum in court before the trial started again. She came over with Teresa Hunter, carrying a big bunch of carnations which she tried to hand to me, but the police wouldn't let her.

After she'd introduced me to Teresa, I said, 'I thought I'd heard the last of you last night.'

'Oh, Carole,' Mum laughed. 'I thought the same. They chased me all the way round the building – with their guns out, too! They didn't stop till I got to the bridge. I thought I'd break my ankles with those high heels. Tonight, though, I'll be ready for them. I'll put my jeans and trainers on.'

Teresa was laughing, too. She seemed a nice girl.

'Carole,' Mum leaned closer, 'Mr Masi says you're not to smile so much. He thinks it's giving the judge the wrong impression.'

'Mum,' I sighed, 'I've been told that many different things—'

The door behind the bench opened.

'Good luck, Carole,' Mum whispered. 'Remember, no smiles!' She hurried out with Teresa.

The first witness of the second day was Emanuela Ricci.

She swept into the court like a film star, wrapped in an ankle-length fur coat, and tossing her hair back.

Before the judge could say a word, she snapped into the witness's microphone: 'I wish to make a formal complaint! We have been shut up in a cold room for two days, without so much as a cup of coffee offered as refreshment! This is after having to travel to Livorno at considerable personal expense. It really is too bad!'

There were chuckles from the gallery at the back. Mr Minervini raised his eyebrows; Mr Valenti was grinning and shaking his head. The judge did not look pleased.

Having got that off her chest, Emanuela sat down. The judge began his questions. He asked if she had suspected me after the first fire in Ortisei.

'No,' she said. 'I couldn't believe Carole had anything to do with it.'

'Was it true that Compton did not like being away from her boyfriend and cried every night?'

Emanuela nodded. 'On one occasion I spoke to her on the phone and she told me she was very unhappy and that she had no friends.

'I also saw letters in which she spoke ill of our family. In one of them she said she had been disgusted when she saw a young couple making love behind a beach hut.

'Every time she telephoned her boyfriend in Rome – you know, of course, he jilted her – she told him she didn't like the family and that the little boy did not like her. She used to cry when making these telephone calls.'

I stared at her, incredulous. The fact that she admitted reading my private letters, too, made me even angrier.

The judge asked how I'd got on with little Emanuele.

'He sobbed whenever Carole was near him. Every time she touched him he cried, "*Mamma, brucia!*" She's burning!'

I shook my head. This was crazy. Mr Minervini leapt to his feet.

'Would the judge confirm with Mrs Ricci that the boy was burnt as a baby and this is simply a phrase he uses for anything he dislikes?'

The judge put the question. Emanuela nodded.

'He didn't mean she was actually burning him, just that he didn't like her.'

I sighed. The judge began asking about Rosa, the maid.

'Rosa told me of one occasion when a large picture of the Holy Mary fell off a wall and then a vase fell down,' said Emanuela. 'Rosa said Carole did it, and she asked me several times to give Carole the sack. Rosa didn't like her.'

I grunted. That much, at least, we agreed on.

'The picture was on a wall in a dark corridor. It may have

been knocked down accidentally by someone. I did not regard it as a paranormal occurrence.

'Carole once told me she was unlucky and that something strange had happened to her in Scotland. She didn't know what this strange thing was. I didn't always understand her because of her strong Scots accent.'

I shook my head. She obviously believed what she was saying; I just worried what the judge might think.

'After the picture fell,' Emanuela went on, 'any strange episodes were blamed on Carole. When I returned from Paris Rosa told me that the water boiler was making funny noises and that the electric meter had been spinning when Carole had been standing near it.

'But, of course, Rosa is a Sicilian and very superstitious.'

There was a burst of laughter from the courtroom.

'You can ask her yourself,' said Emanuela, turning round.

The judge shook his head. 'I don't think that will be necessary,' he said.

Emanuela turned again to look straight at me. 'I was very disappointed in this girl,' she said.

It was all I could do to stop myself leaping up at her.

The judge dismissed her, and she got up and swanned out with a flourish. Several of the reporters came down from the press seats and hurried after her. She was obviously enjoying their attention enormously.

The next witness was Nicole, Grandfather Ricci's maid. Apparently she'd had the flu on the first day. As she was called, I glanced round the courtroom.

In the gallery upstairs I noticed Dr Bender, the psychiatrist who'd examined me in September. I asked Mr Minervini if he was going to be a witness.

'Mr Valenti and I have decided not to use him, Carole,' he said. 'We think it's going well enough as it is. We should have another forensic expert this afternoon, who will be even better for us.'

There was a stir at the back of the courtroom. I turned my head. Nicole was coming in.

She looked sensational.

She was wearing bright red leather trousers, high-heeled boots, a leather jacket and a silk shawl wrapped round her shoulders. Her long black hair hung right down her back. I saw all the reporters perk up as she went by.

When she'd settled in front of the microphone the judge asked her what had happened just before the fire in the Ricci's house.

'I was coming home from the village at eight o'clock on July the eleventh,' she said, 'and I saw smoke coming out of a window. Carole was standing outside with the child. She was in tears and shouting, "Fire! Fire!" She hadn't told anyone about the fire. Although the grandfather was in the house she hadn't told him, either.'

It was worse than with Emanuela. The more she went on the more bizarre it got. I just shook my head in disbelief.

'Everything,' I told the interpreter, 'practically everything she says is wrong. That's not the way I saw it at all.'

The interpreter translated this for the judge. I was pleased when he told me to sit up at the microphone next to Nicole, so he could question us both at once.

But it didn't make any difference to Nicole. She still insisted she'd come back on her own from the village at eight o'clock, and been surprised little Emanuele wasn't in bed.

'He *never* went to bed before half past eight!' I said.

'He was very excited and calling, "Fire, fire", as if he'd seen it close up,' Nicole went on.

I was getting more and more upset. 'That's a lie!' I cried.

Then she said she'd taken Emanuele and followed me inside to warn Grandfather Ricci. But I'd insisted we all go upstairs to the grandfather's bedroom. When the grandfather had gone to open the bedroom door, I'd cried out 'Don't open it! Don't open it!' as if I'd known there was a fire there.

'*Bugie, solo bugie!*' I cried, unable to contain myself. 'All lies. She never came into the house, and of course I knew there was a fire in the bedroom – there was smoke pouring out!'

'No,' Nicole said flatly. 'It wasn't like that.'

'It *was!*'

By now I was so upset my anger was getting the better of me. It was ridiculous. It was turning into a slanging match. At one point I was so incensed I snatched the microphone away from her; she snatched it back.

The judge's arms went up. The jurors obviously didn't know what was going on. Finally the judge stood up and adjourned the trial for lunch. Nicole stalked off. I sat there, seething, annoyed most by the fact that I'd let myself get annoyed.

I stood up for my guards, and caught Mr Minervini looking at me. His eyebrows shot up in a kind of mock horror, as if to say, 'Is this really my Carole?'

At least I hadn't smiled too much.

In the afternoon an expert on fires, Professor Vitolo Nicolo from Pisa University, gave evidence.

He said he'd examined the mattresses on the grandparents' bed in Elba and on little Agnese's cot. He hadn't found any trace of suspicious stains, smells or inflammable substances.

'It was very strange that the mattresses burned only on the surface at the same spot and not on the inside at all,' he said. 'Although they were made of different types of material – one of wool and one of much more inflammable horsehair – they were both burned in the same way.

'Both fires had the same characteristics – great heat but no flames. The fire had also moved downwards rather than up, which I find phenomenal.'

That was what the fireman from Ortisei had said about the other fires. I could see the press people stirring, biros flying over notebooks.

Dr Cindolo asked if a hot iron could have set fire to the mattresses.

'The burn marks could have been caused by an overheated iron,' said the Professor, 'but not by a cigarette lighter, a match or any naked flame.'

Mr Minervini sprang up. 'Would the Professor agree that there is nothing to link the defendant with either of these fires?'

The Professor agreed.

'So the Professor's evidence is, in fact, completely negative with regard to this case?'

The Professor agreed again.

'In my forty-five years' experience of this kind of investigation I have never seen fires like these,' he said. 'They were created by an intense source of heat, but not by a flame. I cannot explain what caused them.'

Mr Minervini sat down with a satisfied smile. Dr Cindolo did not look very pleased.

The court was adjourned until the next day. As I went out with my guards, Mr Minervini smiled at me, put his finger to his cheek and turned it backwards and forwards. It was what Italians did when they meant to say, 'Good!'

Just after the cell doors were locked I heard Mum outside again.

'I've got my running shoes on, Carole!' she called. 'They won't catch me tonight!'

We laughed together.

'I had to complain to Mr Masi today,' she said. 'The witnesses were coming back into the witness room after they'd given their evidence – they were talking with the others who haven't even been in yet. I couldn't believe it! I shouted for Mr Masi to come and see. "You're right, Mrs Compton," he said. "I'll do something about this." He did, too.

'But it's a right circus, Carole. You can wander in and out to the café. Buy yourself a coffee or rolls – your Mrs Ricci even offered me one. Can you believe it?'

'Did you take it?'

'Aye, why not? If she's willing to pay for it. Then she sat there, chatting about me and Teresa in Italian to the others, right in front of our faces. Meanwhile there's reporters all over the place, talking to everybody. Can you imagine that in a court back home?'

I told her what had happened with Nicole.

'I shouldn't have lost my temper, Mum.'

'Don't be ridiculous, Carole! You give them what for! The Italians love a bit of drama. They'll respect you for it.'

'You be careful they don't catch you there, Mum.'

'I'm getting used to it,' Mum called. 'Now I've got some fellow chasing me all over my hotel.'

'What do you mean?'

'Some fellow who works in the hotel – buying me cappuccinos and brandies! The other day I came in and found him sitting on my bed. I told him: "You! Out!" Actually I said it a bit stronger than that!'

I had to laugh. 'What's he like?'

'Horrible! He's nearly fifty and he's got no teeth!'

'Oh no!'

'Trouble is he can't speak a word of English, so he can't take no for an answer. Thank God I've got Teresa with me.' She paused. 'Uh-huh. Here comes my escort. I'll have to give myself a head start. See you tomorrow, Carole!'

'Take care, Mum!' I yelled.

I didn't hear her go, but I did hear two pairs of heavy footsteps thudding down the street after her.

'I was well ahead of them,' she told me in court the next day. 'I think the guards are beginning to enjoy it!'

The first witness of the third morning was the Cecchini grandfather, Mario. The judge asked him about the fire in Agnese's cot.

'I saw Carole standing in the sitting-room,' he said, 'and asked my daughter-in-law where the child was because she was not with the nanny. Daniela pushed open the door to the bedroom and I saw flames coming from the cot where it touched the bed where the baby was sleeping.'

I murmured to Mr Minervini: 'That's not the way *I* remember it.' He nodded.

Then, said the grandfather, Daniela had picked up Agnese. He had thrown the burning mattress out of the window. When his wife had seen what had happened she had grabbed hold of me. I had run away, crying, and hidden in the cellar.

The judge asked if he had ever seen me with matches or a lighter. He said he hadn't.

I looked at Mr Minervini. He didn't seem too unhappy with what the old man had said.

Next was the grandmother.

The court stirred when she was called. This was my chief accuser, the woman who'd started the whole 'witch' business. She didn't meet my eyes as she came in. Sitting by the microphone in her old, dark green coat, wrinkled stockings and lace-up shoes, she looked like a little wizened dwarf.

The judge asked her what she had said when ornaments had fallen over before the fire in Agnese's cot.

'I said, "Heavens, there must be spirits in the house".'

'Were you joking?' asked the judge. 'Or did you really believe in ghosts?'

'Oh, you know, you say these things from time to time.' She shrugged. 'It doesn't mean you believe in abnormal powers. It was just one of those things people say when something strange happens. I told the police about it, but only because they asked me to tell them everything. It was not said with malice.'

I grunted; it hadn't felt like that to me.

When the fire had been found in Agnese's room she said she had taken hold of my arms and shaken me. 'I said, "It was you. It was you". I blamed her because she was the only stranger in the house.'

Mr Minervini stood up. 'Would the judge ask Signora Cecchini what she thought of strangers in her house?'

'I liked them,' said the grandmother. 'They are nice. I have never been against them.'

I shook my head and smiled.

Then the judge asked how the fire in Agnese's room had been discovered.

'My husband went into the room first. The flames were half a metre high. I could see them from the kitchen.'

'Isn't it true that you turned off the electricity immediately you heard there was a fire?'

'Yes, but there has never been a short circuit in the house.'

The judge was frowning, looking down at some papers.

'If you were turning off the electricity in the kitchen, how could you see flames in the bedroom? According to the plan there is no direct line of sight.'

The grandmother blinked. She didn't say anything.

I glanced at Mr Minervini. He was smiling.

The judge asked the grandmother if she smoked.

'A few cigarettes, but never in the bedrooms.'

'Didn't your daughter-in-law complain that you left burning cigarette ends about the house?'

'No, never.'

The judge went back to what she had actually seen when Agnese's cot caught fire. She began to hesitate. 'There was a lot of smoke,' she said. 'It was difficult to see exactly.'

The judge was frowning. 'One moment you say one thing, and the next you say another,' he said. 'You keep changing your story.'

The grandmother didn't reply.

When she was dismissed Mr Minervini and Mr Valenti slapped each other on the back. Mr Minervini gave me a broad grin.

Daniela was called.

The judge asked her to describe Agnese's cot fire.

'When I opened the door and saw my daughter half enveloped in flames I thought she was dead. But when I snatched her up she opened her eyes and I realised she was alive.' She said I hadn't gone into the bedroom until she had left it with Agnese.

The judge asked about her impressions of me.

'What struck me about her was her complete air of indifference, even after the fire in Agnese's bed,' she said. 'Carole is a person who moves without making any noise. I told her that mysterious things only happened in my home when she was present.'

'Did you ever complain to your mother-in-law about leaving lighted cigarette ends about the house?'

'Now and again I did.'

'Would you say your mother-in-law felt jealous of Compton or Teresa Hunter, or was she sympathetic to them?'

'She does have this approach which gives the impression that she has no sympathy for British girls. She has a closed personality, but I exclude any ill will from this. We had one British girl who stayed with us for two summers. She still sends us postcards.'

Mr Minervini got up. 'Could the judge ask Signora Cecchini what burns little Agnese suffered as a result of being "half enveloped in flames"?'

'None, thank God,' said Daniela. 'I was in time to save her.'

'Did Mrs Cecchini have the same long hair at the time of the incident that she has now?'

'*Si.*'

'And was this hair also undamaged despite Mrs Cecchini having to bend over a raging inferno in order to save her daughter?'

'Yes, but I had to be very quick.'

Mr Minervini smiled and sat down as Daniela was dismissed. He leaned towards me. 'Things are going very well for us, Carole,' he said. 'I'm confident about the outcome now.'

Immediately there was a flurry at the back of the courtroom.
Someone was shouting – a woman. Everyone turned, but all I
could see was something dark being waved in the air. I heard,
'*Spiriti . . . Inghilterra . . .!*'

There was laughter. Mr Minervini shrugged. Everyone
settled down. The judge called for Luigi Cecchini, Daniela's
husband.

He said he thought the fire in the grandparents' bedroom had
been caused by a cigarette end dropped on the carpet, or
perhaps thrown through the window.

'I never saw my mother smoking in the bedroom,' he said.
'She denied it when I asked her if she had, and I believed her.'

The judge was obviously interested in the idea of a short
circuit causing the second fire. He asked Luigi about the lights
in Agnese's bedroom – a globe-shaped lamp next to the little
girl's cot, and a night-light on a table near the door.

Luigi said that, after the fire, both had been working
normally.

Then he was asked about the incident at the beach when
Agnese had fallen off her lilo.

'I grabbed her and pulled her out of the water,' he said.
'Carole didn't do anything but just stood there on the beach.
She didn't rush to save the child. She was completely passive.'

I looked down, shaking my head. Now I was blamed for not
having hysterics when there was nothing I *could* have done.

After Luigi had finished, there was a brief recess. Mum
suddenly appeared at my side.

'Hello, love,' she said. 'I'm on next.'

My guards glanced away, and let us chat.

'You know what they're calling you at the back?' Mum said.
'*La poverina*. Masi says it means "poor little girl". I've said
some hard things about the Livorno people in the past, but I
think they're on your side now, Carole. Let's hope the judge
hears, eh?'

Something caught my eye over her shoulder. An odd little
figure was walking down the courtroom towards us. It was a
tiny old lady dressed completely in black. She had a black
crucifix about seven or eight inches long in her right hand.

As I looked at her, she lifted it up to shoulder-height and
pointed it at me, mumbling something.

Mum turned where I was looking. 'What the hell—?'

People were pointing from the gallery and the press seats, but no one near us seemed to have noticed the woman. Then Mr Pirie from the Milan consulate stepped up behind her.

'*Scusi*,' he asked, '*Che cosa fai?* What are you doing?'

The woman's free arm shot out. Liquid splashed over mum's suit.

'*Jesus*—!' Mum jumped up in shock. The old woman snatched at me, tugging at my hair, pulling my head back. The police grabbed her. I saw a little bottle in her hand.

'Please!' the woman cried. 'I only want to save them – I must touch them to cleanse them! They're possessed by a demon! The devil told me in a dream last night – they have the power of fire!'

She burst into tears as the police took her away. Mr Minervini shook his head, then twisted a finger against his head. 'Bats!' he said loudly. 'She is bats!'

There was laughter from the press seats; reporters hurried after the woman.

Mr Pirie was asking if Mum and I were all right.

'I think it's just water, thank God,' Mum said, brushing her suit. 'Bloody mad woman!'

'I think she was trying to exorcise you,' said Mr Pirie. 'It's probably holy water.'

'Are you all right, Carole?' Mum asked. 'Did she hurt you?'

The woman hadn't, but she had got to me. I was shaking like a leaf.

15

Verdict

DECEMBER 1983

I gave Mum a quick smile before she sat down in front of the microphone. She looked tense, but raring to go. The woman interpreter was sitting next to her.

'I must warn you,' Judge Galligani told her, 'that you are bound to tell the truth like any other witness, despite the fact that you are the defendant's mother.'

'Yes,' said Mum. 'I'll do that.'

'I would also like you to speak clearly and simply in order to help with the translation.' Mum nodded. 'Can you tell me if you ever quarrelled with your ex-husband in front of your daughter?'

The interpreter repeated the question in English.

'Can I have that again?' said Mum. There was a chuckle from the press seats.

Flustered, the interpreter tried again.

'No,' said Mum. 'Like many married couples, we had arguments, but Carole has never seen anything bad between me and her father.'

'Even when he had been drinking? Didn't your ex-husband have an alcohol problem?'

'No, he just liked his little drink. When he got a bit tipsy I tried to keep him quiet. If there was going to be a row, I sent Carole and her brother to their grandmother's four doors away. I didn't want them to hear any shouting.'

The judge nodded. 'When was your daughter's first menstruation? Did you remember when it happened?'

Mum looked taken aback. She frowned.

'I remember it very well, as mothers do. It was just before her fourteenth birthday.'

The judge was flicking through some papers. 'Don't you mean sixteen? That was the age the defendant gave.'

'She makes mistakes,' Mum snapped. 'I make mistakes, *you* make mistakes. Does this make us stupid?'

The judge cleared his throat. 'Do you remember what she said when she first saw the blood?'

'No, I do not!'

Mum was dismissed. As she went past me, she hissed loudly, 'I call questions like that degrading!'

Teresa Hunter was the last defence witness.

She said she'd left her job with the Cecchinis after just fifteen days.

'My presence was obviously resented. I was worked very hard, and the former au pair left because she said they made her life hell as well. I was doing every piece of domestic work for the grannie.'

She said she had invented an excuse that her father was ill so that she could leave. She said that the Cecchinis had never paid her. When she offered her gold watch as security for a loan to buy her fare home, she said they had refused.

Mr Minervini asked if she had an explanation for the fires.

'I believe they were caused by short circuits. The wiring in the house was always overloaded. If fires had started while I was there I think I would have been accused because I was the only stranger in the house.'

We swapped little smiles as she left the microphone. I could see Mr Minervini was pleased too.

'Nearly there, Carole,' he said to me as the court was adjourned for the day. 'Tomorrow we start the summing up.'

Thursday opened with a surprise announcement by the judge. He said that a telegram had been delivered to the court by one of Nicole's former employers in Rome. It advised the judges to reject everything Nicole said because, it claimed, she was a 'pathological liar'.

Mr Minervini and Mr Valenti smiled at each other.

The judge called the last two witnesses. They were the psychiatrists who'd first examined me.

'Could the defendant have deliberately built up an atmosphere of witchcraft for some purpose or for her own amusement?' the judge asked them.

'I can't give the court a definite answer to that, I'm afraid,' said the woman psychiatrist, Dr Bertocchini. She turned and spoke quickly with her colleague.

'That type of behaviour could be consistent with the defendant's personality. She has an abnormal personality in that she shows signs of profound immaturity, emotional instability and a weak and inefficent willpower. She is both inhibited and introverted. I could say she has a naughty personality.'

I heard chuckles from the press seats. Were they trying to make me out as some kind of practical joker?

'The subject cannot be described as psychotic,' said the male psychiatrist, Professor Inghirami. 'She is responsible for her actions, but her personality does coincide in many ways with the profile of a pyromaniac – juvenile age, non-cohesive family, first years spent in an alien environment with signs of alcoholism, premature separation from parental figures, and so on.

'Such personalities can suffer from what we call an "impulsive short circuit" at a time of crisis, when they are not in full control of their actions.'

'Could this "short circuit" have occurred five times in such a short space of time?' asked the judge.

The two psychiatrists said not. 'Short circuits only happen once in a lifetime,' said Professor Inghirami. 'They are normally only associated with a psychotic character.'

'Do you consider the accused to be socially dangerous?'

'We feel we should express no judgement on that,' said Dr Bertocchini. 'The subject cannot be described as a pyromaniac unless it can be proved she started any of the fires.'

Mr Minervini was smiling again.

It was the end of the evidence. The judge shuffled his papers, then turned to Dr Cindolo.

'Will the prosecution now make its summing up?'

Dr Cindolo got to his feet. He took a deep breath.

'This trial is two-fold,' he said. 'There is a trial taking place here and there is a trial taking place in the newspapers.

Someone labelled Carole a witch and this has been blamed on the prosecution. But we are here to judge calmly, to consider facts, not fantasies.

'There has been too much talk of objects falling down, and of the paranormal, and not enough about a child about to die in a fire.'

He turned to me. 'Just because the accused has a nice face, an innocent face, it is not enough for people to sympathise with her. It is mere appearance; people should not be influenced by that.

'They should realise that Carole Compton is a liar! She lied to her boyfried and to the families she worked for – she showed them a face that was not her true face. She has lied in the trial and to the experts.'

I felt my cheeks burn. I glimpsed Mum, sitting behind the lawyers, bite her lip.

'I took the responsibility for Carole's arrest,' Cindolo went on. 'I would not have done so unless I had thought she was guilty. However, I was not responsible for the seventeen months she spent in gaol. This period was necessary because of the special examination by psychiatrists and forensic experts and the transfer between courts.'

He went through the details of the fires, saying in each case I had ample time to start them.

At the Ricci's house Nicole's evidence contradicted my statement that I was never alone on the evening of the fire. When the grandparents' bed had caught fire in Elba, Daniela had wondered why I was taking so long to wash little Agnese's hands.

When Agnese's bed had caught fire, I was found 'in a suspicious position outside the door. She had the attitude of someone looking round to make sure no one was approaching.

'Carole never took responsibility for being the one who discovered the fires. She was always said to be looking out of windows, or standing with an absent-minded appearance.

'I cannot produce a witness who can say they saw her starting the fires. There isn't one. But she is the common factor. It is too much to speak of coincidence. It could only have been her.'

Perhaps I had done what I had to get back to my boyfriend in Rome, he said, or perhaps not. That shouldn't affect the jury's decision.

'We know from the evidence of the psychiatrists who examined her that she could have the personality of a pyromaniac. But, even if we cannot say exactly why she did what she did, the facts are there. Lack of motive is not equivalent to lack of responsibility.

'There is uniformity in her attitude throughout the different circumstances which cannot be accounted for by "short circuits" in her personality. Her actions were carefully planned.

'But justice is not a vendetta. The results of Compton's psychiatric examination, her unhappy childhood, her young age must carry some weight in the guilty verdict which the court will have to return. I demand a sentence of seven years imprisonment.

'Free this girl today,' he thundered out, 'if you would trust her with your own children!'

My heart stopped. A murmur went through the court as Dr Cindolo sat down again.

I saw Mum's face. It was white. What had happened to Mr Minervini's maximum of four years? I stared at him.

He was frowning. Then he glanced at me and quickly shook his head.

Dr Cindolo had spoken for nearly three hours. Mr Valenti got to his feet.

'We are not judging a witch,' he said. 'Carole's arrest was illegal and wrong and a mistake. The public prosecutor wants to see her in gaol, and he is obviously prepared to make highly emotional and blatantly unfair statements to make sure she goes there. But the court is running the risk of convicting a young girl for acts for which there is no scientific explanation. I would prefer an acquittal based on the paranormal to an unjust verdict that left it out.'

He went over the fires in Ortisei. 'How can a young girl described as backward manage to time these events so exactly that she is never detected, and leaves no incriminating traces?' he asked. 'It is not possible – unless she is telling the truth.'

I wasn't so sure about the 'backward' part, but I felt a little better after Dr Cindolo's attack.

Mr Minervini didn't start until the afternoon.

'I want to show,' he said, 'not only to Italians but to whoever wants to know, that Italian justice is not a farce. There have been mistakes and misinterpretations right through this trial.'

He turned towards me. 'When she was thrown into gaol on August the second last year, Carole Compton was a nervous girl a long, long way from home. The only Italian she has learned has been through a small book I lent her in prison.

'The public prosecutor has referred to things being at the mercy of a stranger. Well, that is how it has been for Carole Compton all along. Carole came to this country a stranger and she has been blamed for everything that has gone wrong.'

Then he began to review the fires in Elba in every detail. He was passionate, he was angry – he was the most impressive I'd ever seen him.

Eventually the judge stopped him at eight in the evening. Mr Minervini had been talking for four hours and he still wasn't finished.

'Tomorrow, Carole,' he told me. 'Tomorrow will see the end.'

Yes, I thought, *but what exactly will that end be?*

The next morning I put on my best things: my new black shoes, a dark blue pinstripe skirt, a pale blouse with a cardigan over the top, and a beige jacket.

When I got into court, the first thing I saw was that the TV and film cameras had been allowed in. There were tripods and batteries of fierce lights all over the press seats.

Mum came rushing over as soon as I'd sat down. She was back in her new suit. With her was a very thin man in his thirties with dark, curly hair and thick glasses. I thought I recognised him from the press seats.

'Carole,' Mum said quickly, 'this is Ramsay Smith from the *Daily Star*. The paper wants to buy your story. They're offering five thousand pounds!'

'Hello, Carole,' said the reporter. 'Your Mum's right. I've told her that's as high as we can go. But we've got to have your agreement pretty quick.'

I looked at Mum. 'It's your chance to get something out of this mess, Carole,' she said.

I only paused for a second. I'd no idea how much money I had left in my appeal fund, but I knew it couldn't be much, and

Mr Minervini and Mr Valenti still hadn't been paid any fees.

'OK,' I said.

'Great!' said the reporter. 'Now don't speak to anyone else, and I don't want you and your Mum photographed together. When you get out. I'll have a car waiting. Get in the back and keep your head down. Got that?'

I nodded. As he went away, I said to Mum, 'Do they really think I'm going to be let out today?'

'God, I hope so, hen,' Mum said. 'I don't think I could stand another twenty-four hours of this.'

There were bags under her eyes. She looked really tired. I knew exactly how she felt.

The judges and jurors took their seats on the bench. The judge asked Mr Minervini to go on.

He spoke for another hour and a half.

'The circumstantial evidence is wholly unconvincing,' he said towards the end. 'Carole Compton was present, but so were others who saw nothing incriminating. Exhaustive scientific tests have come up with no shred of proof of inflammatory substances or anything else.

'Which leaves us where? The normal and paranormal – what do these things mean? I don't believe in the paranormal as it is accepted today. But you have to be modest when considering this subject, and accept that you don't know everything. The human field is immense and not completely explored.

He paused. 'The fact remains that Carole Compton had no motive for these fires. There is no witness and no evidence to say that she had anything to do with them. There is nothing to show Carole wanted to kill. If she did she had other ways and means and other times to choose which would have made the task far easier.

'There is nothing to show that Carole is other than what she has always claimed to be: an innocent victim of circumstances.'

He sat down. The judge was expressionless. He turned and spoke quietly to the second judge, then he looked at me.

'Would the defendant like to make a final statement?'

I glanced at Mr Minervini, who gave a slight shrug, leaving it up to me. I stood up and went over to the microphone.

'Everything I have said is the truth,' I said. 'I have nothing more to add.'

The judge nodded. He said the court would now consider its verdict. The judges and jurors got to their feet; so did everyone else. As soon as the members of the bench had left, my guards led me out.

I gave Mum a last quick wave. The whole courtroom was in a hubbub.

We went down the corridor and into a small, plain, dingy room with only a few chairs in it. I sat and waited.

It was just after a quarter past eleven.

By lunchtime nothing had happened. The guards seemed to be wondering whether or not I should go back to the Domenicani. Eventually someone brought coffee and some rolls.

Two o'clock came, then three, then four. It was cold in the room, but I was beginning to sweat. If Mr Minervini was right, if they were going to let me go, why spin it out? They only had two choices – release me, or lock me up again. So there *was* a chance I was going back to prison.

It started to get dark. Five o'clock passed. This was getting crazy. It looked like I'd be spending another night in the Domenicani.

Then at a quarter past five there was a knock. The court was sitting again.

My heart jumped in my chest as I was taken back down the corridor. I tried to take deep breaths. Seventeen months of disappointments, seventeen months of hopes raised and dashed – I mustn't count on anything; anything could happen.

Patience and strength. Patience and strength.

I said a prayer in my head as the door to the court opened.

I walked into a blaze of television lights. Cameras began flashing. The whole room was seething with excitement, just like the first day.

The guards made me stand between them just to the left of the bench. I blinked in the bright lights, trying to catch sight of Mum. I glimpsed her sitting up on the press seats.

Then I saw Mr Minervini. He gave me an enormous, gap-toothed grin and pulled his robe aside to show me his jacket pocket. A dark blue booklet was sticking out the top.

A passport.

Almost at once the door behind the bench opened. Everyone

else in the room stood up. The judges and jurors filed in. I saw
the cameras move to follow them.

They took their places. Everyone stayed on their feet. I saw
Mum pressing forward. Judge Galligani looked down at a piece
of paper in front of him. I couldn't breathe.

'*Il verdetto della corte d'assise di Livorno*—'

The words came out in a mumbled rush. Then the judge
snatched up the paper, turned and went! The others followed
him.

I blinked, totally confused. No one seemed to know what
had happened. I saw Mr Minervini turn to Mr Valenti; both of
them turned to the clerk of the court.

Then there was a roar from the back of the room. Cheers,
clapping. I saw a handbag go flying up in the air. *Mum*'s
handbag—.

The reporters charged towards me.

It *had* to have happened – I *had* to be free!

My two guards caught my arms and quickly pulled me back
the way we'd come before the press got to me.

We hurried down the corridor. I was weeping and laughing
at the same time. We turned corners. I didn't know where I
was. There were more police, then court officials. I went
through a door. Mr Masi was there.

'What's happening? Am I free? Can I go?'

Mr Masi looked flustered. 'The judge obviously believed
what the families said. They found you guilty on two charges
of arson, Carole, and one of attempted arson. You got two and
a half years imprisonment, but because of the time you've
already spent in prison the sentence was suspended. And the
attempted murder charge is not proven.' His face broke into a
smile. 'You're free, yes. It's all over. You can go home.'

So I was free. I burst into tears.

16

Home

DECEMBER 1983 – AUGUST 1984

'I'm so glad it's worked out this way, Carole,' Mr Masi was saying. 'But first we must get you out of the court. There are formalities, release papers to sign, we have to fetch your things from prison – and we have to get through all those reporters.'

He grinned as he took my arm. 'A good day, eh?'

I nodded. I couldn't speak.

He ushered me out of the room. More corridors – more doors – then a broad, echoing space, packed with people. There were shouts as they saw me – camera flashes exploding everywhere – reporters pressed toward me.

'Carole! . . . Carole, how do you feel? . . . What's it like to be free? . . . Carole, *this way* . . .!'

Mr Masi caught my arm, squeezing me through the crush. Police came to help him. Microphones, cassette recorders were pushed towards me, questions shouted from every side.

'Carole, are you pleased?'

'I'm delighted at getting free. All I want to do now is go home and start my life again.'

'Do you think they were wrong to arrest you?'

'I'm just an ordinary girl who's maybe a bit naive and found herself in deep trouble through no fault of her own. It's been a nightmare—'

'Are you bitter towards the Italians?'

'Oh no, I've nothing against the Italian people.'

We were through the main door. The narrow street was full of jostling, shouting people. Television lights lit up the darkness. It was pandemonium.

I looked round for Mum and the *Star* reporter.

I saw a police car parked by the pavement. A carabiniere stood by the back door.

'Carole! Carole, over here!'

Mum was squeezing her way towards me from the side. The *Star* man's head bobbed behind her. I grasped her hand.

'Oh Mum!' Her face was shining. There was no room to hug. 'I'm free! I can go!'

'I know! I know!' We were both shrieking. A face I knew appeared out of the crush. It was Mrs Vitulano.

'Carole,' she said. '*Mi dispiace.* I'm so sorry.'

'Who's this?' called Mum.

'It's Marco's mother,' I said.

'Tell her it's too late to be sorry now!'

'Where's Marco?' I asked.

'He's away — on a cruise.' She pushed something into my hand. I looked down. It was a Christmas card. Then the crowd swept her away.

Mr Masi was clutching at my arm, pointing towards the car. 'Go with them, Carole,' he shouted above the hubbub. 'Both of you! I'll see you at the gaol!'

Mum turned, gesturing helplessly towards the *Star* reporter. I tumbled into the back of the car. The carabiniere who'd been standing beside it squeezed in beside me, slamming the door.

Mum jumped into the front. Faces pressed against the windows. I was laughing. This whole thing had started in madness — it was ending the same way.

The car's siren wailed. Nothing happened. No one would move.

The car inched forward, and stopped; inched forward and stopped. The driver was swearing. It was five minutes before we got clear of the crowd.

As the car finally moved away, I gasped as a reporter sprawled across the bonnet and rolled off into the darkness.

We turned right, drove along the street and came out at the end of the canal bridge. There was an even bigger crowd in front of the Domenicani.

The carabinieri had blocked off the road in front of it. But the crowd still swarmed round the car when we stopped beside the main door.

The police held people back as I got out. Immediately there were shouts and whistles from above. I looked up. Hands were waving out of the windows. Mugs were banging against the bars. The prisoners were cheering me!

The police hurried Mum and me inside. Mr Masi was already there with guards and prison officials.

'Go and fetch your things, Carole,' he said. 'I'll have your papers ready when you come down.'

Two guards went with me. I climbed the stairs in a dream. After all the tension and the excitement nothing seemed real any more.

I heard banging and shouting from the top landing. Then we went into the male section. The noise was tremendous. They were jumping up at the windows, pushing their hands through, blowing kisses.

'*Carolina! Bella Carolina!* . . . We see you on TV . . . *Buona fortuna!* . . . You are beautiful!'

Laughing, I went through to the women's section. Anna opened the door.

'Well done, Carole,' she smiled.

Lori and my cellmates were behind her. They crowded round; we hugged and kissed.

'They showed it on TV,' said Lori. 'You were fantastic!'

Everyone was chattering away, grinning, patting me on the back. We all went into the cell. I began to empty my cupboard.

I gave away the food I had left, my stamps and soap – all the odds and ends I wouldn't be needing any more.

Then I began to pack my clothes. Lori's eyes lit up as I got to my suede boots.

'A promise is a promise,' I grinned, and handed them over.

'*Grazie, Carolina, molte grazie.*' She hugged me.

'God,' I said, 'look at all these letters.'

I filled a giant-sized Pampers box, and there were still another couple of carrier-bags full. I couldn't carry it all on my own. The male guards had to help.

I glanced round my cell for the last time. The window *still* not repaired, the doorless loo, the little wooden cross over Lori's bed. I couldn't believe it wouldn't all be there when I woke tomorrow morning.

There were more hugs. I was starting to cry again.

The male guards wanted me gone. They were worried about the fuss I was causing.

They hustled me out. There was no time to say everything I wanted.

'I'll write to you, Lori,' I called. 'I won't forget you.'

They were all shouting goodbye. The steel door slammed shut.

Downstairs the *Daily Star* reporter was waiting with Mum and Mr Masi.

'My God, Carole,' Mum said, when she saw all my things, 'how are we going to carry this lot?' Then she frowned. 'Are your boots in your case? The suede ones I got you because you were cold?'

'I gave them to Lori, Mum. It was the least I could do.'

Mr Masi drew me away to sign some papers and collect some more of my things that had been kept in the prison office.

The *Daily Star* man was twitching, looking at his watch, then out at the crowd. A photographer had joined him, a much younger man in a leather jacket and flannels.

The guards were taking my stuff outside.

'Follow the police to the carabinieri station,' said Mr Masi. 'You'll get your passport back there, and your deportation papers. I'm afraid you'll have to leave the country within twenty-four hours, Carole. It's normal practice with foreigners in your position.'

'That's soon enough for us!' Mum cried.

'We've really got to go,' said the *Star* reporter.

'I haven't said goodbye to Mr Minervini,' I said. 'I haven't even thanked him – after all he did.'

'I'll thank him for you,' said Mr Masi.

'OK, the car's outside,' said the *Star* man. 'Mrs Compton, get in the front, Carole in the back. And keep your heads down!'

Mum and I called our goodbyes and thanks to Mr Masi as we were hustled out. Instantly the reporters were all around, tumbling over each other to get at us.

'Carole, can you give us a comment?' 'Mrs Compton, what are your feelings?' 'Where are you going, Carole?'

'Keep going!' the *Star* men yelled. 'Don't say anything!'

It was another madhouse, like something out of a cartoon.

Guards were still putting my things in the boot of the car. The reporter slammed it shut. Mum and I piled into the car.

'No comment! She's no comment!' the reporter called, pushing his way round to the driver's seat. The photographer crawled in beside me, locking the doors.

The police car I'd come in was in front of us. Its siren hiccuped. It drew away. We started after it. Faces fell back from the windows.

The car speeded up. Photographers were running alongside us, cameras still flashing.

The car turned, and turned again. And suddenly the photographers, the crowd, the lights were gone. We were in a quiet, dimly lit city street, early in the evening – an ordinary street, an ordinary evening.

I sat up, my head still ringing with the noise of the crowd. Mum twisted in the front passenger seat and looked back at me. She was grinning.

'Well, that's that, then, eh, Carole?'

'Yes.' I gave a great shuddering sigh that almost turned into tears again. 'That's that.'

Then we both burst out laughing from sheer relief.

I'd thought my problems were over, but it wasn't going to be that easy.

As soon as we'd picked up my passport and deportation papers from the carabinieri station, we headed straight for the autostrada. Ramsay Smith said the rest of the press would be waiting for me at Pisa and Glasgow airports. We'd avoid them by sticking to the roads and driving up the coast to the border with Monaco.

Once we were out of Italy we could relax a bit, and they could interview me properly and take some photographs of Mum and me together.

By now the excitement was beginning to wear off. I started to realise how tired I was; poor Mum was exhausted. It began to rain.

Eventually, around ten o'clock, we pulled off the motorway and ran into a café for a coffee and something to eat. Neither Mum nor I had had more than a bite all day.

While we were sitting down Ramsay Smith said he ought to call his newspaper, and went to find a phone. About ten minutes later he came back, looking embarrassed.

'Look,' he said, 'I don't know how to say this, but I think the deal's off.'

'What do you mean?' Mum said. 'How can it be off?'

Ramsay Smith blinked at us through his thick spectacles. 'I think they were counting on an acquittal. We're not supposed to pay people for their stories when they've been convicted of crimes—'

Mum and I looked at each other.

'God,' she said, 'this is another nightmare! Where does that leave us? I don't even know where we are. We're stuck out here!'

The reporter shook his head. 'No, it's OK. I've been informed to take you further on. I'm sure we'll sort something out.'

'You'd better,' said Mum.

This time she sat in the back with me. As we drove off a thunderstorm began. I'd never seen so much rain. There were cracks going off like bombs, right overhead, and forked lightning was flickering about the roofs of the cars on the autostrada.

Mum and I were terrified. We ended up hugging each other. What made it worse was that Ramsay Smith didn't seem to be able to see through the windscreen. He was crouched over the wheel, peering through the rain from behind his thick lenses.

Eventually, around midnight, we reached the border. I handed over my deportation papers to the guards. Then we crossed into Monaco. I had finally put Italy behind me.

I hardly remember the hotel we stayed in – all I was aware of was a room with an enormous bed. Mum and I collapsed on to it, and fell fast asleep.

In the morning, straight after breakfast, we drove on again into Nice, and booked into another hotel. Both Mum and I were still very uneasy; so was Ramsay Smith and the photographer, whose name was Ciaran Donnelly. No one seemed to know what was happening.

The two newspapermen had the room next door to us. 'I don't trust these two,' Mum told me. 'Whatever they do don't say anything. Keep your mouth shut until we know what's what.'

After we'd settled in, Mum had it out with them.

'Is this deal on or off?' she asked.

Ramsay Smith just looked sheepish. 'I think it's off,' he said.

'So what's going to happen to us?'

'I'm not sure, but I think you'll be getting a bill.'

Mum's face just dropped. Here we were in a luxury hotel in a foreign country with nothing in our pockets, and, as far as I knew, no money anywhere else to bring us home.

We couldn't do anything but sit in our room, and worry. By now we were starting to row. I couldn't help it. After being locked up, with no hope of getting home, for two years, the same thing was happening all over again!

Then Ramsay Smith came back to us. 'I've had another talk to the editor,' he said. 'You'll be pleased to know the deal is on. That'll be a big weight off my back.'

'Ours too!' Mum snapped. 'But I'll be happier when we've signed some sort of contract.'

'Oh, we'll take you down to London and do all that there,' said the reporter. 'That'll be taken care of.'

Ciaran Donnelly took a lot of pictures of Mum and me, then I went next door and Ramsay Smith spent a long time interviewing me.

On Sunday we left the hotel and drove to Paris, where we caught an afternoon flight to Manchester. Apparently they were still worried about rival reporters waiting for us at Glasgow airport.

Another *Star* reporter, a big Scotsman from Glasgow called Stewart McCartney, met us when we landed and drove Mum, Ramsay Smith and me north. Ciaran Donnelly left us then. We stopped that night at a hotel in Carlisle, and Stewart McCartney asked me a lot more questions.

While I was there I lost my watch and the crucifix on the gold chain my father had given me. It seemed extraordinary, after managing to keep those things through all my time in prison, that they could go so easily. Later Mr Hosie rang up the hotel for me to see if anything had been found, but nothing ever was.

On the Monday the *Star* published a big story on me. Ramsay Smith said he was sorry it hadn't been on the front page, but it had been pushed off by the IRA bombing at Harrods.

The next morning, Tuesday 20 December, we finally drove over the border and up to Ayr. Even then I couldn't go straight home. We had to meet another photographer at the Station Hotel, and more pictures were taken.

Mum and I turned up on Gran's doorstep with the three newspapermen in tow. Little Sean opened the door to us.

'Hello, Sean,' Mum smiled. He blinked at her, then stared at me. He looked so much older than I remembered him.

'Oh Carole!' he cried. 'I'm that glad to see you!'

I was astonished by how well he was talking.

Gran appeared and we all hugged and hugged. Then she rushed straight into the kitchen and put on some of my favourite tatty soup. I'd spent nearly two years dreaming about it. This was the moment when I'd felt I'd truly come home.

I spent my twenty-second birthday and a quiet, family Christmas in Galloway Avenue. We had a big tree, lots of decorations and all the presents my mother had wrapped for me before she'd flown to Italy for the trial.

There was a sour ending to the *Star* story. Once we were home the phone rang continuously. We were afraid to answer because we knew it would be other press people, wanting interviews, and we thought we were under contract. Eventually, though, Mum did pick up the phone. It was a local newspaper reporter. According to her, there was no contract with the *Star*.

Mum rang up Stewart McCartney, who confirmed it. He suggested we get in touch with a solicitor. They claimed no formal contract had been made. Both sides disagreed with each other. It took over a year, and almost went to court, before we decided to settle.

Over the holiday I telephoned Marco's flat, thinking he would be home for Christmas. His mother answered, but said he was out. I spoke in Italian, and I don't think she recognised my voice.

I don't know what I would have said. I didn't expect anything from him, but I still cared, and some kind of explanation would have been nice. We could still have been friends. It was the last time I tried to get in touch.

Now I just wanted to be normal again, to forget the whole nightmare, and to *be* forgotten.

But things weren't that simple.

One evening I was finally persuaded to go out to the disco I'd promised myself once I got free. As I sat listening to the music, a punk came over and said very clearly to one of my friends: 'Aren't you frightened what might happen with *her* sitting next to you?'

It wasn't the first time I heard remarks like that. The 'witch' label was like a stain that wouldn't wash out.

I thought seriously about changing my name. In the end I told Mum I'd come back to Aberdeen and live with her. Gran was upset, but I needed a fresh start. And Ayr had memories I could do without.

In January the Livorno court published the reasons for its verdict, which in Italy it is obliged to do. It had decided that I had started the fires out of 'pathological nostalgia' – the desire to get back to Marco at whatever cost. The judges had accepted what Dr Cindolo had believed from the start.

They thought I'd probably used spirits to start the fires, which explained why no trace of inflammable substances was found. And I'd deliberately knocked over the statue and the cakestand and other objects, then pretended I didn't know why they'd fallen, to create 'an atmosphere of unease'.

I laughed when I read it. It was all so ludicrous. The only part that made me feel any better was that the court completely rejected any suggestion of witchcraft.

Both Mr Minervini and Dr Cindolo were planning to appeal against the sentences. Dr Cindolo wanted my sentence increased to at least eight years!

Mr Minervini wrote, insisting that I would have to attend the appeal hearing for it to have any chance of success. *No way!* I thought as I read it. *Absolutely no way!* The hearing was held, without me, in Florence on 8 November. Both appeals were rejected. My sentence stood.

At the start of 1984 I moved in with Mum and little Sean at Mum's place in Glenbervie Road in Torry on the south side of Aberdeen. Mum was now back in 'the fish'. There was a vacancy in the factory where she worked. I had to work, so I tried for it and got the job. My life seemed to have turned full circle.

The Friday before I started the girls in the factory were

having a hen night. Mum invited me along to meet them. We
began at a pub with a disco and planned to move on later to
another disco called *Effusion* which was just off Union Street.
But, by the end of the evening, the other girls decided they'd
had enough.

Mum, though, was in a party mood, so we went to the disco
on our own. When we got there, we went upstairs to drop our
coats off in the cloakroom. As we came down again, Mum's
foot slipped on the stairs and the heel of her shoe broke off.

We asked a couple of bouncers if they could do anything to
mend it, but they couldn't. Three young men were standing
nearby, watching what was happening. Mum asked jokingly if
they had any suggestions. One of the boys, who turned out to
be Spanish, took some chewing-gum out of his mouth and tried
to stick the heel back on with that. Of course, it didn't work
at all.

'Oh well,' said Mum. 'We'll have just one dance and then
we'll go away home.'

We went through on to the dance floor. A few minutes later
the other two boys we'd seen outside came up to us. One who
was slim and dark with glasses asked me to dance. His friend,
who was Welsh, asked Mum. When the music stopped, we all
sat down and chatted.

My partner's accent was an odd mixture of Aberdeen and
Yorkshire. He told me he'd been born in Kashmir, but he'd
been brought up in Bradford and spent some time in Aberdeen.
Now he was an industrial chemist, analysing oil samples on a
BP oil rig. He should have been on the rig that night, but he'd
missed his flight.

His name was Zaroof Fazal, but all his friends called him
Faz.

He was pleasant and funny and very easy to talk to. I didn't
realise how the time was passing until Mum announced that
she'd had enough and was going. Faz asked her if she minded
me staying on and offered to bring me home.

'All right,' Mum said, 'but you make sure it's in a taxi.' Faz
promised he would.

Talking and dancing with him was the first time in ages I felt
normal again – just an ordinary twenty-two-year-old enjoying
herself on a night out, like thousands of other girls all over the

country. Then, as we chatted, a girl I'd never seen before came over to me.

'Carole Compton?' she asked. 'I thought I recognised you. Could I have a few words?'

She took a notebook out of her handbag. She was a local newspaper reporter.

Faz sat and looked bemused as I answered questions I'd answered a hundred times before. I didn't want to be rude and tell the girl I wasn't interested. I was too embarrassed that she'd picked me out in the first place. Eventually she went away.

'I didn't know I was talking to a celebrity!' Faz joked.

He said he'd heard about my story, but he'd never have recognised me. I couldn't avoid telling him what had happened to me.

We got the taxi he'd promised and he took me home. He asked if he could see me the next day and I gave him my phone number. After the business with the reporter I didn't really expect him to call. But he did. We went out the next night. We began to see a lot of each other.

It was curious. With Marco it had taken us a long time to become close. With Faz it wasn't like that at all. Perhaps when you are older you know your mind and your feelings that much better. Things just felt right between us. It felt natural being together. The more we saw of each other the stronger that feeling grew for both of us.

We became engaged just after St Valentine's Day. We were married at Aberdeen registry office on 31 August 1984. I wore a white gown. My mother wore pink. Little Sean was dressed in a kilt. Both families were there. Faz, who had been brought up as a Moslem and normally never touched alcohol, managed to get tipsy on the two glasses of champagne he had for the toasts.

My only sadness was that my father couldn't give me away; he was in hospital in Ayr, recovering from a cancer operation.

The press were there, and so were the TV cameras.

This time they were giving me the kind of attention I was more than happy to share.

Afterword

Was Carole Compton the unwitting victim of a poltergeist attack? Were the five fires that so mysteriously broke out around her caused by paranormally induced spontaneous combustion?

Many of the world's foremost authorities on poltergeist phenomena believe there is a strong possibility that this did occur.

One of them is Guy Lyon Playfair, a leading British writer on and investigator of the paranormal. He is the author of several classic works on the subject, including *The Flying Cow*, *The Indefinite Boundary* and *This House is Haunted*.

Playfair first became interested in Carole Compton's case shortly after her arrest. With fellow investigator Dr Hugh Pincott (founder of the Association for the Scientific Study of Anomalous Phenomena) he offered his expert services to Carole's defence lawyers.

At the same time both men appealed to the world's most prominent authorities on the paranormal to contribute to a dossier testifying to the considerable body of well-documented evidence that exists on poltergeist phenomena – in particular those forms involving fires.

As Carole's own account makes clear, none of this testimony was used in her defence – not least because such evidence has never been accepted in a court of law. What difference – if any – it would have made to the verdict must remain a matter of speculation.

Eight years after his initial involvement Guy Lyon Playfair

presents his summation of the case and concludes with the address he would have made to the Livorno court, had he been given the opportunity to appear in Carole's defence.

Extracts from the expert dossier are included in the Appendix.

Gerald Cole, 1990

'Everything I have said is the truth. I have nothing to add,' said Carole Compton at her trial. Everything she has said in this book reads to me like the truth, told by a brave young woman who lived through an ordeal I would not have thought possible in a civilised country in the 1980s – and one I hope will never be repeated anywhere.

Her story may have a happy ending, with 'what I've always wanted – a loving husband, children, a home of my own'. Yet she still has to bear the stigma of a guilty verdict on charges of arson and attempted arson, which I am satisfied she did not commit or contemplate committing. I have something to add: an explanation of why Carole does not deserve a criminal record, which technically she has, and why she is not and never was a witch.

Like Sergio Minervini, I do not 'believe' in the so-called paranormal. How can one believe in something that by definition can only be described in terms of what it isn't? Likewise, I can hardly be an 'expert' in it. I am merely a writer who is interested in any area of nature or human experience that remains unexplained, and I agree with Minervini's understatement that 'the human field is immense and not completely explored'.

It certainly is both, but, unfortunately, when we come to those corners of it labelled 'psychic' or 'paranormal', we find those who believe that any attempt to explore them (let alone claim that they actually happen) is in itself a sign of mental instability and a wish to return to the superstitions of the Dark Ages.

What I do believe in are *facts*. I am not a lawyer, but I will now present some evidence in the form of well-documented facts that, had I been on jury service at Carole's trial, would, I hope, have persuaded my fellow jurors to throw the case out of court.

Much of law is based on precedent, and here are some previous cases which seem to me to be particularly relevant.

- *Suzano, Brazil, 1970.* A total of sixteen fires broke out for no identifiable reason in a modest family home in this small town in the state of São Paulo. Objects burnt included mattresses, a sofa, clothing inside a wardrobe and the wardrobe itself. This case is of special legal interest, because part of it was witnessed at first hand by the local police chief and his forensic expert. The chief gave a detailed statement shortly after the event to Brazil's leading parapsychologist Hernani Guimarães Andrade. I later interviewed the expert at length in 1975. He described how a mattress began to smoulder in front of his eyes, noting that it seemed to be combusting from inside. Then, he told me, he hung a calendar on a nail on the wall, stood back and challenged the whatever-it-was to start another fire for his benefit. 'If I live to be a hundred,' he said, 'I'll swear that calendar hanging on the wall in front of my nose caught fire by itself.'

- *Holloway, London, 1978.* Firemen were called seven times to the council flat of a (childless) couple where things were catching fire on their own – a sweater, a dishcloth, a pile of newspapers, and a bed. Partially burned objects included a box of kitchen matches, but not the matches themselves, and two pound notes. The case was thoroughly investigated by Maurice Grosse, with whom I was working at the time on the Enfield poltergeist case described in my book *This House is Haunted*. (There, too, several objects combusted spontaneously.) Grosse recorded on-the-spot evidence from a fireman, who stated 'I've never seen anything like it', and from the local chief fire prevention officer, whose conclusion was 'There's no explanation at all – no indication of how they started'.

- *Séron, France, 1979.* This case surely belongs in the *Guinness Book of Records*. No less than ninety-eight fires broke out during August in the Pyrenees village in front of dozens of witnesses, including twenty gendarmes. Here, too, there was no explanation as to how any of them started. One eyewitness noted that all fires seemed to start with a small charred spot on a bed or piece of clothing which would eventually burst into flames. Like Carole Compton, two young people were jailed, tried and convicted (in that order) on the flimsiest of evidence, despite the absence of witnesses or motive. They were later pardoned or freed.

● *Birmingham, 1980.* An open verdict was recorded at the inquest into the death of three-year-old Cassandra Wickenden, who suffocated in her smoke-filled bedroom. The coroner's unlikely sounding suggestion that the fire was started by a cigarette left burning in *another* bedroom drew an angry outburst from the girl's mother. 'No,' she shouted, 'nobody had been up there all day. Why won't you believe us? It didn't start like that!' An unusual feature of this tragic case is that both parents insisted that some kind of unknown force *was* responsible for the fire, and they mentioned several incidents of poltergeist-type phenomena that had occurred in Cassandra's presence.

Alan Gauld, a leading historian of psychical research, has compiled a list of 500 poltergeist cases dating from the sixth century AD, in fifty-three of which there were reports of 'incendiary effects'. Outbreaks of fire on cases in which other inexplicable phenomena are reported are not exactly new. True, the quality of evidence on many early cases is poor, but as I have indicated the recent evidence is much better. Three of the cases mentioned above were witnessed at first hand by either police or firemen. (In the French case, both.) By coincidence, on the day I began to write this Afterword, a letter arrived from Hernani Guimarães Andrade describing two new Brazilian cases of what he calls 'parapyrogenesis', or spontaneous combustion for which there is no normal explanation. One is of special interest because it was captured, I believe for the first time, on film. It was shown on Brazilian television.

'You can see the fire begin and develop rapidly on a mattress,' Mr Andrade writes. 'A Jesuit priest then appears on the scene and, in front of the camera, gives a "scientific explanation" of the phenomenon, showing much erudition. He then tells the open-mouthed victims of the poltergeist that he is going to do away with it.' He blesses the family, asking everybody to forget their internal problems, assures them that the problem is solved and leaves. 'As soon as he is out of the house, fire breaks out again, causing panic and despair. The whole thing is on film.' Perhaps it will convince those who only believe something if they see it on television.

Things can, of course, catch fire all by themselves quite normally. Rags soaked in linseed oil can easily start burning if left in confined spaces in hot weather, as can all kinds of substances, from grass clippings to certain foodstuffs. A ball of steel wool once burst alarmingly into flames in my own home. Yet it should be emphasised that normal spontaneous combustion has never to my knowledge been put forward as an explanation for any case of the kind I have mentioned.

This is not to say that all inexplicable fires have the same cause. Indeed, we can understand how some of the fires in Carole Compton's case, particularly the first one, could have seemed quite normal at the time. We are told here of lighted cigarettes being left around regularly, and of overloaded electrical circuits. Yet we hear no evidence of earlier fires in the houses concerned. I would have expected them to have burned down fairly often if their occupants were so careless. And here we suddenly have five fires in just over three weeks. The first one may have been normal, and possibly the second, but all five? I doubt it.

As described in Chapter 14, Ortisei chief fire officer Teodoro Comploi stated that in his thirty-eight years' service 'I've never seen fires like those before'. Referring to the Elba fires, Professor Vitolo Nicolo from Pisa University tells Minervini 'In my forty-five years' experience of this kind of investigation I have never seen fires like these' (Chapter 14).

Some interesting evidence emerged from the testimony of these two experts. The Ortisei officer noted that a fire broke out on a stool and then went out, while another began in a nearby wardrobe. Both men described fires burning downwards rather than upwards. Their testimony would, I believe, have been even more interesting if heard together with evidence from the cases I have mentioned. At Suzano, fire broke out inside a closed and empty wardrobe a few minutes after a mattress had combusted, in the presence of the police. There were many other coincidences: six of the sixteen Suzano fires involved beds or sofa-beds, four of the five Italian ones were also on mattresses, while at Séron witnesses lost count of the number of times that their bedding was burned. In the Birmingham case, the sole, fatal blaze was on a bed.

Another coincidence is that on at least three of the four cases I have cited, the inexplicable fires were accompanied by standard tricks from the poltergeist repertoire. Again, the evidence is not at all bad: the Suzano forensic expert told me how stones whizzed round the room while it was quite plain that nobody present was throwing them. Strange incidents in Cassandra Wickenden's short life described at the inquest – presumably under oath – by her parents included bangs on the ceiling that shook the house, a chair sliding across a room (as at Enfield, witnessed by two police officers), and objects jumping off shelves. At Holloway, lights switched themselves on and off, fruit jumped out of a bowl, doors opened and closed on their own and books flew off shelves – one of them always landing open at the same page on which was a recipe for something called American Devil's Food!

Carole admits that she found the brief outburst of small object movements at Elba 'weird', and that it gave her 'the shivers'. There seem to be only two normal explanations for the breakage of the glass vase and the movements of the statue and the cake stand. One is that old favourite, coincidence, which always explains everything. The other is that Carole entered what one of the psychiatrists called an 'impulsive short-circuit' state and threw the objects without knowing what she was doing, having no memory of having done so. However, the second psychiatrist tells us that such states only occur once in a lifetime and are normally associated with psychotics, and Carole was definitely not psychotic.

Professor Inghirami did touch on the kind of evidence I would have presented when he referred to her 'non-cohesive' family background and the 'alien environment' she was in at the time of the fires. These, he said, fitted the profile of a pyromaniac. They also fit the profile of a poltergeist victim very well indeed. In such cases there is always a history of divorce, separation or infidelity, or a comparable cause of prolonged stress. This in itself is obviously not enough to activate poltergeist phenomena – if it were, it would be happening all over the place nearly all the time – but it is an essential condition. I know of no poltergeist case involving a united and happy family. What triggers off the activity is a matter for speculation, but I am only concerned here with facts.

It was the late Eilean Ross, a freelance journalist from Ayr, who first had the idea of mobilising the international para-psychology community in Carole's defence. Since she did not know any of them, she phoned around, and among the first to hear from her were Dr Hugh Pincott and me. I had known Hugh for many years, and he had been a valuable colleague on the Enfield investigation. An oil company executive with a PhD in chemistry, he was also the founder of the Association for the Scientific Study of Anomalous Phenomena (ASSAP). He and I had both been following Carole's case since her arrest, and had been doing our best to publicise her plight.

'I am appalled that in this enlightened and technological age we come up against a solid wall of bigotry, ignorance and superstition,' Hugh told *Psychic News* (18 December 1982), while my position was made clear in the *News of the World* (12 December): 'She is certainly not a criminal or a witch – I and many other researchers are prepared to go out to support the girl, even if it has to be at our own expense.'

Eilean Ross had got in touch with Carole's Euro MP, Mr Alasdair Hutton, and suggested we should channel our efforts through him instead of jumping on the next plane to Italy and trying to drag Carole out of jail ourselves. We agreed, and set about contacting all the experts we knew and asking them to submit written opinions. A sample of these is included in the Appendix.

Were we all leaping to the wrong conclusion – that Carole was a poltergeist victim? This seemed quite possible at the time, and the least we could do, we felt, was make the facts known to her defence lawyer. This we did, through the good offices of Mr Hutton, and we were naturally disappointed that neither Carole nor Minervini was sympathetic to our approach. However, Carole could be forgiven for thinking at the time that we were just another bunch of 'interfering busybodies', as her mother was quoted as calling us, while Minervini had every reason to feel confident that he would get his client off without becoming involved in parapsychological arguments. There was, after all, an impressive lack of evidence, motive or witnesses.

I am glad, therefore, that some of the expert testimony that

Hugh and I collected has been published here. In the Appendix, the reader will find a good deal of informed opinion from specialists in many fields, from psychology, psychiatry, physics and statistics to criminology. It is especially good to have the statements of Professor Hans Bender on record, for he was and still is unquestionably the most experienced researcher in his field.

He had been approached independently by my Italian colleague Paola Giovetti, one of the few journalists in her country who was prepared to come to Carole's assistance, and he was the only one of our team to meet Carole and attend her trial. He was confident that she would go free. 'She will probably be acquitted without the need to argue about the paranormal cause of the fires,' he wrote to me shortly before the trial. 'If the verdict should be guilty (which I do not think will be the case) we must unite to mobilise the whole world.'

The verdict was guilty, at least on two counts. Carole's name needs to be cleared once and for all, and this is what I would like to have said at her appeal:

'We were told at the trial that Carole's background and situation fitted the profile of a pyromaniac. Yet we were offered not a scrap of evidence that she was one, and all the evidence I have heard fits another profile perfectly – that of somebody who serves as a focus for what is called poltergeist activity, and which has nothing whatsoever to do with witchcraft. In any case, witches were never noted for starting fires. Nor are young women today except in the purely fictional works of Stephen King.

'The word "poltergeist" is one we use for something we don't understand. It is an emotive and misleading one, for we are probably not dealing here with a "noisy spirit", which is what the German word means, but with a syndrome – a collection of symptoms that combine to produce certain effects. So let us forget about poltergeists and adopt the term used by parapsychologists: Recurrent Spontaneous Psychokinesis, or RSPK.

'Professor Bender has studied sixty such cases in three countries, and has found they show what he calls trans-cultural uniformity – meaning that exactly the same things happen in different cases. Even minor details are often identical. He also reports that paranormal combustion is a well-established, if relatively rare, symptom in the RSPK syndrome. I have produced independent testimony from police and fire officers that identical, inexplicable fires have been well observed on cases in which other RSPK symptoms such as stone-throwing or small object displacement have been reported, as they were at Elba.

'Now, if Carole is an RSPK victim, which is what the facts suggest to me and many of my colleagues, then she cannot be found guilty of any crime at all. The whole point of RSPK is that the epicentre – the person around whom the activity takes place – has not the faintest idea what is going on. Such people have no conscious involvement with the phenomena, and are usually scared stiff by them. In many cases they have fled their own homes, something most people will not do without good reason.

'All we could say about Carole is that she suffered a brief personality disorder brought about chiefly by continuous stress. This in turn had a number of possible causes, from the separation of her parents, her own separation from her mother and her own country to her third enforced separation from the young man she hoped to marry. And her feelings of discomfort on first arriving in Elba undoubtedly helped increase the level of stress. Indeed, it may have been her employers' attitude that raised it above the critical level.

'Was she guilty of this? Is it a crime in Italy to have a psychosomatic disorder, which is all she had? Do you arrest people for catching German measles? Then why arrest somebody for suffering from a condition caused by external factors over which she has no conscious control at all? She is not insane any more than she is a witch. RSPK syndrome only affects people of sound mind who are undergoing a period of disturbance that is usually very brief. When the conditions that led to it are removed, the disorder cannot develop. As a loved and loving mother and wife, she will never have any more experience of it. All the evidence indicates that RSPK syndrome is a disorder you can only have once. That is the good news.

'It is true that damage was done and a life was in danger. Mercifully, little Agnese survived, unlike Cassandra Wickenden in Birmingham. Yet even if she had not survived, how can we blame Carole for an accident in which she had no conscious involvement at all?

'We have no idea how RSPK causes its effects, and many of us prefer to pretend that it does not exist. Yet it does exist. There is too much well-documented evidence. There is even evidence that it can be created to order, as I have experienced for myself in the company of Kenneth Batcheldor, a clinical psychologist who spent more than twenty years experimenting in his own home with a procedure based on the traditional table-tapping seance. He has not only succeeded in producing RSPK in various harmless forms, but he has gone far towards explaining why it occurs, if not how.

'His theories are not at all easy to summarise briefly, but one important feature of them is that RSPK can only develop in a group – people cannot produce it by themselves. In fact, there is not a single case of RSPK on record in which there was only one person involved. Carole could not have started fires on her own, except by normal means, even if she had wanted to.

'Let us all concentrate our minds on the facts and the precedents. Your own experts have testified that these fires were not normal. English, French and Brazilian experts have come to the same conclusion on similar cases. Naturally, I cannot prove that the Elba and Ortisei fires were started by group-generated RSPK, but it is possible to disprove this by finding a more usual explanation – which nobody has yet done.

'If ever a case had an element of reasonable doubt, this is it. I ask you to do three things: declare Carole innocent on all charges and compensate her for her seventeen months in jail; rule that the causes of the Ortisei and Elba fires are unknown but strongly suggestive of group RSPK; and urge that some serious and long overdue research is done in this baffling but real corner of the human field.

'Whether we choose to believe in it or not, there will be more cases of RSPK. More of its innocent victims will find themselves accused of crimes they never committed. Spare a thought for them, and those defending them. Carole Compton's long ordeal need not have been entirely in vain.'

Guy Lyon Playfair, 1990

Appendix

Thirteen leading authorities on the paranormal responded to the appeal by Guy Lyon Playfair and Dr Hugh Pincott to provide evidence of poltergeist phenomena.

Their contributions included personal testimonies, addresses to learned bodies and press reports of cases that appeared to be similar to Carole's.

Their letters were addressed either to Playfair or to Alasdair Hutton, Member of the European Parliament for the South of Scotland, who took up Carole's case and collated and arranged for the translation of the dossier for use by Carole's lawyers.

Also included here is a letter written to Sergio Minervini by Professor Hans Bender after his examination of Carole in Livorno prison in September 1983 and outlining his conclusions. Professor Bender attached an article by Giuliano Ferrieri from the Italian journal *L'Europeo*, describing a similar case involving fires which occurred in Italy at about the same time.

The contributors were:

Professor ARG Owen, Faculty of Medicine, University of Toronto
Professor DF Lawden, Head of Mathematics Department, University of Aston in Birmingham
Professor Hans Bender, Institute for Border Areas of Psychology and Mental Hygiene, University of Freiburg
Dr Alfred Krantz, a leading French psychiatrist and forensic expert
Dr Hernani Guimarães Andrade, electrical engineer, founder of the Brazilian Institute for Psychobiophysical Research (IBPP)
Dr J Beloff, Senior Lecturer in Psychology, University of Edinburgh, Ex-President of the Society for Psychical Research
Professor AJ Ellison, Head of Department of Electrical and Electronic Engineering, The City University

Professor JB Hasted, Head of Department of Physics, Birkbeck College, London

Professor AE Roy, Head of Department of Astronomy, Glasgow University

Mr Arthur North, Senior Lecturer, Polytechnic of North London

Dr JF McHarg, Consultant Psychiatrist, Honorary Senior Lecturer in Psychiatry, University of Dundee

Dr AO Gauld, Senior Lecturer in Psychology, University of Nottingham

Dr Jean Dierkens, Head of Faculty of Educational Psychology, State University at Mons, Belgium

Grateful thanks are made to all those who gave their permission for their contributions to be reproduced here.

Faculty of Medicine
Department of Preventive Medicine and Biostatistics
University of Toronto
Toronto, Canada

7 February 1983

Dear Guy

I am writing to say that I am quite concerned about the case of Carole Compton whom you mention. From the facts you give, I am much inclined to believe that the girl is guiltless, and is in fact one of the very many persons of both sexes who have been, to their own misfortune, centres of what is now described as 'RSPK' – recurrent spontaneous psychokinesis. These cases have been documented in numerous books by highly sophisticated and knowledgeable scientists – medical doctors, physicists, psychologists, etc., as well as by senior police officers, administrators, legislators, judges, and other persons experienced in practical affairs. The number of such impeccably witnessed cases now amounts to hundreds.

The phenomena embrace a wide range: movement of objects, production of strange noises and, interestingly enough, effects of heating and production of fires. Often these fires occur in relatively unpromising sites (e.g. wallpaper catches alight) that would not be selected by an arsonist, sane or insane, for the simple reason that, with the worst will in the world, to actually ignite them is a matter of the utmost practical difficulty – indeed, impossible by normal means. As a case in point, may I mention that of Matthew Manning, whom I have known since he was eleven years old when he became the centre of psychokinetic happenings. These came to my attention when I was a professor at Cambridge, England. As with Miss Compton, strange happenings recurred when he was fifteen at Oakham School (1971). One of the most interesting of the occur- rences – amply testified to by masters, boys, the school matron, and the headmaster (a retired army brigadier general) – was the fact that areas on the interior walls of some of the rooms became luminous and were hot to the touch. (He says this in the film *Matthew Manning, Study of a Psychic*, which would provide an excellent overview of RSPK phenomena for use in court, if admitted.) Doubtless this was a related phenomenon to that of ignition of wallpaper, bedding, the fabric on furniture, such as sofas, chairs, etc.

I should stress that these happenings are in no way 'supernatural' – they have no relation to superstitions (now rightly obsolete) concerning the devil, evil spirits, witchcraft, or the spirits of the dead. The subject has been assessed over the last seventy or eighty years by a variety of savants, the weight of whose opinion has fallen unambiguously on the side of affirming:

(a) the phenomena are *not* the result of fraud or trickery on the part of the principal person concerned (e.g. Miss Compton).
(b) the phenomena are *not* the result of 'supernatural' influences.
(c) the phenomena are 'natural' ones, though rare.
(d) the person concerned, though the centre of the forces which are operative, is *not consciously* intending of them.
(e) the person concerned, though doubtless subject to some psychological tensions, or stress, is not insane.

With warmest good wishes

Yours sincerely

Professor ARG Owen, M.A. Ph.D. (Cantab).

The Department of Mathematics
University of Aston
Birmingham

14 February 1983

Dear Mr Hutton

<u>Miss Carole Compton</u>

I was disturbed to read in my newspaper recently that the above named children's nurse had been imprisoned in Italy and was awaiting trial on charges of arson and attempted murder of one of her charges.

I was instantly alerted when it was mentioned that unaccountable movements of objects had been observed in her presence. These phenomena, together with outbreaks of fire, the casting about of hot coals and sometimes the appearance of pools of water, are well attested indications of a poltergeist disturbance, often associated with a young woman (called the 'focus') subject to mental stress. In these circumstances, the woman has no conscious knowledge of the effects she is causing and no control over them.

I fear that this poor girl may very well be unjustly treated due to the authority's ignorance of these facts established by recent psychical research and hope that you will be able to intervene to ensure that they are fully enlightened as to the range of possibilities.

Yours sincerely

Professor DF Lawden
Head of Mathematics Department

Institut für Grenzgebiete der Psychologie und Psychohygiene
Freiburg

15 February 1983

Dear Mr Playfair

I appreciate very much that you take part in the campaign to ensure the release of the twenty-one-year-old Scottish girl, Carole Compton, who has been held in an Italian prison since 2 August 1982.

I am fully informed of the facts by Paola Giovetti in Modena whom I assured that I would do my best to help this unfortunate girl.

I have investigated more than sixty poltergeist cases in Germany, Switzerland and France and have published many reports on exceptional phenomena which mostly depend on a young person. Inexplicable movement of objects, removal of pillows and bed linen, sudden change of temperature, aggressive actions against persons (such as throwing of knives and so on) are often reported and show a trans-cultural uniformity: the same poltergeist patterns are in evidence all over the world. Among these patterns paranormal combustion has also been observed. This happened for example in a case in Freiburg, West Germany, where dependent on a 15-year-old boy, fires broke out: curtains, cushions, books, etc., were involved. It was a clear case of poltergeist, the psychological motivation for which was a protest of the boy against the drunkenness of his father. The case led to a legal suit: inhabitants of the house in which the family in question had an apartment took the boy to court on account of arson. The State Attorneyship, Freiburg, arranged for a testimonial in the department of juvenile and child psychiatry of the Heidelberg Clinic of Psychiatry. The director of the department, Professor Müller-Küppers, drew up a testimonial in which he claimed that the boy's statements that he had not started fires intentionally were trustworthy.

I have very good reason to believe that Carole is not a criminal but the victim of a condition in which outbreaks of 'recurrent, spontaneous psychokinesis' occur. RSPK is the scientific term used in parapsychology for poltergeist phenomena.

Should it come to criminal proceedings, I should be prepared to take part as expert counsel. No costs will be incurred if I have to stand in court.

With best wishes

Yours sincerely

Professor Hans Bender, Ph.D. M.D.

Doctor Alfred Krantz
Pau, France

15 February 1983

Dear Sir

The fact that movements of objects without physical contact (telekinesis) took place in the presence of [Carole Compton] suggests that this could involve 'paranormal' fires. The phenomenon has been described many times. Its origin is, however, unknown. It occurs in the vicinity of a person, usually young, who is called its 'epicentre', but it is not produced voluntarily. It might lead to a miscarriage of justice if (as is normally the case) the judge were ignorant of the existence of paranormal fires.

In our area, in 1979, there were ninety-eight fires in three weeks at Séron (Hautes Pyrénées). A girl in her twenties was arrested, and also a young man, then they had to be released. To this day there has been no conviction. The costs were borne by the fire insurance.

In 1970 at Suzano in Brazil, a similar case was reported. In another case at Piraporinha in Brazil in 1977 a child was burnt to death.

I enclose a few extracts from newspapers and a study from the Instituto Brasileiro de Pesquisas Psicobiofisicas.

I would be glad if these few data could avoid a miscarriage of justice.

Yours faithfully

Alfred Krantz

Instituto Brasileiro de Pesquisas Psicobiofisicas
São Paulo, Brazil

4 April 1980

The Suzano Poltergeist

A report given by Mr Hernani Guimarães Andrade to the second International Conference for Psychotronic Research, at Monte Carlo, Principality of Monaco, from 30 June to 4 July 1975.

The case we have chosen includes three interesting factors:

1 A large number of uncommon incidents, involving paranormal spontaneous combustion, or parapyrogenesis; sixteen incidents of

this type occurred of which nine were within the space of two hours.

2 The large number of witnesses who were involved in this case and the fact that three of the people we interviewed were members of the local police force: the Commissioner of Police, Mr João Lazaro Rodriguez, a police officer, Mr José Carlos Soares, and a police technical expert, Mr Natal Samuel de Lima.

3 The possibility accorded to my colleagues and myself to confirm the facts a short while after the manifestation of the phenomena, while the events were still fresh in the memories of those who had been present.

Cases of poltergeists accompanied by parapyrogenesis (spontaneous paranormal combustion) are very important because they leave typical traces. These traces or signs permit better documentation of the event and mean that the paranormal nature of the phenomena is more evident.

Among the thirty-five poltergeist cases which our Institute has been able to study, thirteen were characterised by paranormal fires.

I should mention that three members of the Institute are engineers of high calibre and are familiar with the effects of normal combustion.

The phenomena occurred in three rooms of the house of Mr Ezequias Valerio de Souza, 508 Padre Eustaquio Street, at Suzano, a town of 65,000 inhabitants situated forty-seven kilometres east of São Paulo. It all began in 1968 and ended two years later on 28 May 1970.

In 1968, Ezequias deserted his wife and children to live with another woman, named Thereza. A short time afterwards he left her and returned to his own family. Judith, his wife, worked in order to help her husband keep the family. The eldest daughter, Ivanil, who was thirteen in 1968, looked after the house and the young children. There is evidence to suggest that Ivanil was the epicentre of the poltergeist we are about to describe.

One day Thereza met Judith in the street, behaved with great hostility, and told her she would 'destroy her house'. From that moment, stones and bricks fell frequently on to the roof of the house and the broken tiles had to be replaced.

In May 1970 the falling of stones on to the roof increased, breaking a total of 176 tiles. Mr Ezequias decided to file a complaint with the Commissioner of Police.

After this, at about midday on 20 May, while Judith and her children had gone to a spiritualist seance to ask for help, a violent explosion was heard in their empty house. Ivanil was washing some linen in a neighbour's house. When she and some neighbours rushed to get in, they saw that fire had broken out in the locked wardrobe in the largest bedroom; the clothes were on fire.

The fire was put out immediately. The clothes were taken out of the wardrobe, put into a bag and left in a lavatory built outside the house.

A little before this episode, the fire had reached the sheets of the baby's cot which was near the wardrobe. There was nobody in the room and Ivanil was about ten metres away.

The same day at about 6 pm, the bag of clothes was destroyed by a spontaneous fire. During the night of 22–23 May, more than nine similar fires were recorded, beginning at midnight and lasting more or less two hours.

The first was extremely bizarre. Four children were lying in a double bed in the smallest room. They were huddled together for safety, very afraid due to the three previous incidents. At around midnight, while two of the children were still awake, a ball of fire, which appeared to have come down from the ceiling, fell on the mattress of the other, unoccupied bed, which burst into flames.

One of the girls recounted that, just before this incident, she had heard a noise outside like a dog's baying, which did not seem to come from their own dog.

Ten minutes later the fire reached the double bed where the children had been sleeping a few minutes before. They dragged the double bed into the yard and threw water on to it. Even when it was still wet, its padding continued to burn.

Just then a police patrol called by; Officer Soares and two others. They had stopped to find out what had caused so much noise, because a crowd had gathered in front of the house. One of the policemen phoned the commissariat to report the incident. He also called Commissioner João Lazaro Rodriguez, who remembered the address as being the one from where the complaint of the stones falling on the roof had come.

Commissioner Rodriguez decided to lead the investigation himself and went to the scene immediately accompanied by Mr Natal Samuel de Lima, a police technical expert. When they arrived, as Lima told us later, they had the impression they were seeing a family moving out. All the furniture was scattered in the yard and the family was very afraid.

The police ordered everybody to leave the house and began to examine it. Almost immediately the mattress of the largest bed caught fire.

A few minutes later the sheets, which had been folded and placed on top of the slatted wooden frame of the bed, caught fire. Once more the fire seemed to come from inside the bundle.

Then a calendar fixed to the kitchen wall by a nail began to give off flames, in the presence of Police Officer Soares.

Mr Lima and Mr Soares decided to see if they could repeat the phenomenon. They found another calendar on the floor and hung it up by a nail, this time in the bedroom. They remained outside for a while watching, and then, in the presence of the Commissioner and of at least three other police officers, that calendar also began to burn. Mr Lima put his hand near the flames to be sure they were real and was burnt. He described the flame as of a bluish colour, like that of a gas burner, and stated that the fire rapidly destroyed the entire calendar, except the metal bar at the top.

Lima nailed half a page of newspaper to the kitchen wall and this too began to burn in the presence of several witnesses. He and the Commissioner tried other experiments with cheques pinned to the walls, but these were not burnt.

Then, when at least four police officers were in the largest room, smoke began to come out of the closed wardrobe door. The Commissioner, a man used to fighting all sorts of dangerous criminals, became visibly nervous at this point. Despite this Mr Lima opened the wardrobe door and everyone saw quite clearly that one of the internal balancing partitions of the wardrobe was bright red. This piece of wood was taken away later and is today in the possession of the IBPP, part of the collection gathered in the investigation of poltergeist cases.

The very moment that this was taking place, a small bundle of notes placed nearby on a table in the kitchen also began to burn. This was the last phenomenon of that night.

While all this was happening, stones fell again twice. The first time, a stone came violently into the master bedroom in front of several witnesses; according to one of them, it bounced against the wall like a soft ball. Immediately afterwards, a shower of stones fell in the kitchen.

Several witnesses have recounted later that a stone rose from the floor and passed through the kitchen window, breaking the glass. Nobody had actually seen the stone rise from the floor, but they all knew that it had been there and was no longer. According to one witness the stone had hit a child who was in the yard.

A similar incident took place in another poltergeist case in the presence of an IBPP investigator, and we know how difficult it is to document exactly spontaneous occurrences of this sort.

The paranormal phenomena stopped on the morning of 23 May, after Commissioner Rodriguez and police expert Mr Lima had said some prayers inside the house. The children went to sleep with a neighbour and a policeman stayed on guard all night.

The sole incident of 23 May took place at 4.30 pm: sudden flames came out of a cupboard door in the kitchen. Ivanil, the eldest daughter, had gone a few days before to stay with an aunt, at the express request of a Catholic priest who had been called to exorcise the house. The phenomena stopped.

On 28 May two other incidents coincided with Ivanil's return home: at 9 pm the sheets of the baby's cot in the largest room began to burn. At 2.30 in the afternoon, the mattress of a single bed which a neighbour had given them began to catch fire. From that moment, the phenomena ceased.

Hernani Guimarães Andrade
Director-President

Excerpt from the French local newspaper *Eclair Pyrénées*, Monday 13 August 1979

WHERE DO THEY COME FROM?

SEVENTY-TWO CASES OF SPONTANEOUS FIRES ON A FARM AT SERON

Gendarmes and a whole village mobilised in vain

The little village of Séron, a piece of Bigorre broken off into Bearn, has been getting to grips for a week with the mystery. That is a weak word for what the inhabitants of one of the houses there are experiencing. Since last Monday their washing has spontaneously caught fire. How? Why? Nobody knows . . . Only one thing seems certain in the current state of police enquiries: it is difficult to see how the hand of a criminal could cause such destruction. So what is it?

It all began on Monday afternoon at the Lahore farm. There live Edouard Lahore, a robust farmer of fifty-nine, his wife and the rest of the family. The farmstead consists of two dwelling blocks separated by a yard. One of them, prim and proper with its green blinds standing out from the ochre of the walls, is the main building – the 'new house' built some ten years ago. The other, the 'old house', is where they all lived before the 'new house' was built. It is an old family house, with no special history. Edouard Lahore was born

Superstition

there. Until now, it was a store for materials, for furniture or linen,
with two of its rooms still occupied.

On Monday afternoon, while the members of the Lahore family
were busy repairing the roof of a shed, a neighbour passing by raised
the alarm. Smoke was coming from one of the rooms and a strong
smell was evident. Some washing in a cupboard had caught fire,
setting light to the furniture.

That was only the start! The same day, other fires broke out all
over the 'old house'. On Tuesday there were thirteen. On Wednesday
ten. It began in the morning, and finished in the evening. The latest
fire broke out a little before two in the morning.

'It's always washing which catches fire,' explain the Lahores. One
of the children, Roger, a lorry-driver of twenty-nine, well-built and
self-assured, a thin beard lining his jaw, saw the phenomenon occur
before his eyes. 'It was a face towel which was hung up still wet.
Suddenly there was smoke, then a glow at the centre, then it began
to burn. The flames were about forty centimetres high. I grabbed it
to smother the flames. I didn't feel the heat, and the jersey I was
wearing bore no marks afterwards.'

The strangest thing is that these fires which break out so easily are
extinguished with just a little water. Another curious thing: the fire
always begins at a certain spot, where there seems to be an intense
heat. However quickly it is extinguished, the part of the cloth the
flames reach is completely burnt. 'You'd think it was a laser beam or
a blow torch!' That is indeed the comparison which comes to mind:
as if a ray of flame had touched the cloth, or as if a giant, invisible
magnifying glass had concentrated the rays of the sun to one point!
And at night, as well as during the day . . .

Stranger still, the smell: strong enough to be distinguished from
afar: 'Even with a cigarette under your nose, you smell it. A strong,
burnt smell, difficult to define.' Some people have thought at times
that they could distinguish the smell of sulphur . . .

Speak of sulphur and the devil isn't far away! Washing piled on
top of the furniture burst into flames. Some more did the same inside
a cupboard on a hanger. 'You would pass by any piece of cloth a few
times; suddenly you felt a burning sensation, you turned round, it
was on fire!' Two kilogramme bags of sugar piled on a floorcloth on
top of a heap of rubble in the yard did the same. The cloth suddenly
caught alight, setting fire to the wrapping of one of the packets and
producing red blocks of sugar. That was all in the time it took to
throw a bucket of water over it.

Now, indeed, there are buckets of water everywhere. The neighbours have brought reinforcements. Linen, mattresses and furniture

have been brought out into the yard. The interior of the 'old house' has been hosed down. Night and day they are on the lookout for the fires which have continually appeared since Tuesday, in the yard and even in the 'new house'.

Thursday was a real paroxysm, with thirty-three during the day. 'From ten o'clock until just after noon we did nothing but run. To eat, we had to divide into two teams. One sat at table while the other watched and put out the fires.'

The fear that haunts them, if one may put it like that, is that a fire might escape notice and spread to the house.

On Friday the gendarmes are there. It is a calm day, then, towards evening, the cloth covering of a sofa flares up in the 'old house'.

The gendarmerie take the decision to mount guard for forty-eight hours. The adjutant-chef of the Ossun brigade spends part of the night between Friday and Saturday patiently and methodically picking out on the plans of the houses the times and the positions of the outbreaks.

More seriously, for the first time the cloth affected by the flames was worn by a person. Four times during the afternoon, Michele, twenty, a girl who lives with the Lahores, saw her clothing scorched after feeling 'a sensation of heat'. Once it was the bottom of a dress lent by a neighbour. On another occasion the event took place in a car she was being driven in. On that occasion the dog, which belonged to the woman who was driving, behaved strangely, hiding under a seat. Until then the animals on the Lahore farm had remained calm.

Yesterday evening the gendarmes came back to mount their guard. Reinforcements from Tarbes will help by taking turns with the Ossun brigade.

Mystery requires analyst

What explanation can be found for these mysterious fires? Are they the work of a criminal? The frequency of the phenomenon, and the conditions in which it occurs, make the investigators shy away from this explanation. What then? A layer of gas underground? Fissures in the earth do not cause fires in the inside of drawers. And where would the spark come from? Perhaps it is chemicals which have been deposited on the cloth and which are of the kind which spontaneously combust? There have been no works carried out in the houses.

But there are other explanations. As yet we only roughly understand all the capabilities of nature, and all the powers of man. And that is without acknowledging that it does not take much for the supernatural to reassert itself. In whispers, at Séron, people can sometimes be heard putting forward theories to do with parapsychology.

Excerpt from the French newspaper *Nouvelle Republique*, 22 August 1979

SERON: A PARAPSYCHOLOGIST AT THE FIRE

Séron: it's starting again, and nobody understands why

After forty hours of respite, mysterious fires have once again begun to break out at the Lahore farm at Séron.

It was thought they were over. The furniture was put back so that the family could resume the course of their everyday lives. In the bedroom, the bedstead was put back, and they were about to replace the mattress.

Then the bedstead began to emit thick smoke. It was 7.20 pm.

Adjutant-chef Carrère, who is in command of the brigade of gendarmes at Ossun, was there. It was he who put out the nascent fire with his hands.

A little later, towards 9.30 pm, in the cellar (statistically the place where the highest number of blazes have appeared), there was smoke again, then fire. This time it was the hat belonging to Mme Marie-Louise Lahore which bore the brunt.

That night the Lahores took it in turns to keep guard so that one person should permanently be awake. A cousin from Gardères came to keep them company. The gendarmes from Rabastens were watching outside.

A third way?

During this time, the radio bulletins and those of a certain press agency were announcing constantly that the arrest of the arsonist was imminent.

In fact, the only conclusion the investigators have been able to reach – but not to prove – since they began, is that the fires cannot have been produced by a person, either deliberately or accidentally.

An arsonist who was able to light fires without being noticed, in spite of the constant presence of gendarmes, members of the family, and journalists, would be a magician capable of walking through walls. He would be wasting his time at Séron, and would be better off entering the armoured vaults of the Banque de France or Fort Knox. Nobody could suspect his presence. He could carry off gold ingots and banknotes without fear. That would be worth far more to him than setting fire to old hats at Séron.

The fires are neither deliberate nor accidental. Could there be a third way? Hypotheses of physico-chemical phenomena have been definitely ruled out, which means we are left with ... The planet Pluto – put forward as an explanation this morning by a pirate radio station – made Mr Edouard Lahore burst out laughing.

At the Palais de Justice in Tarbes, it is impossible to get any information. The magistrates, be they judges involved in the preliminary hearing or the deputy public prosecutor, hide behind the shield of judicial secrecy. If you try to get hold of them by telephone, they are always busy.

But an important fact could give a new lead for the judges to follow; if only through a desire to exhaust all possibilities.

A new expert has just been appointed. He is a psycho-physiologist, M. Eric Vexmann, who discharges these functions at the faculty of science of the University of Paris.

At the scene M. Vexmann joined up with Professor Kaplan, Director of the laboratory at Serres-Castets. Both have carried off fragments of cloth, of burnt material, and of earth from the garden.

M. Vexmann is a paragon of discretion. But news of his position gives us reason to think that the investigation could now be turning towards a combination of psychic, organic and physical factors as explanations for these astonishing happenings.

It is an area where one can only proceed delicately – precedents are lacking.

Excerpt from the French newspaper *Hautes Pyrénées*, Friday 24 August 1979

SERON: SIX NEW FIRES HEIGHTEN THE TENSION

After the eighteenth episode of the 'Séron affair' we cannot really say that we are any further along the road to an epilogue, as we announced a few days ago. Among the observers present, there is a suspicion that the curtain which must eventually fall on this real-life drama will itself go up in flames.

A Hypothesis from the CNRS (Centre National de Recherches Scientifiques)

Paris, 23 August

The CNRS states that 'the mysterious spontaneous combustions at the farm at Séron could be explained by a process of auto-ignition, which happens when several substances are put in the presence of certain others'.

This hypothesis was put forward last Thursday by the CNRS's Centre for Research into the Chemistry of Combustion and High Temperatures. They gave examples of substances producing 'auto-ignition': among these are sulphur-powder (used against dogs who foul pavements) and iron filings. The mixture produces a slow combustion which can ignite.

Perchlorates, used as weedkiller, and powdered sugar produce quite a dangerous reaction when mixed with acids. These phenomena were minutely described in 'joke chemistry' manuals at the beginning of the century.

The principle behind these experiments is that of auto-ignition: a slow reaction gives off energy after a 'latent period', the temperature rises and speeds up the phenomenon and the reaction becomes ever more violent until a flame appears and what is called the 'explosive phase' begins.

When sodium comes into contact with humidity it turns into sodium monoxide, giving off hydrogen, a highly inflammable element. The mixture may then detonate at any moment and give off an intense heat.

Nuclear reactors use sodium as a fluid heat conductor, and are equipped with safety systems which are protected like military secrets. In the same way, white phosphorus, which looks like a whitish chalk, dissolves in carbon sulphide and produces small fragments, after the moisture has evaporated. The substance produced by this process reacts violently on contact with air and detonates, producing a flame. This is, in fact, the principle behind the phosphorus bomb.

Sodium is kept in the form of shiny bars, softer than lead, in tanks of petrol to shelter it from air and water. Phosphorus is simply kept in water to avoid it coming into contact with air.

So, very many natural elements and their compounds can, when properly mixed, auto-ignite spontaneously, though after a long latent period. The 'spontaneous combustions' on the Lahore farm could, then, be explained by processes well known to chemists.

. . . and the opinion of an agricultural engineer

We asked an agricultural engineer for his opinion on the matter:

It is not a case of criminal arson, but is due to an occurrence of will-o'-the-wisps, following exceptional circumstances.

If you don't believe in witchcraft, you can imagine two hypotheses:

it's either a physical phenomenon (electrical or magnetic), or a chemical one.

The first hypothesis does not seem valid, because there has been nothing exceptional (such as the construction of new structures, for example). The chemical hypothesis remains. We must explain:

1) the nature of the effect
2) its occurrence on clothing, etc.

The nature of the effect

We are on a farm; we should naturally look for chemical products which are used in agriculture and could give rise to spontaneous combustion.

We know that agriculture uses products which contain phosphorus and magnesium. One thinks naturally of manure, and especially of manure containing phosphates which come from ground bones.

We see immediately a link with will-o'-the wisps which are produced in cemeteries on hot and humid evenings.

But what is the reason for this exceptional reaction and what could have produced the dispersion of this substance?

On the Lahore farm, it must be remembered, there was a fire in the spring in a shed which contained manure. The manure was then dispersed throughout the farm. Did it by chance impregnate clothes which were drying, or did the dust penetrate into the house and on to materials which easily catch fire, such as cloth or paper? That would explain the dispersal of the substance, and the conditions of temperature or humidity might have caused combustion – as in the case of will-o'-the-wisps . . .

SERON: THE FIRES MULTIPLY

Michèle is held by the Gendarmes

Having got away once from the Lahore farm, Michèle was the 'star' of the day yesterday at Séron. It was the eighteenth day of an affair which we are beginning to doubt will ever end. The tension has clearly been heightened. After two fires had broken out during the night, four more appeared during the afternoon. After the last of these the gendarmes suddenly seized the Lahores' adoptive daughter to interview her in the old farm building where they have established their HQ. Marie-Louise Lahore protested: 'They want to make us break down'. And then night fell on Séron without any real further development. This is the first time the gendarmes have started an interview straight after a fire. Meanwhile special correspondents from the American and German press were making their way to this enclave of the Haute Pyrénées . . .

M. Lagarde, Mayor of Séron, 'in consideration of the particular conditions prevailing at Séron, and with the assent of the Public Prosecutor of the Republic, has issued a decree forbidding the parking of any vehicle on all the public roads of the commune of Séron. The Mayor will take all measures necessary to assure that these decisions are enforced, and the colonel of the gendarmerie has been charged with putting this decree into effect.'

This affair is far from becoming monotonous. This eighteenth day has not escaped from the pattern now effectively established: two fires broke out in the night between Wednesday and Thursday. The first was at 9.40 pm in the cellar; the second in the bathroom in the middle of the night. Then there was a lull, which everyone knew would sooner or later be broken.

Indeed, a little after 2 pm at the 'fire time', as journalists familiar with the case now call it, the alert went out again. The first time, it was the table napkins which had remained untouched by a fire the previous afternoon. Then, at 2.30, a bath towel placed on a washtub in the cellar. A third fire appeared on another towel at 3.40. At 4.40 it was a new towel hung in the bathroom. The room was locked and the fire was again inexplicable. Then a fifth fire, the last of the evening, at 6.10. This one was remarkable because of the reactions it provoked in this mini-society, but also symptomatic of the ambivalent atmosphere which pervades the Lahore farm.

Suddenly, the last fire . . .

At about 6.10 in the evening, in the dining-room in the new house, Marie-Louise Lahore was talking with her eldest son André, his wife, a neighbour, Pascal Marsan, and with Michèle, in the corner by the door in the corridor leading to the kitchen. A group of journalists were waiting outside and the uniformed sentries were on guard when a fire broke out among the towels which were on top of a bread bin. A strong smell of burning spread through the house. At the very moment when the fire started, a gendarme took hold of Michèle and led her decisively to the old house where the division of gendarmes has its HQ. At that moment, tension animated all the actors in the drama: the gendarmes and the family. As the gendarmes recorded the girl's statement, we could see the Lahore family go up to her one by one, as if to protect her from the chain of events which Marie-Louise Lahore summed up in a lapidary phrase, 'They want to make us break down'. Edouard, the father of the family, said, 'We are here to protect you, Michèle.'

As soon as this latest alert was over, the farm took on a reassuring appearance of calm. That was the end of the eighteenth episode of an affair whose epilogue, near or far, was still unknown last night.

M MAHLER

Department of Psychology
University of Edinburgh

16 February 1983

To: Alasdair Hutton MEP

Memo on 'Fire-raising Poltergeists'

Poltergeist cases involving incendiary incidents are unusual but by no means unknown. Gauld and Cornell (1979), in an analysis of 500 historical cases ranging from 530 AD to the present day, identify some fifty-three cases (eleven per cent) as involving such incidents. Owen (1964) devotes the whole of Chapter Seven of his book to cases of this sort, some of which are curiously reminiscent of the Carole Compton case that is currently causing concern. Gaddis (1967) has published an entire book devoted to this topic and deals with some striking cases of recent vintage from the United States.

I can do no more than put on record my own considered opinion that, in cases where there is no circumstantial evidence implicating a suspect in deliberate incendiary activity, and no pathological symptoms suggesting insanity, the possibility of the fires being due to a paranormal cause of the kind associated with poltergeist agents is one that should not be overlooked.

Signed

John Beloff Ph.D.
Senior Lecturer in Psychology
Ex-president, Society for Psychical Research
Ex-president, Parapsychological Association

Refs
A Gauld & AD Cornell *Poltergeists* (Routledge) 1979
ARG Owen *Can We Explain the Poltergeist?* (Garrett Publications: New York) 1964

Vincent Gaddis *Mysterious Fires and Lights* (D McKay: New York)
  1967

The City University
Department of Electrical & Electronic Engineering
Northampton Square
London EC1

16 February 1983

Dear Mr Hutton

From what I have heard, it seems to me perfectly possible, if it is
accurate, that Carole Compton is the focus of what is sometimes
called Spontaneous Recurrent Psychokinesis or, in old-fashioned
terminology, of poltergeist phenomena. The evidence for such
phenomena occasionally occurring is very good, and sometimes they
appear to be the result in a young adolescent person of stress which,
for reasons not at all understood, appear to be discharged in this
inconvenient way. In genuine cases the person acting as the focus
would not be at all conscious of what was happening. I have heard
of more than one case of spontaneous fires starting, but usually
objects fly about in the traditional way.

Yours sincerely

Arthur Ellison

The University of Glasgow
Department of Astronomy
Glasgow, G12

18 February 1983

Dear Mr Hutton

I would like to say that in the history of Psychic Research, especially
in the type of case called poltergeist cases, there is evidence that in
some of these, a human being is associated with the spontaneous
outbreak of fires; there is no evidence that a human being has
deliberately begun these fires.

  I myself had a case in 1974 where a family was troubled by

poltergeist type phenomena. At one stage there is evidence to believe that one of the members of the family was present when inexplicable fires broke out, usually of an electrical nature, even though the house had been rewired twice. In that case there was no reason to believe that the boy was starting these fires deliberately.

To anyone who has not studied psychical phenomena of this nature it is, of course, against commonsense that such things can happen and certainly one must try to follow up all 'normal' explanations before resorting to any 'paranormal' ones. Nevertheless the possibility of such things occurring is supported by a large number of psychic investigators who have made a study of such things.

Yours sincerely

Archie E Roy

AE Roy
Professor of Astronomy
Head of Department

European Foundation for the Arts
19 Cranley Gardens
London N10 3AA

20 February 1983

To Whom It May Concern

I have been asked to support representations which are to be made for the release of the British girl Carole Compton.

I write sincerely on her behalf, for it is my long experience that the circumstances in which such cases occur are often related to paranormal 'poltergeist' phenomena, over which the subject has no control, and I feel that this is most probably such a case.

I was personally sceptical about such phenomena until eight years ago when they began to occur in my own family.

My son, Stephen North, has during those eight years been the subject of a variety of psychic phenomena which are being thoroughly studied, confirmed and recorded by scientists at the highest academic level in Britain and the USA.

As a consequence, I have developed a serious interest in the subject and have investigated a number of cases, in particular those at Enfield and Archway, London where poltergeist energies were claimed to be causing spontaneous outbreaks of fire daily.

In both cases the police and fire services were called in and they confirmed that the cause was unknown. No legal charges were made against the young girls around whom the phenomena occurred and they were regarded as innocent.

I have since found considerable evidence on an international scale that poltergeist fires of this kind are widely recorded by reliable witnesses and I have no doubt whatsoever that these effects are of random psychic origin and not deliberately caused by the person involved, usually a young girl.

Arthur North
Senior Lecturer, Polytechnic of North London

The University of Nottingham
Department of Psychology
University Park
Nottingham

24 February 1983

Dear Mr Hutton

Incendiary Poltergeists

I am the co-author, with Mr AD Cornell, of *Poltergeists* (Routledge & Kegan Paul, 1979), a book which contains an historical survey and a statistical analysis of past poltergeist cases, together with accounts of various cases which we investigated personally.

'Poltergeist' phenomena, as you probably know, are peculiar physical happenings, not readily explicable, which tend to centre round particular individuals, often adolescent children. The kinds of happening most commonly reported are percussive sounds (volleys of raps, little explosions) and movements of objects, ranging from displacements of small objects to movements and even levitations of quite large pieces of furniture. Where such phenomena centre round a young person, the most obvious explanation of them is trickery. But there have been not a few cases (several are described in the book mentioned above) in which this explanation seems very hard to entertain. For example, in the Miami poltergeist of 1966/7, two very competent witnesses, Professor JG Pratt and Mr WG Roll (both known to me) were able to sit at either end of a long warehouse room and dictate into tape recorders details of phenomena, and the positions of all persons present, during or immediately after the occurrence of phenomena. I have been present myself on a number of occasions when poltergeist phenomena took place for which I could find no explanation.

The staple poltergeist phenomena of raps and object movements are not uncommonly supplemented by other peculiar happenings, for instance the spontaneous breakages of objects, 'apports', the carrying rather than projection of objects through the air, and among these additional phenomena are two classes which seem rather often to go together, and which may also be reported on their own without the usual background of raps, object movements, etc. These are cases of mysterious inundations of water and of the mysterious outbreak of fires.

I have notes of well over sixty poltergeist cases in which incendiary effects are said to have taken place. The earliest dates from AD 738, the most recent from the 1970s. I think it would be fair to say that while the evidence for incendiary phenomena is by no means so strong as that for raps and object movements, there is enough of it to merit consideration, especially when it is borne in mind that incendiary effects often occur in a context of other kinds of poltergeist phenomena for which the evidence is really quite strong.

I am also impressed by the fact that similar *patterns* of phenomena have allegedly happened at times and in places very distant from each other. Let me give some examples of this (I must emphasise that I am not selecting these cases for the strength of the evidence, but as examples of the recurrence of a pattern):

1. According to the *Annual Register* for 1820, a servant girl aged ten, named Elizabeth Barnes, was accused in court of having reputedly set alight to the clothes of her employer's mother. The mother suffered serious injury, but did not blame the girl, stating that 'something supernatural' was responsible. However, phenomena ceased and the girl was sent away. Consequently, her employer accused her before magistrates; but what happened to her does not appear.

2. In 1963 my co-author, Mr AD Cornell, investigated a case near Bath, in which phenomena centred around a married lady of thirty-two. There were various object movements, inexplicable inundations and overflowings of water, and spontaneous outbreaks of fire. The lady, when alone in the house, would find crumpled balls of paper smouldering in corners of downstairs rooms; on other occasions a rug, a table, and a tablecloth were found smouldering.

3. To take an Italian case, the *Tribuna* of Rome reported on March 5 and 21, 1904, a case which took place in Calabria in

December 1905, in which an old lady of eighty, who had with
her a niece of sixteen, was allegedly persecuted by outbreaks of
fire, sometimes dangerous, and by inundations of water. No
explanation was forthcoming.

One could multiply such examples. My own feeling is that while, as
I said, the evidence for incendiary poltergeists falls short of
conclusiveness, there is enough of it to require that, where this pattern
of happenings recurs yet again, one should not immediately jump to
the conclusion that a particular person *must* have deliberately and
directly caused the fires, despite the fact that he or she denies it and
was apparently not in a position to have started them. There is,
furthermore, some element of what may be called psychopathology
in some poltergeist cases. By this I mean not that the phenomena were
produced by fraud, but that they express the 'poltergeist agent's' own
inner conflicts and feelings in a way that is outside his or her
conscious control. There are some curious instances of this in the
literature and I have come across one or two examples myself. In
some cases the phenomena may assume the appearance of an assault,
either against another person or, in some instances, on the agent
himself. I cite a number of instances in the book already referred to.
This could hold true of incendiary cases also.

Yours sincerely,

Dr AO Gauld, M.A., Ph.D.
Senior Lecturer in Psychology

Université de L'État à Mons
Rue des Dominicains
Mons
Belgium

25 February 1983

Sir,

Every researcher in parapsychology knows that the so-called 'poltergeist' events take place usually when a young girl or boy, under
psychological tension, is present. Though Carole Compton is already
twenty-one, it seems that the most probable origin of the fires is
paranormal – indicated for instance by the fact that she was not

always present when the fires began and that she was never seen trying to set fire to any place.

Centuries ago such fires were considered as signs of possession by the devil and religious authorities have many records of such cases.

Since that period, happily, science has much progressed and it is now possible to record objectively, and without any doubt, to prove the existence of the events. It is even possible to suppose that events occur at a distance of one to five metres, that the movements of objects will be more circular than straight, etc.

I should therefore suggest that at the trial itself, experts in parapsychology would be called, whose experience in parapsychology and psychoanalytical knowledge could help the judges to discriminate between reality, unconscious pathological movements and parapsychological facts.

It would be an unbearable crime to allow, in 1983, someone to be condemned for parapsychological events for which she is not responsible.

Sincerely yours,

Dr Jean Dierkens

Professor Dr Hans Bender
Institute for Border Areas of Psychology and Mental Hygiene
Freiburg im Breisgau,
West Germany

12 December 1983

Illustrissimo Avvocato Sergio Minervini
Livorno

Dear Avvocato Minervini

As Professor Emeritus of Psychology and Border Areas of Psychology at the University of Freiburg and Director of the Institute for Border Areas of Psychology and Mental Hygiene at Freiburg, I feel obliged to comment on the case of your client Carole Compton. I am famous as a representative of parapsychology, the science of so-called 'occult manifestations', for which in Europe there is a Professorship at the University of Utrecht, in addition to the Chair at Freiburg. In the USA there are a number of institutes for this research; the John F Kennedy University in California now offers a full course in parapsychology.

However, general recognition of parapsychology in the 'scientific community' has not yet come into full being.

The Carole Compton case has been under discussion for a long time in the Italian press, and internationally. There is reference in the reports to analogies apparent between fires in the vicinity of the girl (five in the course of fourteen days in two places where Carole worked as a nanny), and unexplained fires in the vicinity of people who are triggers for so-called 'haunting' phenomena. In particular, there was reference in the Italian press in August this year to the analogies between the Carole Compton case and the case reported from Formia of the sixteen-year-old Benedetto Supino. A number of fires broke out in the vicinity of this carpenter's son, without it being possible to establish the intention to commit arson. Italian television carried reports on this. In the end, the family turned to the Italian President with a request for help in clearing the matter up. (See the magazine, *L'Europeo*, No. 35, 27 August 1983: 'This Boy Makes Sparks . . .').

There are numerous cases of this sort, where in connection with a so-called 'Focus Person' (mostly young people who are completely normal), phenomena are observed, which are as yet unexplained in the material world of physical objects: knocking noises, or footsteps with no recognisable cause, objects moving, doors opening, electrical fuses blowing, bulbs exploding, pictures falling off the wall, etc. These also include spontaneous fires. At the congress of the 'Centro Studi Parapsicologici' at Bologna in May, 1983, Dr Anna Maria Bononcini, psychologist and psychotherapist of Florence, and Professor Aldo Martelli, biologist and pharmacologist at the University of Turin, reported a 'poltergeist' case of this sort in northern Italy, which was triggered by a thirteen-year-old boy. Dr Piero Cassoli, President of the Centre at Bologna, and Professor Emilio Servadio in Rome, have pointed out the analogies between the Carole Compton case and such poltergeist cases.

Paranormally triggered fires rank as a well-observed phenomenon in parapsychology. Cases of burning which led to burn marks on the body have been observed in the instance of the Soviet medium Nina Kulagina; a classic Brazilian case (in 1970 in the town of Suzano), which was confirmed by the public police, has received a great deal of publication coverage (cf. Guy Lyon Playfair's *The Flying Cow*, Souvenir Press, London 1975). In a case in north London in 1978, firefighters were present when fires broke out in a poltergeist case. Dr Andres Barros of the Southern University of Chile reported a sensational case of spontaneous combustion in the vicinity of a fourteen-year-old girl some time ago. I myself, together with collaborators, investigated a poltergeist case at Freiburg in 1976, where numerous fires broke out over a period, and other classical poltergeist phenomena were associated with a fifteen-year-old boy. Curtains caught fire, clothes were singed, bedlinen and mattresses were burnt, but it was possible to extinguish the fires before major damage was caused. Other residents of the house where the boy lived with his family reported him for arson.

The Public Prosecutor was informed of the incidents and instituted an investigation which took several weeks at the Department for Children and Young People of the Psychiatric Clinic in Heidelberg. Professor M Müller-Küppers, the psychiatrist heading the department, came to a positive verdict on the boy's credibility when he insisted that he had not caused the phenomena intentionally, and the Professor did not rule out a paranormal cause.

A detailed interview with Carole Compton in the prison for those in investigative custody at Livorno on 8 September 1983 strengthened my suspicion that in this case as well, there was a paranormal triggering of the five fire phenomena observed in fourteen days, and that her affirmation that she did not start the fires intentionally in any of the cases is credible. An analysis of the accompanying circumstances adds to the argument for a paranormal triggering: in the Ricci family house in Rome, a picture of the Madonna fell from the wall suddenly without any ascertainable reason, which caused the housemaid to make the sign of the Cross. When Carole went past a hot water tank, it hissed and sizzled (personal statement by Signora Ricci). At the Cecchini family home on Elba, a silver vase which had been standing on the table fell to the ground without explanation, whilst Carole was asleep. A glass vessel also broke into pieces. A smouldering fire in the refuse bag in the kitchen, which took place on 13 July 1982 in Signor M.'s house, is comparable with analogous phenomena in poltergeist cases.

In the files accessible to me, I found no indications of the presence of pyromania, nor of any investigation results which could prove intentional arson, let alone attempted murder of the child Agnese Cecchini. The charges seem to me to have arisen as a result of the impression that five fires in fourteen days in the vicinity of Carole Compton, employed as a nanny, could not have broken out by chance, but were connected with her. It is understandable that such an accumulation in the vicinity of one person has a 'social perception' as a consequence, which suggests suspicion of intentional arson and, in the last case, of the burning of a child's bed, of intent to murder.

I conclude with the declaration that I regard as credible the repeated affirmation by the girl that she did not start the fires, and that I see the solution of the puzzle of five consecutive fires, which are apparently connected with one person, as being in a probable paranormal cause for which she is not responsible. This probable paranormal cause is, however, just as impossible to prove in the strictest sense as is the assumption of intentional arson with intent to murder which underlies the charge. Hence the High Court probably cannot be expected to issue an acquittal by accepting the poltergeist argument which is familiar only to experts, but not to the whole scientific community.

Professor Hans Bender, Ph.D. M.D.

Bibliography
L'Europeo, No. 35, 27 August 1983: 'This Boy Makes Sparks . . .'
Sixth Sense: Clairvoyance, Telepathy, Ghosts: Hans Bender, Feltri-
    nelli Editore, Milan, 1974.
Telepathy, Clairvoyance and Psychokinesis: Hans Bender, Edizioni
    Mediteraneo, Rome, 1981
Can We Explain the Poltergeist? ARG Owen, Helix Pr. Garret, New
    York, 1964.

Extract from *L'Europeo*, edition No. 35, 27 August 1983

THIS BOY MAKES SPARKS . . .

Giuliano Ferrieri

The electric boy from Formia, the incendiary baby-sitter of Trento, and so many other inexplicable cases. Are they tricks, or phenomena which science can verify?

'Medicine has grown difficult these days, because it has become so convoluted: we have to know everything that has been learnt over four thousand years, and at the same time we have to be able to repudiate it all, bit by bit, in order to reinstate it, bit by bit. And we have to take into account that mankind – "lay" people as well as "scientific" people – is changing its ideas, its languages and its rhythms. And it is also changing science itself.'
    The man who smiles quietly as he expresses these concepts, which are as simple as they are revolutionary, is Professor Carlo Sirtori. A medic with a rigorous academic background (he has specialised in radiology, physiology, pathological anatomy, and oncology, and he was a candidate for the Nobel prize), Carlo Sirtori is at the same time

a very cultured humanist, open to unorthodox science and medicine.

The topic of the conversation stems from the case of the so-called 'electric boy' of Formia, Benedetto Supino, to whom a series of paranormal phenomena is attributed. Professor Sirtori moves on to many other analogous 'medical histories', where a human being shows characteristics, behaviour or reactions (psychic and also biochemical) which appear anomalous from the point of view of orthodox scientific norms.

In each of these cases, at least three questions arise. The first: is it a trick? Have the phenomena been faked (consciously or unconsciously)? The second: is there a 'scientific' explanation of the facts, or for those aspects which seem impossible to the layman and so raise the case to the level of a miracle? The third: where official science remains silent, is there an opinion which is in line with research and studies today labelled as 'heretical', but which are perhaps destined to be recognised as valid tomorrow?

Let us turn to the events of recent days. Benedetto Supino is sixteen and a half years old, he lives at Formia with his family, and he studies electrical engineering (by correspondence). The events with which he is involved started several months ago. The boy – so he himself and his family relate – unintentionally causes the fuses in the meter-box at home to explode, and sets fire from a distance to newspapers, sheets, plastic, rubber and wooden material. It is as if a charge of energy within him were turned towards the outside, transforming Benedetto into a sort of flame-thrower with an invisible jet.

In many aspects, Benedetto's story recalls the recent case of Carole Compton, a Scottish girl who came into service as an au pair. But, as a woman, a servant and a foreigner, Carole was less fortunate: she is now in prison at Trento, and has been waiting over a year to stand trial for 'intentional arson' (or do we want to call it witchcraft?) The magistrate's court is accusing her of starting five fires which broke out in two houses where she was in service.

Advocate Sergio Minervini, Carole's defence lawyer, maintains that the girl is innocent of everything. She had no responsibility, either direct or indirect, for the fires; furthermore, she had no motive, and on each occasion was far away from the place where the flames broke out. The alternative, then, is that, without being to blame at all, Carole was the victim of 'poltergeist' phenomena; these are psycho-physical disturbances which can occur at the age of puberty, with physical manifestations (objects which move about, bells which ring, flames which burst out from nothing).

Science has not yet given its verdict on Benedetto Supino. In the end, President Pertini has been entrusted with the problem (the boy's parents requested him to intervene so that scientists 'above all suspicion' might study the case and give their verdict) but, at the moment, the academics are all at sea – through no fault of their own. Benedetto has been approached in turn by magicians, healers, and exorcists who are convinced that the boy will have a great future, as a sideshow attraction or a 'paranormal' phenomenon.

But two other men have visited the boy as well: a neuropsychiatrist, Dr Sandro Bartolomeo ('There is something within him which normal medical science cannot explain') and a medical physics specialist, Professor Pierluigi Ballesio, who is currently director of the Institute for Medical Physics at the University of Rome. Ballesio measured Benedetto Supino with an ohmmeter (to verify the body's electrical resistance), and conducted a series of other specialised tests on him. He says: 'All the readings have come out as normal. I stepped in principally for humanitarian reasons, in order to calm both the boy and his family. A definitive scientific judgement on this case requires various tests at different times, and a more accurate verification of the events (or presumed events) which have taken place around the young man.'

If the data are normal, the phenomena most definitely are not – or only with reference to the standards of parapsychology. Massimo Inardi, a doctor at Bologna, and a fairly well-known student of paranormal phenomena, thinks of Benedetto as an 'unwitting medium', and, without having visited Supino, he conjectures that there are 'frustrations, complexes and character instabilities' at the root of the energy disharmonies.

Dr Carlo Cassoli, another respected interpreter of parapsychology in Italy, has this to say on the subject: 'Phenomena of this sort are mysterious aetiologically – that is to say, with regard to what causes them – but there is no longer any argument about their existence and distribution. The theory of the poltergeist (literally, 'joking spirits') has by now been accepted by science, after the scientific experiments by Professor Hans Bender of the University of Freiburg, and by the technical experts from the Max Planck Institute; the hypothesis is that of the presence of a 'naughty little girl' (who could, of course, also be masculine) whose aggression is released through these energy conversion phenomena.'